D1287465

CISTERCIAN STUDIES SERIES:
NUMBER ONE HUNDRED EIGHTY-SEVEN

Charles Dumont OCSO

PATHWAY OF PEACE
Cistercian Wisdom according to Saint Bernard

CISTERCIAN STUDIES SERIES:
NUMBER ONE HUNDRED EIGHTY-SEVEN

Pathway of Peace
Cistercian Wisdom according to Saint Bernard

by

Charles Dumont OCSO
ℳ
Monk of Scourmont

Translated by

Elizabeth Connor OCSO

Cistercian Publications
Kalamazoo, Michigan — Spencer, Massachusetts

Original title:
Au chemin de la paix. La sagesse cistercienne selon saint Bernard
Pain de Cîteaux, série 3, n° 13

Cistercian Publications (Editorial and Business Offices)
WMU Station
Kalamazoo, Michigan 49008

Cistercian Publications (Distribution)
Saint Joseph's Abbey
Spencer, Massachusetts 01562

The work of Cistercian Publications
is made possible in part by support from Western Michigan University
to The Institute of Cistercian Studies

Library of Congress Cataloguing-in-Publication Data

Dumont, Charles.
    [Au chemin de la paix. English]
    Pathway of peace : Cistercian wisdom according to Saint Bernard /
By Charles Dumont ; translated by Elizabeth Connor.
      P. Cm. — (Cistercian studies series : no. 187)
    Includes bibliographical references.
    ISBN 0-87907-687-9 (alk. paper). — (SBN 0-87907-787-5 (pbk. : alk. paper)
    1. Bernard, of Clairvaux, saint, 1090 or 91–1153. 2. Cistercians—
Spiritual life. I. Title. II. Series
    BX4700.B5D8513   1999
    248.8'942—dc21   99–30965
                                        CIP

Typeset by BookComp, Grand Rapids, Michigan
Printed in the United States of America

TABLE OF CONTENTS

Abbreviations

Mich	*Sermo in festo sancti Michaëlis*
Miss	*Homelium super* Missus est *in laudibus virginis matris*
Nat	*Sermo in nativitate domini*
Nat BVM	*Sermo in nativitate BVM*
1 Nov	*Sermo in dominica 1 novembris*
O Epi	*Sermo in octava epiphania domini*
O Asspt	*Sermo dominica infra octavam assumptionis*
O Pasc	*Sermo in octava paschae*
OS	*Sermo in festivitate Omnium Sanctorum*
Palm	*Sermo in ramis palmarum*
Par	*Parabolae*
Pasc	*Sermo in die paschae*
P Epi	*Sermo in dominica 1 post octavam epiphaniae*
Pent	*Sermo in die sancto pentecostes*
Pl	*Sermo in conversione sancti Pauli*
Pre	*Liber de praecepto et dispensatione*
6 p P	*Sermo in dominica sexta post pentecosten*
PP	*Sermo in festo Ss. Apostolorum Petri et Pauli*
Pur	*Sermo in purificatione BVM*
QH	*Sermo super psalmum* Qui habitat
Quad	*Sermo in quadragesima*
Rog	*Sermo in rogationibus*
SC	*Sermo super* Cantica Canticorum
Sent	*Sententiae*
Sept	*Sermo in septuagesima*
Tpl	*Liber ad milites templi (De laude novae militiae)*
V And	*Sermo in vigilia sancti Andreae*
Vict	*Sermo in natali sancti Victoris*
V Mal	*Vita sancti Malachiae*
V Nat	*Sermo in vigilia nativitatis domini*
V PP	*Sermo in vigilia apostolorum Petri et Pauli*

PERIODICALS

ABR   *American Benedictine Review*. Newark, NJ; Richardton, ND, 1950–

ASOC/AC *Analecta Cisterciensia; Analecta Sacri Ordinis Cisterciensis*. Rome, 1945–

Coll   *Collectanea Cisterciensia; Collectanea o.c.r.*

CSQ   *Cistercian Studies Quarterly; Cistercian Studies*, Chimay, Belgium; Caldey Island, Wales; Trappist, Kentucky; Vina, California; Huntsville, Utah, 1961–.

NRT   *Nouvelle Revue Théologique*. Tournai, 1969–

COLLECTIONS

PC   *Pain de Cîteaux*. 3rd series. Oka, Québec, Canada, 1989–.

PG   J.-P. Migne, *Patrologiae cursus completus, series graeca*. Paris, 1857–1866.

PL   J.-P. Migne, *Patrologiae cursus completus, series latina*. Paris, 1844–1864.

SCh   *Sources chrétiennes series*. Paris: Cerf, 1941–.

Introduction

A NEW BOOK ON SAINT BERNARD. And we mean new, not simply in the sense that it is another book, but that it is a book capable of communicating the bernardine good news in all its freshness, the newness (*novitas*) that inspired the abbot of Clairvaux.

We know that Cîteaux was known from the beginning as the New Monastery. Even if this name was soon set aside, the reality to which it points remains. A two-fold reason seems to explain it: Saint Stephen's charism for organization and Saint Bernard's mystagogical charism. The *Charter of Charity* and Saint Bernard's literary work are the ripened fruits of the graces received by these two Fathers, these two saints.

The charism the first Fathers had as founders gave form to the primitive documents and found expression in numerous treatises, letters and sermons which conveyed its spirit, grace, and life. These documents are not in themselves the cistercian charism, of course. The charism, as an experience of the Spirit who configures us to Christ in a very particular way, is found in human hearts; it dwelt in the hearts of the first Cistercian Fathers and it dwells in the hearts of all those who follow Christ along the cistercian way.

The cistercian charism, as an evangelical form of life, the thrust and transforming gift of the Spirit, is found in the hearts of each and every Cistercian. The vocation to a cistercian monastery can in fact be considered the discovery of the charism in one's heart and the desire to see it reach its greatest fulfillment. Although this may seem to be an exaggeration, we can say that whenever, after serious discernment, a young man or woman comes to the monastery, it is because he or she already possesses the founding charism of Cîteaux as it was at its origin and birth.

The charism of the founders has been transmitted to every monk and nun to enable us to live according to this charism, to preserve it, deepen it and unceasingly develop it, always in growing communion with the Body of Christ.

But we do not all have the same graces. It is one thing to have the experience, another to be able to conceptualize and communicate the grace we receive. Saint Bernard received the grace of mystical experience and also the grace to introduce others to its mystery. He was an authentic mystic and mystagogue.

Father Charles has penetrated the bernardine mystery as few others have done and, as few others, he has received the grace to communicate it. The reason for this is very simple. Father Charles, like Saint Bernard, has lived by and reflected on the fundamental and profound realities of human and christian experience. Both communicate it with a note of humanism which brings them close to all men and women of all times and places. Both possess the same vocational charism: holiness in contemplative and cenobitical charity lived to its fullest.

This work by Father Charles Dumont will be helpful to all of us who want to read Saint Bernard's works fruitfully. Still more, reading this work will nourish and motivate a generous self-giving, and will enlighten and guide the offering of our life. The author knows how to put the permanent values presented by Saint Bernard alongside our present-day experience. He knows how to distinguish what is obsolete from what is enduring, and he has re-translated the abbot of Clairvaux in a contemporary idiom, to help us understand it.

The cistercian charism, received by pure grace, is a gift of the Spirit for the Church and, through it, for the world. *Pathway of Peace. Cistercian Wisdom according to Saint Bernard* attains a three-fold goal: it is an excellent instrument for our formation in the spirit of Cîteaux; it opens to all Christians the wisdom contained in our tradition; and it proclaims to all men and women of good will a message of peace.

And finally, may the Lord grant that this book help strengthen the bonds of communion among all the members of the cistercian family who live in the same school of charity as Saint Bernard.

Bernardo Olivera, Abbot General

Rome, 26 January 1997
The Feast of the Holy Founders of Cîteaux

Author's Preface

AM VERY GRATEFUL to Dom Bernardo for his letter, which so well expresses the purpose of this book. My thanks to him also for having wanted this book and having encouraged me to pursue this work in spite of poor health and other trials which have postponed its publication.

The attempt at a synthesis of Saint Bernard's spiritual monastic teaching which the reader finds in this volume took form slowly. During the 1970s the idea was suggested during a series of talks on bernardine texts both in Europe and North America. Two booklets of selected texts were printed at Laval Abbey. It struck me as helpful for understanding Saint Bernard, to compose a synthesis built around the major themes of his teaching. In March 1990, I was invited to present to my own community of Scourmont a kind of overview of the abbot of Clairvaux's thought and cistercian life as he lived it. The same series of lectures was given in twenty-five communities of the Order, and I sincerely thank them all for the interest they took in them. It was during a session at Notre-Dame-du-Lac, Oka, in Québec, Canada, in September, 1991, that someone suggested I write a book on this material. *Pain de Cîteaux* offered to publish it. On the advice from various persons, however, I felt it would be preferable to change the style of these lectures, to quote the texts differently and to increase the number of references given in the notes. The result of this postponement of publication was that instead of this volume, two others appeared in the same series: *Sagesse ardente* (3rd Series, no 8, 1995) and *Une éducation du coeur* (3rd Series, no 10, 1996). These volumes are collections of articles on benedictine and cistercian spirituality which appeared in various periodicals, principally *Collectanea Cisterciensia*. This third volume, then, completes the other two in an unexpected way.

The manner in which this synthesis was composed gives it a unique character. It is not to be classed among the many works which have appeared since the eighth centenary of Saint Bernard's birth. In spite of the temptation to provide parallel texts from the works of other cistercian authors, I considered it necessary to limit myself to Saint Bernard's writings. As for ancient authors, we must believe him when he says that he is simply repeating what they said, but differently (*aliter*). Is it necessary to quote them, since it is this 'differently' which gives the texts their persuasive charm and beauty? Allusions to modern or contemporary philosophers and poets are intended not so much to accentuate present-day resonances of Saint Bernard's thought as to indicate the enduring features (the constants) which can be discovered in the works of great thinkers once they set out on the profound trail of their search for God. In spite of numerous differences of language and culture, at this depth one is always dealing with the same human being, with human greatness and misery, with the same God in his humanity and mercy, and with their reciprocal seeking by grace and liberty.

This synthesis is not an anthology, a *florilegium*. When I was choosing and presenting the various quotations, it seemed to me that I was rediscovering the craft I learned before entering the monastery. In those days I had to trace measured lines on cloth so that from it pieces could be cut which would be fitted together and sown into a garment. I wanted, therefore, to compose a work of art (or craftmanship) rather than a work of erudition. Saint Bernard, I believe, will not be among those who perhaps reproach me for this.

A recent review of Father Pacificus Delfgaauw's dissertation on Saint Bernard[1] points out that it is already out of date, but that 'attempts at synthesis are too rare to be neglected'. Here, then, is a new attempt.

I wish to thank Sisters Elizabeth Connor of Saint Romuald, Gaëtane de Briey of Clairefontaine, Marie-Bernard de Wilde of Soleilmont, and Gabriela Scanavino of Hinojo, and Brother Pierre-André Burton of Scourmont for their help in completing this work.

C. D.

---

[1] Pacificus Delfgaauw, *Saint Bernard, maître de l'Amour divin* (Paris: FAC-éditions, 1994).

Saint Bernard

His teaching instructs us and leads our steps on the pathway of peace.

Sermon for the feast of Saint Benedict 7

Some went ahead and prepared the way:
they were the ones who prepared the Lord's path in your hearts,
who lead and guide your steps on the pathway of peace.

Sermon for the Palm Sunday Procession 2.5

I

GOD AND HIS SPIRITUAL CREATURE SEEKING ONE ANOTHER

1. THE THEME 'SEEK-FIND'

CHRISTIANITY WAS BORN by love, under the sign of the covenant between the Creator and his spiritual creature. The mystery of Christ brings to realization and reveals within him an accord of two wills: divine and human. For Saint Bernard, the wisdom of love consists in this accord.

To those who desire it, a cistercian monastery offers a place where by means of a community, a rule, and an abbot, they may participate in this mystery of love in Christ. Little by little, imperceptibly, peace will fill their hearts.

When Saint Benedict asks monks to seek God 'truly', he means that they should concentrate all their attention on seeking him and devote their whole life to it. When, on the other hand, he portrays God seeking someone who takes this pursuit seriously to heart, he tells us it is because God wills to be loved. This mutual seeking by the Creator and his spiritual, loving, and rational creature forms the principal and constant object of Saint Bernard's teaching. He felt passionately about this throughout his life, and through all his works he retold this love story and marked the highpoints in this life of friendship. The ultimate goal of such agreement is peace, as we see in the benedictine Rule; but for Bernard this peace is the fruit of love, in the sense of being wisdom, the art of acquiring a taste for truth. The wisdom of love means specifically a creature's free acquiescence. In following his most profound desire, a human being accepts the Creator's offer and, by doing so, finds peace.

In our present attempt at a synthesis of the abbot of Clairvaux's cistercian monastic doctrine, we have chosen this mutual seeking as the guiding thread. It is presumptuous, of course, to propose a synthesis when dealing with a mind as unsystematic as Saint Bernard's. Did he not compare himself to a hound or a hunter, always ready to follow a new scent?[1] Like Pascal, he follows the order of the heart.

> Jesus Christ and Saint Paul followed the order of charity, not of the mind; they wanted to kindle our fervor, not to instruct us. Saint Augustine was the same. This order consists principally in developing each point and linking them all to the goal, so as to make it evident at all times.[2]

Christ our peace is the goal Saint Bernard constantly puts before us, and the way he points out to us is above all the doctrine of the image of God, that ineffaceable mark on the soul which, in spite of its disfigurement, holds out to us a divinely revealed assurance that we are capable of finding God. At the heart of this divine image, the love innate within us is the principal dynamic force in our search for God who is Love.

The soul's voice murmurs: *I have sought the One my heart loves* (Sg 3:1). On this verse of the *Song of Songs* Saint Bernard wrote ten sermons which summarize his entire message. For him, this song of love is the celebration of our spiritual search, its essential theme. First come five sermons (75–79) in which he comments on Christ's meeting with the Church; then five sermons (80–85) on the search by Christ and the soul. In a way, the last sermon (85) sums up love's

---

[1] Bernard of Clairvaux, SC 16.1 (SBOp 1:89–90). Saint Bernard also says in the same passage: 'For me it is not so much a matter of explaining words as touching hearts.'

[2] Blaise Pascal, *Pensées*, edited by Brunschvicg, n°283. [*Pensées. The Provincial Letters* (New York: Modern Library, 1941)].

adventure and its perfect fulfillment in a total union of spirits human and divine.

Of the many passages which refer to this theme of seeking God, two in particular stand out. The first, which dates from the end of Bernard's life, reveals one of his profound convictions:

> Seeking God is the supreme good. It is the first gift, and also the final stage of our progress. What value would life have if a person did not seek God? What limit can be set to this kind of seeking?[3]

The other text is found in one of his first treatises, where he marvels at the fact that no one can seek who has not already been found.[4] By this, Saint Bernard means what he often affirmed elsewhere: to seek God, we must first have been found by grace. Speaking to God, he says: 'You want to be found to be sought, to be sought to be found. And you can most certainly be sought and found, but no one can ever take the first step'. All seeking is, in reality, inspired by divine grace, because in this mutual love it is certain that God has loved us first, as Saint John tells us (1 Jn 4:19). Saint Bernard exclaimed: 'Seek the person you love, Lord, to make of that person someone who loves and seeks'.[5]

All the same, it is important to distinguish carefully the nature of this seeking and meeting. The divine love which precedes the soul's entire search is first and foremost the grace of redemption. It is part of the theological mystery of salvation. God set out in pursuit of the soul and acquired it at the price of his blood.[6] Whatever meaning Pascal gave in his *Mystery of Jesus* to 'You would not seek me if you had not already found me,' Paul Valéry was right to point out that, for Bernard—who coined this famous phrase—'the soul's search for God depends on God's search for the soul; you would

---

[3] Cf. SC 84.1 (SBOp 2:303). See also SC 84.5 (SBOp 2:305).

[4] Dil 7.22 (SBOp 3:137). See also: 'What a surprise to be sought by God, what a dignity to seek God', Adv 1.7 (SBOp 4:166).

[5] Asspt 4.2 (SBOp 5:245). 'He comes to seek Lazarus, to be sought and found by Lazarus.' See also And 2.5 (SBOp 5:437).

[6] SC 68.4 (SBOp 2:199).

not seek if you were left to yourself alone.'[7] Sometimes a verse from the psalms inspired Saint Bernard to develop an entire commentary. Verse 6 of Psalm 23—*This is the generation of those who seek the Lord*—prompts him to identify the generation of those who seek God as monks,[8] even if he does not explicitly say so. Seeking is possible only for Christians, who have been born again in baptism. Those who seek him further, after being found and saved, are those who receive the second baptism of monastic profession.[9] Saint Bernard could say then that the surest proof of having found God is to seek him.[10] In some way, a monk's progress will consist in the growing conviction that it is God who is seeking him and not he who is seeking God; that it is God who has found him and not he who has found God.

Because this seeking can be identified with love—which is desire in constant search of its object—in describing it Saint Bernard made use of the insights of the psychology of human love.[11] Even so, we must never lose sight of what he considers the theological foundation of the reciprocal seeking by God and the soul, by grace and liberty: the mystery of the redeeming Incarnation. In its initial thrust, seeking God is almost identical to the desire to love and to be loved. Saint Bernard tells us this almost as a confidence:

> Why should I be ashamed to admit that quite often, and especially at the beginning of my conversion, I experienced dryness and coldness of heart? My soul sought the one it was going to love, because it could not yet love someone it had not found; or, at least, it loved less than it wished, and wondered what it should do to love more. It would not have sought if it did not already love at least a little.[12]

---

7 Paul Valéry, *Variété. Oeuvres* I (Paris:Gallimard, 1957) 472.

8 *In labore messis* 3.4 (SBOp 5:224).

9 See Pre 17.54 (SBOp 3:288–289).

10 *In labore messis* 3.3–4 (SBOp 5:224–225), where an allusion is made also to second baptism.

11 'For us, in the meantime (*interim*), God has granted us to taste by faith and seek by desire', Ep 18.2 (SBOp 7:67).

12 SC 14.6 (SBOp 1:79–80). He mentioned to his novices the coldness of his heart: SC 63.6 (SBOp 2:164–165).

In this sermon he also speaks of his need for human friendship to lead him to God. In the passage just quoted we can see how closely interwoven are psychology and the theology of love. In addition, two degrees of seeking are already distinguished: one which has its source in the union with God common to all Christians, and another kind of seeking which urges the soul onward in the way of love. We will come back to these two degrees in Chapter IV.

So it is that a monk's life continues in the search for peace which, according to Saint Benedict, is almost identical to the search for God: 'Seek and strive after peace' (Ps 33:15). This was also to be the curriculum in the school of charity, where the principal teaching was to be the wisdom of love. The monk will be forever seeking this divine identity which, though partially lost, has been restored by grace. Never will he or she be allowed to stop advancing along this Way, which is the way of Truth and Life, because their fullness will always be at the heart of the monk's expectation and desire.

And someone who strays from this path will pray along with Saint Bernard: 'I have gone astray like a sheep; seek your servant' (Ps 118:176). Someone who prays this way, he continues, is not completely forsaken because she remembers being visited and sought by the Word. And yet, so great is the soul's lethargy that to have been sought just once is not enough. And it is not enough to will. To be sought a person needs grace; and no one will even ask for it who had not already been sought.[13]

Reciprocal love gives a particular tonality to a person's life. The same thing applies to the relationship between the soul and God. When Saint Bernard comments on this verse of the *Song of Songs*: *My beloved is mine and I am his* (2:16), he begins by saying that we should add 'He is attentive to me'.[14] And he continues: 'Starting from her personal experience, the soul understands God's ways and, in loving, does not doubt that it is loved. And rightly so, because God's love gives birth to the soul's love; taking it by surprise, his attention to the soul makes it fully attentive to him'.[15]

---

[13] Cf. SC 84.3 (SBOp 2:304).

[14] SC 67.9 (SBOp 2:194). '*Mihi intendit.*'

[15] SC 69.7 (SBOp 2:206)

In phenomenological terms, we would speak of the intentionality of monastic consciousness. But this conscious attention is always a response to God's attention to the soul.

> *Rise in the middle of the night* (Lam 2:19). You will find him near, waiting for you, but you will never arrive first. It would be foolhardy of you to believe that you can precede him or love him more; it is always he who loves more and first.[16]

This attention of consciousness, mind and heart is essential in a spirituality of love. The whole cistercian life, in both its contemplative and active dimensions, has in view maintaining this intentionality in time. Eternal peace is on the horizon in a period of testing, in time-proof eternity. But now, and right from the beginning of conversion, a personal relationship is established between God and the soul who are seeking one another. It develops progressively through increasingly sustained and ardent attention to the point that—according to Saint Bernard in this same passage—a really spiritual person has the impression that in God's eyes his or her soul alone exists, and God alone exists for the soul.[17] In this context, Saint Bernard speaks about the soul's transformation into the likeness of the Word. A monk's true life is interior. Our real personality is found there and nowhere else, and an interior life shines out in a person's whole external existence. The two go hand in hand.

2. EXPERIENCE, LIFE'S TEACHER

The role of experience is very important in cistercian teaching, just as it is in the whole monastic tradition. Saint Benedict's expression *experientia magistra*, in the first chapter of the *Rule*, means experience acquired in a monastery.[18] For Saint Bernard, the fundamental experience is the experience of love, that is to say, the profound and lasting agreement of the human will with the divine will

---

[16] SC 69.8 (SBOp 2:206).
[17] SC 69.7–8 (SBOp 2:206–207).
[18] *The Rule of Saint Benedict* 1.6. Lacking experience, the sarabaites remain without form.

which then penetrates, enlightens, vitalizes and transforms our whole being, our interior as well as exterior life. It is above all the search for God throughout our whole life, by all the different ways God may be sought: dissatisfaction with self and the world, desire, making progress or backsliding, presence or absence, sin and forgiveness, fear or neglect, anxiety or peace. It is first and foremost the experience of the search itself far more than an experience of God, unless we understand this increasingly popular expression as meaning the soul's awareness of being sought by God.

At the beginning of our conversion, there is the experience of the victory of faith, then of the daily struggle against the spirit of evil within ourselves.[19] So experience is like a notebook in which the motions of consciousness, desire for God and interior freedom are written down.[20] We have the impression of embracing Christ's two feet: judgement and mercy,[21] patience and goodness.[22] Experience will help us become aware of our progress, whether slow or rapid, in our journey towards God. It will give us inward confirmation of what we have been taught. Saint Bernard tells his monks that if they are very attentive in a personal way, they will recognize that what he is teaching them corresponds to their own experience.[23]

In his major treatises—those in which he describes the monk's progress—religious experience is usually presented not as something strictly contemplative or mystical, but as an awareness of progress in the journey towards God by the steps and the degrees of truth, freedom and love. By the progressive conformity of the human and divine wills, faith develops to the point of mystical union: it is the experience of a love which gradually penetrates the heart.[24]

Abbot Bernard is very unpretentious when what he teaches goes beyond the possibilities of experience. In a *Sermon for All Saints Day*, after speaking about the peace of the beatific vision, he adds that it surpasses all understanding and consequently everything he

[19] SC 1.9 (SBOp 1:6–7).
[20] SC 3.1 (SBOp 1:14).
[21] SC 6.9 (SBOp 1:30).
[22] SC 9.5 (SBOp 1:45).
[23] SC 21.4 (SBOp 1:124). Cf. SC 39.3 (SBOp 2:19).
[24] SC 67.8 (SBOp 2:193).

has just said about it, and that what no one has experienced, no one has a right to talk about.[25] About his own experience, he admits with simplicity: 'I know by my own experience that it is easier to give advice to others, even many others, than to govern oneself'.[26] Generally speaking, his teaching is sober and prudent. Recognizing that others more favored by grace may have subtler and more sublime experiences, he says, when he teaches in public he limits himself to what he has received from commonly accepted doctrine.[27] Later on, however, in the context of the Incarnation— the foolishness of God—, he says with greater assurance that every truly religious consciousness can experience this mystery (revealed to the Church), because every person who loves God wisely and passionately is a Bride. He continues:

> I myself will not hesitate to say in public what I have been granted to experience in this area, even if it appears to some people to be worthless and despicable. A spiritual person will not scorn me, whereas someone who is less spiritual will not understand me.[28]

When it comes to passing from the first step of truth to the second , that is, from humility and self-knowledge to compassion, the knowledge of others, Saint Bernard insists on the absolute necessity of experience, because no one can understand a hungry person without knowing by experience what it is to be hungry.[29] He then gives us an absolute example: the Word made flesh, God himself, who wanted to experience the human condition in order to know it, to love it and so to save it.[30]

For Saint Bernard, the place most conducive to spiritual experience was unquestionably the reading cloister at the times set aside for *lectio divina* during the course of a day of praise and work. Only when we compare the experiences described in Scripture to our

---

25 OS 4.3 (SBOp 5:357).
26 Ep 87.7 (SBOp 7:229).
27 SC 22.4 (SBOp 1:131).
28 SC 73.10 (SBOp 2:239).
29 Hum 3.6 (SBOp 3:21).
30 Hum 3.12 (SBOp 3:25).

own can we hope really to understand them. 'It is not erudition, but anointing, that teaches us; one reaches understanding not by some science, but in one's conscience.'[31]

The most beautiful example of Saint Bernard's teaching on the superiority of experience over the purely theoretical knowledge taught in the schools is found in his letter to the english academic, Henry Murdach, whom he invited to enter the monastery for the express purpose of understanding Scripture. We could go further and say that what characterizes the monastic approach to theology is this understanding of the text by the experience of what it means for personal conversion and salvation. To understand what Isaiah says about Christ in his prophecies, he says, we must begin to follow Christ even before we finish reading the text. To put what we read into practice, we need only live in a monastery with conviction. Saint Bernard tells us: 'Trust my experience. You will find more in the woods than in books. The trees and the rocks will teach you what you could not learn from professors'.[32]

The trees and the rocks symbolize the struggle of the monastic life. Yet the whole letter is full of very traditional expressions denoting the joys of spiritual experience.

In the search for God, going beyond the first way of seeking God to another, more spiritual, way will be possible (see Chapter IV). Once again, it is as a result of interior experience that a person becomes able to make this step forward.

> How would I not be moved to seek him further when I have already experienced his clemency and am assured of his peace? Brothers, to feel drawn in this way is to be sought by the Word; to be won over interiorly is to be found.[33]

---

[31] Conv 13.25 (SBOp 4:99–100). Later (Chapter II.5) we will describe the fundamental experience of conversion. See SC 36.5–6 (SBOp 2:7–8).

[32] Ep 106.1–2 (SBOp 7:265–267). Concerning this anointing which imparts spiritual meaning: 'The intellect can follow only where experience leads', SC 22.2 (SBOp 1:130). See also the opposition between *cognitio* and *comprehensio*: Csi V.27 (SBOp 3:490).

[33] SC 84.6–7 (SBOp 2:306). *Suaderi-persuaderi*: 'Bernard very frequently plays with prefixes. The new word is sometimes the equivalent of the preceding, but it always adds nuance, insistence or contrast'. J. Leclercq OSB, *Recueil d'études sur*

Saint Bernard made a practical distinction between faith and experience. A good illustration of this can also be found in a conversation about sensible devotional experiences between Bernard's disciple Aelred of Rievaulx and Aelred's novice.[34] Experience, in fact, can be deceptive. When there is doubt, faith alone decides. This is how the abbot of Clairvaux consoles his monks who have not experienced sensible graces in their prayer.[35] Similarly, when speaking about beginners in the monastic life, he uses a clever play on words to tell them that they are not foolish (*insipientes*) because they have already begun (*incipientes*) to seek wisdom. But how can he help them to understand Scripture if they have no experience of the spiritual meaning of what they are reading? Obviously, they cannot learn this from anyone else, because no one can know another person's heart. Let them believe what they read, therefore, because

> these are the words of the Lord himself, and no one is permitted not to believe them. Let them believe what they have not experienced themselves, so that one day they may acquire the fruit of experience as a reward for their faith'.[36]

No doubt experience has such an important place in Saint Bernard's spirituality because his teaching is completely founded on love. At the beginning of his *Sermons on the Song of Songs* he declares:

> Anointing alone teaches this kind of song, and experience alone learns it. Those who have had such an experience recognize themselves in it; those who have not had this experience burn with desire, not so much to know about it, but to experience it.[37]

---

saint Bernard et ses écrits IV (Rome: Edizioni di Storia e Litteratura, 1987) 61. See the same progress by experience in SC 79.3 (SBOp 2:273): *Transire-pertransire*.

[34] Aelred of Rievaulx, *Mirror of Charity* 2.17.41–52. CF 17 (Kalamazoo: Cistercian Publications, 1990) 192–200.

[35] Quad 5.5 (SBOp 4:374).

[36] SC 84.7 (SBOp 2:306).

[37] SC 1.11 (SBOp 1:7).

Towards the end of his commentary, he comes back to this again, repeating that in this song of love it is not the words which count but our feelings. Since it is Love who is speaking in this book from beginning to end, anyone who does not know what it is to love will read it in vain. It would be like reading Greek to someone who does not know the language. The language of love is understood only by a person who loves.[38] It is probably because this priority of love has not been understood clearly enough that experience in Saint Bernard's works has been variously interpreted.[39]

Brother Lode Van Hecke of Orval has skillfully shown in his excellent work that experience is important in Saint Bernard's doctrine because 'it is a doctrine of love,' in which one discovers 'how the believer's relationship with God evolves into union with God. The motive for anthropology's interest in love is both religious and theological, because God is love. Human love is a response to this primordial love. . . . Only the experience of loving can let us know what that means'.[40]

In his introduction to his student's thesis, Professor Antoine Vergote wrote, very much to the point: 'What is so admirable about Saint Bernard's mind is that his theological statements and philosophical concepts meet in a unity of life and thought, so that the ideas seem to spring from experience itself.'[41]

---

[38] SC 79.1 (SBOp 2:272–273).

[39] Feruccio Gastadelli has assembled on one page various studies on this theme of experience in Saint Bernard. 'Teologia monastica, teologia scolastica e lectio divina,' in *La dottrina della vita spirituale nelle opere di San Bernardo di Clairvaux* (Rome:1991) 62. He differs from Jean Mouroux, whose interpretation seems to him to be too narrow in refusing the psychological aspect (J. Mouroux, 'The criteria of spiritual experience according to the Sermons on the *Song of Songs*,' *Cistercian Studies*, 2 (Berryville 1962) 21–36. Gastadelli prefers Dom J. Leclercq's more monastic interpretation in 'Saint Bernard et l'expérience chrétienne,' *La Vie Spirituelle* 117 (1967) 182–198, and Charles Dumont OCSO, 'Experience in the cistercian discipline,' CSQ 10 (1975) 135–138. We should add E. Carlota Rave (Argentina): 'Il Ruola dell'esperienza nella teologia di S. Bernardo,' *Lateranum* 50 (1984) 160–169. See the review in the Bulletin de spiritualité monastique, Coll (1986), n°211.

[40] Lode Van Hecke OCSO, *Le désir dans l'expérience religieuse. Relecture de saint Bernard.* (Paris; Cerf, 1990) 195.

[41] Ibid., 13.

Who could express it better? Saint Bernard himself is the best example of what he teaches. Let us trust his experience, since he has expressed it so clearly and with such burning conviction.

3. THE UNION OF GRACE AND FREEDOM

The mutual seeking of the Creator and his spiritual creature is concretely identical to the search for an ever closer and more stable union between the grace that is offered and its acceptance by free human consent. And so, for Saint Bernard, the symbol of the couple in the *Song of Songs* expresses the whole story of salvation, which is a love story. It is from this point of view that he approaches the problem of grace and free choice, which can be solved in no other way. Yet this solution is situated on the higher plain of spiritual knowledge, close to evangelical purity of heart.[42] He does, nevertheless, describe this inseparable unity with a high degree of precision. Grace, he says, acts together with free choice. Only in the beginning does grace precede, then it accompanies choice, so that the action of the two is always simultaneous and undivided. They form a kind of mixture (*mixtim*) in which grace does everything and freedom equally does everything.[43] This intimate union of grace and freedom is the very foundation of Saint Bernard's whole spirituality of charity. 'What then is the role of free choice if grace does everything?' he asks. The answer he gives has little value in the logical order, but it is the only real answer in the existential order: 'it is saved'. Outside their inter-relationship, they both vanish: 'Take away free choice and there is nothing left to save; take away grace, there is nothing left which saves'. How does freedom work in cooperation with grace? It consents, and for freedom, to consent is to be saved.[44] We can see that the only thing in view here is the

---

[42] John Cassian, *Conference* 13.18: 'How can it be that God accomplishes everything in us and at the same time everything is attributed to our free choice? This is what the sense and reason of human beings are powerless to understand fully'. SCh 54 (Paris: Cerf, 1958) 181. [*The Conferences*, translated by Boniface Ramsey op, Ancient Christian Writers Series 57 (Mahwah, N.J.: Paulist Press, 1997)].
[43] Gra 14.47 (SBOp 3:199–200).
[44] Gra 1.2 (SBOp 3:166–167).

work of salvation. A monk's whole life lies in consent, because it is the very form which his agreement with the divine will takes. This will also be the form of a monk's whole interior and exterior life, of his or her whole life.

Free choice, however, is not freedom, still less the freedom of God's children. Although, by its nature, free choice can never be forced, *freedom* has been impaired, damaged and fettered by sin and its own weakness. Freedom needs to be freed: liberation occurs at every step as a soul progresses in its search for its original dignity as the image of God.

How did the human creature lose the dignity of being free, and of knowing and loving God without error or flaw? In Chapter Two of his treatise *On Loving God*, Saint Bernard has given us a description of the alienation which constitutes the whole drama of human existence. It is significant that, for Saint Bernard, freedom itself provoked the fall. For him, the spiritual creature's dignity resides in its freedom. But instead of recognizing that this freedom was received from the Creator and remains bound to him, the creature attributed it to itself. There was a veritable retort, a refusal. By refusing the relationship of dependence, by this radical autonomy, the soul lost its knowledge of God and can no longer love the One whom it now does not know.[45] The dignity of the human creature could come only from the One who created it in his own image. By freely turning away from the Creator, the soul lost, if not the image, at least the likeness of divine freedom; it strayed from grace. The words Saint Bernard uses to conclude this concise explanation of the fall are very clear:

> It is difficult, even impossible, for someone relying on his or her own strength or on the strength of personal free choice to attribute entirely to God's kindness everything received from him, and not to turn it all back to self-will, so as to keep it for self as though it were one's personal property. It is written: *All seek their own interests* (Ph 2:21).[46]

---

[45] Dil 2.2–5 (SBOp 3:121–123).
[46] Dil 2.6 (SBOp 3:124).

The monk's whole struggle at renunciation of self-will is situated in this perspective: to make it will what God wills (*voluntas
communis*).

An attitude of pride is contrary to grace and makes the soul lose
its vigor;[47] then it has no God. Only the contrasting attitude will
restore its freedom, truth and love. In Chapters II and III, we will
follow in order freedom, truth and love, and there we will see how
Saint Bernard presents to us the restoration of the soul to its beauty
as the image of God.

The most luminous and intense spiritual experience requires
free consent to the divine will. 'Seek the Word to whom you can
consent; it is he who will give you the grace to consent.'[48]

[47] SC 54.10 (SBOp 2:109).
[48] SC 85.1 (SBOp 2:308).

II

THE CONDITION OF THE DIVINE SPIRIT AND THE HUMAN SPIRIT IN SEARCH OF ONE ANOTHER

1. IMAGE AND UNLIKENESS. ESTRANGEMENT AND RETURN

WHEN TWO PEOPLE love and seek one another, they become spontaneously aware of their situation relative to one another. For Saint Bernard, God's love for his spiritual creature is primordial, immense, and gratuitous.[1] Correspondingly, there exists in every human consciousness a sense of innate justice which calls it to love with all its heart the One to whom it owes everything.[2] The possibility of an encounter between these two loves is founded essentially on the likeness that exists between the Creator and his spiritual creature. We can never overestimate the importance of 'the doctrine of the image' to Saint Bernard's monastic teaching. The creation of the human being in God's image, in the first chapter of *Genesis*, was a revelation to him, and it is not too much to say that his whole ascetical and mystical teaching—and for him the two are the same—is based on the way he developed an anthropology totally dependent on this primordial truth. It can be summed up as follows: created in the image and likeness of divine Being, the human

---

[1] Dil 1.1 (SBOp 3:120).
[2] Dil 2.6 (SBOp 3:124).

creature has partially lost the likeness but can recover it, because human beings cannot lose their true nature: creatures made in the image of God. We have retained a radical, a deep-rooted, capacity which cannot be lost; a capacity 'to be like God', but now it depends on him. Having this capacity for God[3] because it is made in his image, the soul can regain by love its original capacity for God who is Love. An affinity exists between God and the soul. The metaphor of the image was charged with meaning in ancient cultures, but today it says less to us. In Antiquity and the Middle Ages, 'image' implied a dynamic and living relationship of causality, not only exemplary but also efficient and formal. To turn away from one's prototype is, by the very act of doing so, to fall into unlikeness. The spiritual capacity to resemble, to be in conformity with (a very important term in Saint Bernard), resides in the original and inalienable imprint of divine Being on the human soul. Yet the image can be disfigured, it can become dis-similar, and this is what happened because of sin at the origin of the human race. Borrowing an expression from greek philosophy used by Saint Augustine, Saint Bernard speaks of 'the region of unlikeness', which was often applied to the gospel story of the prodigal son. It simply provides a way of situating beings according to the greater or lesser distance there is between them, the distance signifying their greater or lesser qualitative, moral or spiritual likeness. In Platonism, especially Plotinus' Neo-platonism, the further away beings are from the One, the Beautiful, or the Good—that is, from God—and the closer they are to matter and evil, the more unlike God they are.[4]

In spite of the great variety of ways in which he applied this

---

[3] '*Capax Dei*': SC 27.10 (SBOp 1:189); Ded 2.2 (SBOp 5:376). We could mention here that in the context of these two quotations, this capacity of the soul is already linked to fraternal charity.

[4] Saint Augustine, *Confessions* VII.10.16; available in English in the Fathers of the Church series, volume 21 (Washington, D.C.: Catholic University of America Press, 1953). Cf. *The City of God* IX.17, where Augustine quotes Plotinus' *Enneads* I.6.8.: 'We must fly to our beloved fatherland . . . But how? . . . Become like God.' And he comments: 'If, then, the nearer one is to God the more like him one is, the only way to be far from God is to be unlike him.' See also the translation in the Fathers of the Church 14 (Washington, D.C.: Catholic University of America Press, 1952)

doctrine of the image—it has even been said that there are *doctrines* of the image in Saint Bernard's works—the abbot of Clairvaux has a perfectly coherent and unified underlying teaching'.[5]

The ancient adage 'like seeks like' expresses a natural phenomenon, says Saint Bernard,[6] and he rejoices in the confidence which likeness to God gives him, because even though God's loftiness keeps us at a distance from him, our likeness to him brings us still closer to him: what would a soul not dare who knows that it originated so close to and so like God?[7]

But this beautiful image of God which is the spiritual creature became damaged in the very beginning and has become scarcely recognizable; it has become disfigured. The soul's vigor, due entirely to its reason, will, and memory, is diminished and weakened. Reason can no longer see clearly, will languishes, and memory is full of unpleasant remembrances.[8] No longer loving its Creator spontaneously because of its desire to claim its freedom for itself, the soul no longer really knows God; but by this very fact, it does not know itself either. It has forgotten its own identity. In this alien region of unlikeness, the soul has also lost awareness of its dignity. It has exacerbated its fallen condition even more by moral wretchedness and let itself sink to the level of animals, even though God's imprint remains like an indelible stamp on it.[9]

The conscience retains a keen awareness of what it is without being able to be it, and because of this it experiences profound uneasiness. Saint Bernard himself felt this acutely and often described it. The clash between these two evident facts—our likeness and unlikeness—is painful, and the spirit which experiences extremes of one or the other will suffer from it even more. It will find itself

---

[5] M. Standaert ocso, 'La doctrine de l'image chez Saint Bernard', *Ephemerides theologicae Lovanienses* 23 (1947) 70–129, esp. 121: 'Nevertheless, *in globo*, this as a whole can rightly be called a "doctrine of the image", the essential component of which can be reduced to the following: a human being is, and always will be, capable of attaining God and becoming like him.'

[6] SC 82.7 (SBOp 2:297).

[7] SC 83.1 (SBOp 2:298–299).

[8] Conv 6.11 (SBOp 4:84–85).

[9] Among approximately twenty quotations on the '*regio dissimilitudinis*', let us note Div 42.2–3 (SBOp 6/1:255–258) and SC 36.5 (SBOp 2.7).

caught between hope and despair.[10] When opposites come close together, the difference between them is sharply obvious, as when white and black are put side by side.[11]

> What a combination of unlike things! If you look at the perversity in yourself, and then at all the good there may be, you have the impression that you must be a miracle to have such ill-matched realities in yourself at the same time.[12]

It is this mixture, this confusion and disorder, which are unbearable. Lack of interior harmony appeared evident to Saint Bernard in the loss of our original simplicity, now inevitably mixed with duplicity, and in the loss of the privilege of immortality, combined henceforth with inescapable death.[13] But it is in the freedom which is now enslaved that Saint Bernard found the most flagrant change, because he believed that by freedom a human being most resembles God. It is also there, in the frustrating sense of a fettered freedom, that we will feel most keenly the conflict between what we are and what we are unable fully to be.[14]

The life of a monk therefore offers a way of return to God, a pathway of conversion. Monastic profession is the sacred sign of this conversion. According to tradition it is a 'second baptism'. When Saint Bernard speaks about this explicitly, he says that the monastic life is called this because of its radical renunciation of the world and the excellence of the spiritual life it fosters, but most especially (*immo*) because it 'reforms the divine image in the human being, configuring the monk to Christ as baptism does'.[15] Speaking elsewhere about this 'second baptism of conversion', he puts the accent on the renunciation of the self-will which led the first human creature to break the original covenant and brought on this loss of freedom.[16] Restoration of the divine image in us will depend

---

10 SC 82.7 (SBOp 2:297).
11 QH 8.9 (SBOp 4:432). Cf. Ep 78.5 (SBOp 7:204).
12 Ded 5.7 (SBOp 5:393).
13 SC 82.3–4 (SBOp 2:293–294).
14 SC 82.5 (SBOp 2:295–296).
15 Pre 17.54 (SBOp 3:289).
16 Div 11.3 (SBOp 6/1:1:126).

essentially on the renunciation of a kind of freedom which has lost its meaning, because it has been cut off from its covenant of love with infinite freedom.

The road back to God through obedience will be long and hard. While we exist in time, liberation from the spirit of slavery can only be progressive. At the beginning, Saint Bernard says, our conscience, our consciousness, oscillates between fear and trust, and the contrast increases its torment. Little by little, however, apprehension diminishes, grace wins out, and a reborn confidence increases until charity finally casts out all fear and the soul falls asleep peacefully in hope.[17]

This is the way of the Gospel and also of the restoration of the covenant: from slavery to the freedom of being children of God, and from fear to peace. The wisdom of love consists in finding the unity, beauty, and interior peace of our being by letting our will be in agreement with God's will. It is, in short, conversion of the heart to God's heart.

2. THE UNFORTUNATE PLIGHT OF FREEDOM, TRUTH AND LOVE

One of the monk's most important occupations, according to Saint Bernard, is consideration. He even identifies it with the essential attitude of all religious life: piety. In the treatise he devoted to *Consideration*, he wrote to Eugene III, once one of his monks at Clairvaux, that consideration is absolutely necessary and that ideally it ought to be given absolute preference over every other occupation.[18] A life without consideration would be a life wasted.[19] Consideration consists in reflecting intelligently in God's sight on our own existence and on the movements of our heart. It is even a way of adoring and worshiping God. Among the advantages of practising it is purification of the mind, because consideration purifies its source. Then follow control of our affective emotions and discernment in judging all our interior or exterior activities.

---

[17] SC 51.9 (SBOp 2:88–89).
[18] Csi I.7.8 (SBOp 3:403).
[19] Csi I.8.11 (SBOp 3:407).

At this point, as we undertake a study of Saint Bernard's spiritual anthropology, it is useful for us to recall the psychological context within which he reflected on this subject. Our emotional life is based on four principal passions: fear and sadness, joy and love. Saint Bernard described them all, showing how they can be orientated towards holiness and life of the spirit.[20] Love, he clearly states, is the most important of these passions of the soul. Then he immediately gives the principle behind the 'natural' ordering of the passions, saying that it is only right that what is natural should be used in the service of nature's Creator, and that this is why we ought to love God.[21]

Nature has become disordered, however, and even though this disorder is most visible in the sphere of love—as he shows it is—the sad plight of the spiritual creature is experienced at the same time in two other spheres of consciousness: freedom and truth. We could call it, as the existentialists do, a situation of unescapable unhappiness. While being accomplices with a kind of duplicity and willing slaves, we still pine for our primordial freedom. In a certain way this is the voice of the image, buried deep within us but still intact. The spirit seeks its truth over and above the deviations of pride's blinding error. Lastly, love—which quickens the two other aspects of the search— desires the object which will fulfill its expectations by assuaging its anxiety and dissatisfaction.

To sum up the situation: even though freedom is its own prisoner, even though truth has been corrupted, and even though love has gone astray, the divine image remains intact, alive, dynamic and active in these three basic desires of all existence. This foundation which has remained intact and incorruptible, Saint Bernard calls 'nature's good'. In his theological vocabulary, nature signifies a being as it exists at birth (*nascitur*), as it has come from God's hands, having perfect likeness to him. This nature, which has remained basically good but has deteriorated, needs grace in order to recover its original beauty. By its freedom it has retained a kind of innate desire to respond to grace. Conversion will consist in consenting to grace,

---

20 Div 50.2–3 (SBO 6/1:271–272).
21 Dil 8.23 (SBOp 3:138).

which is also somehow God's response to freedom's desire. Like two persons who love one another, grace and freedom yearn to be united. Perversity lies in refusing what nature has been inarticulately waiting for.

Disfigurement of the divine image, therefore, is first of all a state of interior division and conflict. This is no doubt why peace—which for Saint Bernard is the goal of the monastic life—is presented in the form of simplicity and unity. Simplicity is the divine attribute which most intrigues him. [22]

Every other kind of unity is an image of this surpassingly-simple unity of God. But it is especially in the sphere of moral life that duplicity makes itself felt. Given his passionate character, the abbot of Clairvaux was particularly sensitive to the radical ambiguity and falseness which exist within the human peson. [23]

It has very correctly been pointed out that in Saint Bernard's work there is 'what can be called the principle of order, or the principle of ordering, that is to say, a fundamental tendency to consider everything, including the human being and the spiritual life, in the perspective of an order which exists or ought to be established'. [24] He often connected the achievement of human unity with order or ordering. And if he spoke a great deal about order and harmony, this was perhaps simply a reaction to disorder, which made him suffer more than it did other people. Like anyone who has a passionate nature, he very keenly felt the ups and downs of his emotive moods and sought a way to reduce the gap between exaltation and despondency. [25] These 'vicissitudes' are linked to time and no one can escape from them in this life. He liked to

---

[22] Csi V.7.15–17 (SBOp 3:479–481).

[23] Saint Bernard is classified as a 'passionate' type in Le Senne's characterology. Pascal, the other great 'passionate', also felt the ambiguity of the human condition keenly : 'This duplicity of the human being is so visible that there are some people who have thought we have two souls. A single simple subject has appeared to them to be incapable of such wide and sudden variations ranging from excessive presumption to horrible dejection', *Pensées* 417. (Brunschvicq's edition).

[24] M. Standaert OCSO, 'Le principe d'ordination dans la théologie de saint Bernard', Coll 8 (1946) 178–216, here p. 178.

[25] When Bernard did not succeed, he felt it very keenly, as one can see when his cousin Robert left Clairvaux (Ep 1 [SBOp 7:1–11] and after the second Crusade

quote from the *Book of Wisdom* the verse which says that *everything has been established with number, weight and measure* (11:20); it was his way of expressing how he longed to transcend this order, outside time.

> O Jerusalem . . . in you there no longer subsist either weight or measure, but only overflowing abundance. No longer do you even have knowledge of number, because in you everyone participates together in him who is Being itself, and who subsists in himself. When will I, who am still delivered up to the vicissitudes of chance and number, come to this unique city which is the object of all my desire?[26]

Throughout Saint Bernard's works we find this eschatological tension, and it gives a definite tone to his entire monastic spirituality:

> Jerusalem, vision of peace! Yes, truly a vision, but a far-off vision, never possessed here, because the Lord has placed it at the end, and not at the beginning or midway. If you do not have peace, and still more, since you cannot have it perfectly in this world, at least look towards it, have it in view, desire it. Let your eyes, your intention and all your activity be directed towards this peace which surpasses all sentiments.[27]

But love has already turned all order and measure upside down. Saint Bernard points this out in discussing the question which the bride abruptly puts to the guardians of the city: *'Have you seen the one my heart loves?'* (Sg 3.3). 'What violent, devouring, impetuous love! . . . it makes no distinction of rank, it defies customs, it knows no measure.'[28] This is the disconcerting wisdom of love because, still in time, it is already in eternity.[29]

(Csi II.1.1–4 [SBOp 3:410–413]). Chapter 12 of Book II of *On Consideration* is entitled: 'How we should conduct ourselves in success or failure' (SBOp 3:429).

[26] Sept 1.3 (SBOp 4:347).

[27] V Nat 2.1 (SBOp 4:204).

[28] SC 79.1 (SBOp 2:272).

[29] See Charles Dumont OCSO, 'L'action contemplative, le temps dans l'éternité d'après saint Bernard', Coll 54 (1992) 269–283. Published also in *Une éducation du cœur*, Pain de Cîteaux 10, 3rd Series (Oka: Editions Abbaye-Notre-Dame-du-

3. ENSLAVED FREEDOM

Let us go back now to the first of the three great themes of Saint Bernard's spiritual anthropology: freedom. As we saw when we were commenting on the end of Chapter II of the treatise *On Loving God,*[30] it is freedom which is responsible for the loss of our relationship of love and knowledge with God. As soon as freedom chose to be autonomous and independent by separating itself from the One whose image it is, it became unrecognizable. Free choice in itself is not liable to the least impairment. It can be defined negatively as the inability of undergoing any determining constraint. It is inalienable and eternal.[31] So the image of God resides above all in the will, which Saint Bernard identifies most often with freedom. Such freedom cannot, however, be reduced to free choice, the use of which is impeded by slavery to sin as well as by the limits of our human condition. Liberation is imperative, and this is the whole theme of the treatise *On Grace and Free Choice.*[32] In Chapter IV of this treatise we see that conversion and holiness consist essentially in liberation from slavery. Its goal is to restore our freedom as children of God. This comes about slowly and imperceptibly, as do God's kingdom and the agreement of our will with his.[33] In the abbot of Clairvaux's teaching, it is important for us to notice this progressive and unobservable conversion which culminates in union with God. Slow and gradual, conversion is very often identified with the whole aggregation of monastic observances which constitute the school of charity, because charity consists particularly in free and persevering

---

Lac, 1996) 57–77. [English translation: 'Contemplative action: Time in Eternity according to Saint Bernard', CSQ 28 (1993) 145–159)].

[30] Dil 2.6 (SBOp 3:123–124). See above, Chapter I.3, p. 31.

[31] 'It is because free choice is the image of an immutable and eternal God that it cannot be subject to anything which would impede or lessen it, and that it is inalienable', L. Van Hecke OCSO, *Le désir dans l'expérience religieuse*, 105–106.

[32] Sr Françoise Callerot's fine introduction to this treatise, published in the Sources chrétiennes series, n⁰ 393 (Paris: Cerf, 1993) 169–227, could profitably be read.

[33] Gra 4.12 and 14.49 (SBOp 3:174–175 and 202). Also, Dil 15.39 (SBOp 3:153). The latin expression is *paulatim sensimque*: little by little and gradually.

acquiescence to God's will.[34] The affections imperceptibly begin to be healed and become spiritual love. Saint Bernard well expresses monastic life's effectiveness in healing freedom. The context shows that he meant the practices of claustral discipline by which—and this is utterly certain—*our interior being is renewed from day to day* (2 Cor 4:16). He mentions three areas in which this renewal is brought about: intention (a healthy mind), sentiments (the conversion of affectivity) and memory[35] (see below, Pacified memory, Chapter VI.2).

Is this not the whole curriculum for the restoration of God's image in the new creature? Spiritual healing is founded on the mysteriously inseparable accord between grace and willed consent. What does free choice do? It is saved, but never without its consent. It seems indeed that free choice is at the source of both will (free) and reason (choice).[36] Reason, therefore, cannot determine the will. Freedom is a central theme in bernardine spirituality. It is likewise at the heart of the existential philosophical reflection which has so influenced contemporary thought. But while it is interesting to note these points of contact, it is still more important to understand Saint Bernard's thought clearly. We can read his definitions in Chapter II of *On Grace and Free Choice* and his description in Chapter VI of how grace works in perfecting the will to the point of true wisdom—which will be attained when to free choice will be joined facility in choosing the good and the already- tasted joy of abiding in good. Free choice lies, not in the freedom to choose between good and evil, but in the choice of one or the other. It is the faculty of choosing without the slightest constraint. The wisdom of the world and God's wisdom can both have a taste. In Sartre's existentialism there is the taste for choosing

---

[34] 'God will be present to anyone who seeks him, to the soul who hopes in him . . . This arouses the will's desire not only to see the place where he dwells, but gradually to enter it (*paulatim*)' (Conv 12.24 (SBOp 4:98). Likewise, a person does not arrive at the summit all at once, but gradually (*gradatim*), and does not become an evil person all at once, but little by little (*paulatim*). Hum 9.26 (SBOp 3:36).

[35] '*Sensim in amorem spiritus convalescit*', Gra 14.49 (SBOp 3:202).

[36] Gra 3.6 (SBOp 3:170).

freely. God's wisdom has another taste: the taste for a love that is infinitely free.

4. FALSIFIED TRUTH

Truth became falsified when the spiritual creature no longer agreed to attribute to its Creator its dignity as a free being. This act of independence put us into a state of falsehood.[37] Created freedom turned in on itself and blinded itself by its autonomy and, by doing so, it lost all desire to seek God in order to love him. Claiming to be somehow absolute and free, just like God, it finds itself swept into a void by its pretentiousness. It wants to choose for itself but it no longer knows what it wants, because being free means, not being able to do anything at all, but knowing what one ought to love and why. Pretending to be everything, all by itself, the human being is completely alone. Without reference to a transcendent being, freedom is condemned to despair. To borrow Sartre's expression, it has become pointless.

In the first part of his treatise *On the Steps of Humility and Pride*, Saint Bernard proposes three steps of truth which are at the same time an analysis of the falsehood pride has introduced into the human heart. The ways in which pride manifests itself are described in the second part of the treatise where, in twelve steps which contrast with Saint Benedict's steps of humility, he gives a phenomenological description of a humble monk. In the first part of his treatise, however, we find a spiritual theology of conversion, that is, a rediscovery of primaeval truth over and above radical falsehood. The three steps of truth are:

> truth about oneself (humility),
> truth about others (compassion) and
> truth in itself (contemplation).

The misappropriation of freedom by the self was due to an error of the intelligence. The mind lost the correct perception of reality. Now it must return to itself; it must leave this state of

---

[37] Dil 2.6 (SBOp 3:124). We commented on this in Chapter I.3.

ignorance and falsehood. This is the first step: accurate knowledge of self, with no harbored illusions. Only on this foundation of the clear knowledge of self can a real and deep knowledge of others be built. Then, from the charity which grows by practising these first two steps of truth, the soul will be able to attain knowledge of Truth—and this is divine contemplation, this is Christ.[38] The three truths, which form in fact one single truth, and the links between them, represent one of the first major intuitions in Saint Bernard's spirituality. Throughout his works this vision was to underlie various aspects of his teaching and would remain the foundation-stone of the cistercian school of charity. Humility is already true love of self, and the compassion which arises almost spontaneously from it is the very form of the communal charity in which divine love grows. Love of truth becomes the truth of love.[39]

Truth here does not mean rational truth (being logical), nor is it moral truth (not telling a lie); instead, it is existential or sapiential truth. In this sense, only Christ is Truth, because he is the Way and the Life.[40] By comparison with this absolute Truth, any reflection on self can lead only to a lowering of our notion of our own self-importance. We need to understand clearly that humility is, above all, the correction of an error of judgment. In defining it, Saint Bernard says that by the virtue of humility knowledge of reality deflates puffed-up pride.[41]

When we consider how striking and preponderant the affective character of Saint Bernard's doctrine is, it may astonish us to see him base his whole spirituality on the search for truth. For him, however, intelligence is always permeated with love. He does, of course, make a distinction between two kinds of humility—depending on whether they come from the bitterness of truth or the sweetness

---

[38] Hum 3.6 (SBOp 3:20–21). '*Veritas in sui natura*', the Truth in its nature; following the context, it is Christ who is meant.

[39] SC 50.6 (SBOp 2:81).

[40] Hum 1.1 (SBOp 3:16–17).

[41] Hum 1.2 (SBOp 3:17). The word '*vilescit*' should not be translated 'debase oneself'. Humility is the virtue which heals pride, the pride which alienates a person from God. See the definitions of pride and humility in Ep 42.19 (SBOp 7:115).

of love—but he does this only to bring them together afterwards. Thus he makes virtue out of necessity, because there is no virtue that is not voluntary and free, and therefore loving.[42]

For a better grasp of the meaning of this truth—love theme in Saint Bernard's work, let us look at a crucial passage of *Sermon 77 on the Song of Songs*. In this text Bernard once again explains his doctrine of the image by commenting on the verse of the *Song of Songs* about the bride seeking the Beloved, that is, the soul seeking Truth. The guards who come to meet her are sent by God to confirm her in complete certainty of truth. But, he says, it is precisely an authentic spiritual love which will make us love truth.

> I am endowed with reason. I have a capacity for truth, but it would be better if I did not if I lack love of truth. The love of truth is the very root of intelligence. I am in danger if I do not have it. There is no doubt that in this love of truth, which makes me superior to all other living beings, the distinctive sign of the divine image shines forth eminently'.[43]

Love and knowledge are more interdependent than some texts would lead us to believe. Saint Bernard says, for example, that without knowledge of truth a soul is dead, whereas as long as it is without love it lacks sensitivity. Truth is the life of the soul and charity is its sensitivity.[44]

Saint Bernard applied each of the three steps of truth to one of the Persons of the Trinity. In the first step of truth, Christ comes to join himself to human reason like a teacher, and from this union is born humility. In the second step, the Holy Spirit joins himself to the will like a friend, and from this union is born compassion. Finally, in the third step, the Father embraces us like sons, and this is contemplation.[45] So contemplation is presented as a normal development of the first two steps of knowledge, that is, knowledge

---

[42] SC 42.6–8 (SBOp 2:36–38). See the excellent article by J.-L. Chrétien, 'L'humilité chez saint Bernard', *Communio* 10 (1985) 112–127.

[43] SC 77.5 (SBOp 2:264).

[44] Div 10.1 (SBOp 6/1:121).

[45] Hum 7.20–21 (SBOp 3:31–33).

of self and of others, but by this opening of the mind the heart also expands and so experiences the truth which is love.

Saint Bernard teaches the same doctrine about the three steps of truth again when dealing with the link between three of the beatitudes: the meek who are humble, the merciful who practise fraternal compassion, and the pure of heart who, after their consciousness has been purified from pride and self–centeredness, see God in contemplation.[46]

Commenting on the verse of the *Song of Songs*: *Who is she who rises like the first break of dawn, beautiful as the moon, choice as the sun, formidable as an army in battle rank?* (6:10), Saint Bernard describes the monastic life as entirely ordered to charity. The dawn at night's end is humility, the beginning of conversion. He specifically mentions that light is dawning because the superstructure of the virtues rises upon humility as its proper foundation.

The moon, which represents the beauty of personal and communal ascesis, receives its light from the sun of charity. The army in its battle line is ordered love, which alone gives the other virtues strength. At the same time it is discernment, the mother of virtues.[47] The dawn of humility breaks in the morning of each of a monk's days until the very last.

5. SELF-KNOWLEDGE, THE BEGINNING OF CONVERSION

True knowledge consists in recognizing that our dignity as free beings is a gift from our Creator. Our ignorance of the created being's dependence which results from this reality has made us forget God. This, in turn, brought about our ruination. It is through knowledge that we will be able to return to God, because clear knowledge of our true being will make us look to a Saviour for help. This will be conversion.

In his long commentary on the Canticle verse: *If you do not know yourself, O loveliest of women, go and follow your flock* (1:8), Saint Bernard has given us a little treatise on conversion. We

---

[46] Hum 3.6 (SBOp 3:20).
[47] Div 91.4 (SBOp 6/1:343).

find it in Sermons 34–39. Sermon 36 is the best-known, because there he speaks about scholastic knowledge, that taught in schools and universities, to which he had strong objections. One passage of this sermon in particular, witty and clever, usually attracts attention—unfortunately—because readers find it either amusing or scandalous. But when this diatribe is taken in the entire context of what he is talking about, we can see that he is protesting against only the kind of knowledge which leads nowhere and gives rise to vanity, a type not at all suitable for monks. Furthermore, he says clearly that the Church will always need learned people and that all knowledge is good as long as it is subordinate to truth. But the abbot of Clairvaux was speaking to monks, and the monks' primary concern is salvation. Life is short and we must be wise with moderation, that is to say, we must *work out our salvation in fear and trembling* (Ph 2:12). The knowledge we must acquire is to choose what we need to know, in the order and to the degree we need to know it, like a sick person taking medicine.[48]

All knowledge is search for truth. What truth does the monk seek, if not the truth of God's image in oneself? Saint Bernard was keen to get to the true meaning of the words God speaks to the soul: *If you do not know yourself, depart* (Sg 1:8). Is the principal ignorance not ignorance of self? Is self-knowledge not the most important knowledge for a monk? This is how the process of conversion unfolds: from knowledge of self to knowledge of God.

First of all, we must know ourselves, because before all else we exist for ourselves.[49] This is also the most useful, because realistic knowledge of what we are leads to humility, the foundation of all spiritual conversion. When the conscience looks itself honestly in the face, it cannot help recognizing that it is in 'the region of unlikeness', unhappy and far from the perfection of its exemplary cause. Conscience is overwhelmed by the realization of the distance between what it knows it can be and what it actually is, but rather than keep its eyes fixed on its own misery it turns to prayer. And Saint Bernard says over and over again that it turns (*convertetur*) to

---

[48] SC 36.2 (SBOp 2:5).
[49] SC 36.5 (SBOp 2:7). Cf. Csi II.3.6 (SBOp 3:414).

the Lord and cries out to him: *Heal my soul for I have sinned* (Ps 40:5). Once turned (*conversa*) to the Lord in this way, conscience will be freed, succored, and saved.[50] In this we observe an action which is the exact antithesis of that of a soul which has turned its free will in on itself, willfully ignoring its condition as a finite and dependent being.[51]

At this crucial moment, the way a person reacts is decisive. As Saint Bernard says:

> For me, as long as I look at myself my eyes remain sad, but if I lift up my head and fix my eyes on divine mercy, the bitterness of seeing myself in misery is immediately tempered by the joy of seeing God. Then I say to him: *When my soul is downcast within me, I think of you* (Ps 41:7). To experience that God is good and answers our prayer is not a paltry thing! By such an experience, and by following this path, we reach salutary knowledge of God . . . So the human person begins by seeing its need and cries out to the Lord, and he will answer: *I will rescue you and you will honor me* (Ps 49.15). So it is that knowledge of self is a step towards knowledge of God. With his image renewed in you, he will make himself visible to you. Contemplating the glory of the Lord with confidence, you will be transformed with ever-increasing brightness into this same image that you reflect. This is the work of the Lord's Spirit (Cf. 2 Co 3:18).[52]

In another passage where he summarizes what conversion means to a monk, he comments on the same psalm verse, *When my soul is downcast within me, I think of you* (Ps 41:7), and gives us an extremely clear, concise statement about the spirit of our vocation.

> Our whole spiritual life can be summed up in this twofold mental attitude: looking at ourselves should fill us with uneasiness and salutary sadness; looking to God will give us a new breath of life in him and consolation in the joy of the Holy Spirit. So

---

[50] SC 36.5 (SBOp 2:7).

[51] See above, Chapter I.3, notes 45 and 46 on the verbs *retorquet* and *intorquet*.

[52] SC 36.6 (SBOp 2:7–8).

on the one hand, let us let fear and humiliation be born in us, and on the other hand, hope and love.[53]

Every monastic life is a spiritual life, and every spiritual life is a life of conversion. At the very outset of such a life, it is essential for the soul to be occupied with two things: knowing itself, and by so doing coming to the knowledge and love of God.

The vision of oneself and God, contemplation is ultimately the nearly complete fulfillment of the essential wisdom of the christian life, and still more, the monastic life. It consists in *knowing oneself and God* in the light of Revelation. The life of the spirit consists in this.[54]

It is a matter of entering into wisdom, just as the existential fear of God is too. But we must go back to Bernard's threefold distinction, where the second step of truth—fraternal charity—is presented in the cistercian school as a necessary stage on the way to the fullness of this christian, gospel wisdom of love.

6. LOVE GONE ASTRAY

In his phenomenological description of consciousness' position before God in the sphere of love, Saint Bernard proceeds by a line of reflection parallel to the one he followed in speaking of freedom and truth. For him, it concerns the movement of a spirit rediscovering its orientation to God. This movement begins at the soul's very real experience of its misery, which is followed by a plea to a Saviour engendered by this experience. This is the first of the four steps of love, described twice by Saint Bernard in his treatise *On Loving God*. A creature endowed with will becomes aware that it has a real and practical need to love God if it does not want its capacity for love to become a fruitless mockery. Saint Bernard's development of this first step of love, the love of self, is not easy to follow. He arrives at a kind of demonstration of why we need to love God.

---

[53] Div 5.5 (SBOp 6/1:104).

[54] P.-Y. Emery, in his introduction to *Saint Bernard. Sermons divers*, Tome I (Paris: Desclée, 1982) 21.

God seeks the soul and wants to be loved by her. This is how it happens: God has established as a law that because he is our nature's Creator and Providence, he should be recognized and loved as such. The creature, who ought to love him naturally, stands in danger of forgetting this and of claiming to be its own master and the master of all it possesses. To avoid such ignorance and arrogance, which would be fatal and issue in unhappiness, the Creator, by a saving plan aimed at the creature's happiness, willed that it should be afflicted by trials and tribulations which will cause it to reflect. When the creature sees that it is powerless, when a prayerful cry bursts from its heart and it experiences liberation from anguish, the creature will give God the love which is due him. Here again, Saint Bernard summarizes this experience by quoting a verse of a psalm: *Invoke me in your troubles; I will rescue you, and you shall honor me* (Ps 49:15). In this way, he continues, the 'animal and carnal man' who was unable to love anyone but himself begins to love God simply for personal advantage, because as he has often experienced, with God one can do all things, and without him nothing. While seeking to love itself, the creature has already tried, by a sort of natural sense of philanthropy, to share with others—but without success. In reality, to love another person in the right way one must first love God. In a logical sort of way, then, the soul will pass to a second step of love: loving God because she sees that it is to her advantageous to do so.[55]

'Life is a trial', said Gabriel Marcel, and this is how Saint Bernard envisions it in the first step of love. Even though it would be rash to try to justify suffering in presence of someone who suffers, this approach to suffering nevertheless has validity, not as an explanation (there is none), but as a motive for facilitating humble acceptance: in some mysterious way, God knows best what will ultimately make me happy. 'When God loves, he wants nothing but to be loved; still more, he loves nothing but being loved, for he knows very well that he will make happy those who love him.'[56]

---

[55] Dil 8.23–25 (SBOp 3:138–140).

[56] SC 83.4 (SBOp 2:301). Cf. 5 HM 5 (SBOp 5:72): our minor faults incite us to have recourse to grace; see also below, Chapter VI.2 (*Etiam peccata*).

Frequently repeating the experience of having recourse to God makes our love increase. The transition from the second step to the third—as we will see further on in Chapter V.2—will come about particularly through the practice of cistercian ascesis. The theme of mercy coming to the rescue of human misery (*miseria-misericordia*), very frequent in Saint Bernard's writings, ought to be taken in an absolute sense: all or nothing. *Deep calls to deep* (Ps 41:8); *the human heart is profound* (Jr 17:9), divine mercy is immense, and through mercy the troubled soul again takes heart. All frivolity or negligence here would signal a fear of reality.[57] Those who pray over-confidently should be told that they are seeking the Lord before they have found themselves. Ignorant of themselves, they do not pray like the publican who implored mercy because he was a sinner, and they therefore put themselves in great danger.[58] The infinite distance between the Merciful God and a creature in peril should not be reduced to a psychological level which it transcends beyond all measure. A desolation of a kind that reaches a sense of distress is necessary if the experience is to be authentic and profound.[59]

Saint Bernard knew the manifestations of human dissatisfaction well and commented on them superbly. Desire lies at the base of the will, and will is the base of our being.

> It is natural for all creatures who have the use of reason to desire what they think is best and most suitable for them, and not to be satisfied with anything as long as they lack something they consider preferable to what they have. For example, someone who has an attractive wife will look with wanton eye and heart at a more beautiful woman, and someone who wears expensive clothes will want to have even more costly ones, and so on. . . .[60]

On the basis of this observation, one writer has said that:

---

[57] 'In [moments of] peril, negligence is a sign, not of security but of despair', QH 10.4 (SBOp 4:446).
[58] Quad 4.3–4 (SBOp 4:370–371).
[59] Epi 1.1 (SBO 4:292).
[60] Dil 7.18 (SBOp 3:134).

It seems that for Bernard the desire which exists in a human being is in a way 'an implicit desire for God', in the sense that, from the initial experience of unsatisfied desire and the continual starting over again which this experience implies, a human being is led to openness to the supreme Good . . . The desire for God is, therefore, a prolongation of our experience of human desire.[61]

This desire for God is set in the perspective of the doctrine of the image and has no limit, because, as Bernard concludes in this brilliant passage: The restless mind

> thinks that everything its famished appetite makes it gobble up is too little in comparison with everything that still remains to be devoured. It is continually tormented by a desire for what is out of its reach, rather than being satisfied and happy with what it possesses.'

So if it were possible to try everything, we would necessarily end up by desiring God. But because life is short and our nature is limited, and because many things compete for our attention, we continue to go round and round in the circle of covetousness. There is only one way out: to break through the circle and take the short, straight, but narrow way of the Gospel.[62]

Though love for God is indispensable to the happiness of the conscience, and though despair threatens anyone who willfully turns away from this love, human love is also necessary for happiness. Dom Anselme Le Bail has said well:

> It is not paradoxical to affirm that Saint Bernard wrote one single treatise on spirituality . . . a treatise on the soul's relationship with God: love. . . . The question of love is (for him) a drama, the drama of a created being who feels that he or she is beyond

---

61 J. Blanpain ocso, 'Langage mystique, expression du désir', Coll 36 (1974) 49. Cf. 'Love of God appeals to the same faculty in us as love of creatures, giving us the sentiment that by ourselves we are not complete and that the supreme Good in which we will find fulfillment is Someone outside ourselves', P. Claudel, *Positions et propositions* I, Oeuvres complètes, tome XV (Paris: Gallimard, 1959) 102.
62 Dil 7.18–19 (SBOp 3:135).

all doubt destined to love. This is the eternal law which creates and governs the universe.[63] At the same time, Saint Bernard found himself faced with the equally necessary law of salvation. Perplexed, he reconciled the two by subordinating human love to divine love, which alone can pacify the heart and make it happy. Was it not for this reason that Dante chose Saint Bernard as guide in the circles of heaven? *The Divine Comedy* and the treatise *On Loving God* are two epics of love.[64]

Not only does the universe depend on the law of love, but God himself lives by it. Commenting on *Psalm 18*: *The law of the Lord is pure* (verse 8), Saint Bernard tells us that it is pure because it is the law of disinterested love, the only love which can convert a soul by turning it completely towards another in total gift and self-forgetfulness. So, he continues, it is not at all absurd to say that this is also the law by which God lives. What maintains the ineffable unity of the Trinity of Persons, if not love? And is this God who is substantial charity not also the source of human love?[65] When, in his most beautiful sermon on love, Saint Bernard exclaims 'Love is the great reality!'[66], he is speaking of the universal law, but then he immediately points out that this love is great only on condition that it ceaselessly returns to its source, so that it can endlessly flow forth from it again. The integration of human love into the mystery of divine love is accomplished by relationships in community, spiritual friendship, and all forms of charity. Before Dante, Saint Bernard saw clearly that it is principally in this reintegration that we find the restoration of the image of the God who is love in his spiritual creature who is a creature of desire.

7. DISFIGUREMENT, CURIOSITY AND APPROPRIATION

The spiritual creature no longer knows itself because it has lost its likeness to its Creator. Its likeness to God cannot be other than

---

[63] Dil 12.35 (SBOp 3:149).

[64] Anselme Le Bail OCSO, article 'Saint Bernard' in the *Dictionnaire de Spiritualité*, tome I (Paris: Beauchesne, 1937) 1474.

[65] Dil 12.34–35 (SBOp 3:149–150).

[66] SC 83.4 (SBOp 2:300).

spiritual. It is in the spirit that the soul's form resides, and the word 'form', used frequently in Saint Bernard's teaching, belongs to the language of beauty. By its unlikeness (and we have seen the sequence of causes which produced it) the human spirit has been disfigured; it has become *de-formed*. In commenting on God's praise of the soul: *Your cheeks are beautiful* (Sg 1:9), Saint Bernard remarks that the plural symbolizes the two sides of the soul's face (that is, the intention): the thing itself and the cause. If one of these two is not pure, we cannot call the face beautiful; instead, it is disfigured. The example that comes to his mind is love of truth. As soon as a person seeks truth for a motive other than love, one of the two cheeks becomes ugly and the soul is disfigured. And if this person is not even seeking truth, both cheeks will be ugly. A monk's falseness will be evident if, under the pretext of seeking God, he is pursuing some other goal.[67]

True knowledge of self is never found without somehow seeking God, because every spirit is made in his image. To know oneself does not mean simply discovering one's wretchedness and ugliness. The drama lies in becoming conscious of the contrast between the ugliness and beauty. Inversely, the soul's ignorance of its greatness or its lowliness—or, more precisely, its ignorance even of its dignity as the image of God endowed with reason—debases it to the level of animals. No longer seeing its own beauty, which is interior, the spiritual creature begins to seek what is beautiful outside itself, in sensible realities alone.

> The soul lets itself be led on by its own curiosity and becomes indistinguishable from other creatures, because it does not understand that it has received more than any of the others. That is why we must very carefully avoid the kind of ignorance which would give us a too low opinion of ourselves.[68]

By the very fact of having lost sight of our relationship of dependence on God and being henceforth 'condemned to freedom', in Sartre's phrase, and all the while aware of not being self-made,

---

[67] SC 40.2–3 (SBOp 2:25–26).
[68] Dil 2.4 (SBOp 3:122).

the person with no one to count on is delivered up to curiosity. Although a good kind of curiosity can be found in Saint Bernard's teaching,[69] there is more often a bad kind which drives us to seek the Spirit's beauty in things which are visible and can be perceived by the senses. The spiritual creature has preserved the form of the Spirit's beauty, but it has been so disfigured that it can no longer recognize this beauty either in itself or in the things in which it expects to find it. Endlessly dissatisfied, curiosity constantly yearns for something new to feed its appetite, and is incapable of remaining calm and peaceful. Is this not proof that it finds no real satisfaction in these various objects of curiosity, since their only charm comes from the fact that they follow one after another?[70] Saint Bernard has left us a very entertaining description of the curiosity which is brought on by intellectual conceit. When he spoke of 'a theologian more curious about what is new than about the search for truth,' he had Abelard in mind. 'He cannot bear to agree with others on any point, or to say something that he is not the only one, or the first, to say. He does not observe moderation in anything.'[71]

Lack of moderation and indiscretion are signs of pride, which, from the point of view of curiosity, comes directly or indirectly from the loss of the awareness that we have been created in the image of God. A relationship with the One whose image we are requires a self-knowledge which is recollective, solitary and silent, because, as Saint Bernard goes on to say, a bridegroom as shy as he is will never go out to meet a soul in the middle of a crowd.[72] Curiosity is the major obstacle to self-knowledge because

---

[69] SC 33.1 (SBOp 1:233); SC 62.3 (SBOp 2:156); Adv 1.1 (SBOp 4:162).

[70] Conv 8.14 (SBOp 4:88). Cf. 'It [curiosity] seeks what is new only to leap from it again to what is still newer . . . That is why curiosity is characterized specifically by an *incapacity to remain* fixed on anything at all which is offered to it . . . By this instability, curiosity obtains for itself the constant possibility of *distraction*. It has nothing in common with admiring reflection. . . .', said Martin Heidegger, *L'être et le temps* I.5.36 (Paris: Gallimard, 1964) 212. [An English translation by Joan Stambaugh is available under the title *Being and Time* (New York, Harper & Row, 1972)—ed.].

[71] Ep 77.11 (SBOp 7:192–193).

[72] SC 40.5 and 4 (SBOp 2:27).

it is not recollection but dispersion in externalization, most of all when it comes to that very beguiling activity of criticizing others. Talkativeness, which inevitably results from curiosity, is an easy kind of evasion because all the fascinating flaws we see in others around us distract us agreeably from our own.[73] A garrulous curiosity has a special significance in a certain type of existentialism, which sees it as an expression of anguish and anxiety (curiosity comes from *cura*: anxiety).[74]

To compare the ways Saint Bernard and Heidegger approach this subject is fascinating, even if they each arrive at a different kind of truth. In Chapter III we will see that Truth alone, Christ, can save the spiritual creature from the predicament in which it finds itself since having been cast out into the world and, supposedly free, having lost its identity by losing its relationship of dependence on absolute freedom. By wanting to be autonomous it became heteronomous, that is to say, dependent on everything, subject to the law of things and subservient to 'the world'. Only God's love can save the spiritual creature from this predicament by guiding it back into the law which is somehow the law by which God, who is love, lives.

The radical ambiguity in a human heart conscious at one and the same time of its greatness and its disgrace is perceptible in the human composite of soul and body which, according to Saint Bernard, reflects this painful contradiction. Only in the soul could God create a human being in his image, and endow it with rectitude and justness. But God also granted human beings the privilege (not given to animals) of having an upright body which enables them to contemplate heaven. Bodily uprightness and physical beauty

---

[73] SC 24.4 (SBOp 1:154–155). Cf. 'Curiosity which leaves nothing hidden, idle talk where nothing is misunderstood, guarantee-that is to say, guarantee to the "being there"—a "life" which pretends to be really "alive". The noise of idle talk and the indiscreet trickery of curiosity feed excitement (in 'being-with'), where every day everything and, basically, nothing "happens' ". Heidegger, *L'être et le temps* I.5.36–37, 213–214. [For an English transation, see note 70].

[74] Heidegger describes anguish and anxiety in the paragraphs which follow those on curiosity and idle talk, and precede his search for 'meaning' and truth, *L'être et le temps* I. 6.39–42. [*Time and Being*, above, note 70].

are therefore a source of shame for the soul, because to a soul of heavenly origin there is no worse degradation than to lower itself by covetousness to earthly things, like an animal. So the body rails at the soul, saying: '*I* have been fashioned by God in *your* image, and *I* have preserved my uprightness, my rectitude and my beauty; and *you*, made in the image of our Creator, have lost them.' God is Spirit, and only by returning to themselves will creatures composed of spirit rediscover their beauty in his image.

Quite apart from any cartesian or even platonic thought, this dialogue between the soul and the body can be interesting to us today, because the expression 'I am my body' lets us see a kind of analogy with Saint Bernard's thought. We can interpret this in the light of the contrast between the body's innocence and the spirit's lack of moral uprightness.[75] The Word must come and restore the spirit's beauty. Then, even in its body, the creature will recognize itself fully as image and will be able to contemplate God. Then curiosity will stop trying to find truth and beauty outside God or without God.[76]

In the doctrine of the image, loss of likeness corresponds quite closely to what contemporary philosophers call 'inauthentic existence'. If there is an inevitable ambiguity between grandeur and slavery, there is also equivocation, and Saint Bernard denounced it clearly while commenting on the words of *Ezechiel*: *You have lost wisdom by your beauty* (28:17). The beauty in question here, he says, is our personal beauty and there is of course nothing dangerous about it. No one can reproach us for having received this gift and being happy about it. The trouble comes from that little possessive adjective. God did not say: 'You lost wisdom by beauty' but 'by your beauty'. Wisdom is not just the soul's form; it is its sole beauty. By wishing to appropriate wisdom and beauty for self, the human person has lost both in one fell swoop. By refusing to recognize its dependence and give thanks, and by wanting to make everything depend on its own will, the creature deviated from truth. It has lost wisdom completely, because to possess it in such a way is to lose

---

[75] SC 24.5–6 (SBOp 1:156–159).
[76] See below, Chapter V.3.

it. And to lose oneself is to lose everything. And who does not lose everything, including self by losing God from sight?[77]

Like deviation towards self and misappropriation of wisdom, intelligence or freedom, severing the relationship of loving dependence on God is also a refusal of truth. It is radical pride, the disfigurement that makes a human being unrecognizable. The grossest type of ignorance occurs in the terrible, equivocal situation of someone convinced that he or she is self-sufficient, has received nothing, and needs no one. The third ignorance is the worst, says Saint Bernard. It is the pretentious claim of total autonomy and inane self-sufficiency. It is deviation and usurpation. Arrogance like this 'denatures' the spiritual creature. It is the fatal illusion which most alienates the creature from its Creator, and consequently makes it most foreign to spiritual beauty, while its desire and capacity for the divine remain ineffaceable, but deeply buried.[78]

8. CONVERSION OF FREEDOM

To summarize the main points of Saint Bernard's spiritual anthropology, we need only restate the description he gave of the soul's loss of likeness to God. The human being is no longer free because it presumptuously chose to usurp freedom for itself by cutting itself off from God's freedom. Therein lies the error and original fault. This refusal of dependence expressed itself in a refusal to obey. Dependence on its only transcendent point of reference gave the human spirit a dignity it is incapable of finding either in its own finite nature or in that of the creatures around it. The loss of the religious absolute of obedience puts a human being in an equivocal situation: the creature takes itself for God. Then its every action becomes a manifestation of self-will and in a way a sacrilege, whereas all obedience is implicitly an act of adoration. The essential conflict, therefore, really takes place at the heart of human freedom. To the extent that a rational creature knows itself, it suffers because of the contrast between what it can be but is not, between its vocation to

---

[77] SC 74.10 (SBOp 2:245–246).
[78] Dil 2.4 (SBOp 3:122–123).

love and its refusal. A person then becomes humble if he or she wants to be, that is to say, if there is an explicit and willing submission to reality. This voluntary and free character of humility is also the characteristic of love, because humility and love go together. Saint Bernard often described the first stirring of conversion. We must have a clear idea of this first step in any monastic conversion, because there is today some confusion on this point. No one has spoken more plainly about it than Saint Bernard: 'It is humility, you see, which justifies. I say humility and not humiliation. A great many people are humiliated but not humble.' He goes on to distinguish three possible attitudes a person can have when faced with the humiliations which are part of our lives, whether they come from God or by way of others: bitterness, patience, and free acceptance. When someone who is offended represses his or her feelings stoically, that person is no humbler than someone else who grumbles about it. Only the person who humbles self is humble. Grace can unite only with the freedom of a humble heart, with the freedom of joyful and absolute humility (*laeta absoluta*). Here we are clearly on the level of the absolute. Only a person who is willingly and joyfully humble will be exalted as a reward for good will; and contrariwise, not everyone who is extolled will be abased, but only people who have exalted themselves and exhibited vain self-will, that is, a will in disagreement with God's will, and in that sense, bad will.[79]

Saint Bernard's approach to humility here in no way contradicts the approach he used in his second step of truth. There he speaks of our need to recognize our real state, which is inferior to what we may imagine; here it is simply a matter of 'making a virtue of necessity', as we say—perhaps because Saint Bernard said it long before we did.[80] Humility which does not result from necessity is freer and therefore more beautiful, as Saint Bernard wrote to his friend, the bishop of Valence, because humility in resplendence is certainly 'a rare bird'. Understood this way, it is not good for us to deny our own value. Rather, we should recognize it and be thankful

---

[79] SC 34.3–4 (SBOp 1:247–248).
[80] Clem 1 (SBOp 5:413); SC 42.8 (SBOp 2:38); Ep 113.1 (SBOp 7:288); 1 Nov 5.3 (SBOp 5:319).

for it, but we should not claim it as our own.[81] Still, whether humility is totally free or accepted through necessity, it requires an intelligent seeking for truth. For Saint Bernard, love of truth is the truth of love. This is how we ought to understand his idea of the relationship between intelligence and will: not theoretically, but as a concrete interaction aimed at conversion. Reason serves will as a companion and, in a way (*quodammodo*), as its follower (*pedissequam*). It is always present as soon as there is a free act, that is, consent to either grace or self-will.[82] This is not a matter of precedence either of value or of chronology, still less of blind willfulness. It is a clear understanding of the essential role in every conversion of a consent which is free and which frees love. Even faith presupposes the will's turning back to God. 'The Apostle says that there are some who have no knowledge of God (cf. 1 Cor 15:34). My opinion is that all those who do not want to be converted lack knowledge of God.'[83]

There is a moral attitude, a fundamental intentional bent, which dominates a person's orientation: and it is love—that is, the dynamic of desire and its search for its own appropriate object. Both knowledge and conscience, each in its own way, contribute to this search. What is important for Saint Bernard is that we should not neglect one for the other. If we do, the penalty is either to fall into error or to cram ourselves with knowledge useless to true life.

> Erudition without love can only puff a person up; love without learning leads into error . . . It is not suitable for the bride of the Word to be foolish, and the Father would not put up with her being proud.[84]

When he speaks of the kiss of the Holy Spirit which communicates love to the soul, Bernard says that the bride ought to offer her two lips: reason—which enables her to understand—and a will

---

[81] Ep 372 (SBOp 8:332–333); Cf. Ep 113.1, to the noblewoman Sophie (SBOp 7:288) and SC 45.3 (SBOp 2:51).

[82] Gra 2.3 (SBOp 3:168).

[83] SC 38.2 (SBOp 2:15).

[84] SC 69.2 (SBOp 2:203). Cf. 'Instruction makes learned, affection makes one wise', SC 23.14 (SBOp 1:147); Asc 6.6 and 10 (SBOp 5:153 and 155); SC 23.6–7 (SBOp 1 111–112).

orientated towards wisdom, because 'neither someone who hears truth without loving it, nor someone who loves it without hearing it, has a right to claim that he or she has received the kiss, because the kiss does not tolerate error or tepidity.[85]

The Spirit is also understanding and wisdom; it is like a bee which produces wax and honey at the same time. We must remember that wisdom is always likened to love and not to understanding, contrary to what we may spontaneously think. The wisdom of love leads us to peaceful harmony within ourselves, with others, and with God. This is the final goal of a monk's journey and the ultimate restoration of God's image in a human being on this earth.

People have very properly spoken about the 'mystical moralism' of Saint Bernard's spiritual doctrine.[86] This ethical side of his teaching should be understood from the point of view of his burning desire as a spiritual father who felt a responsibility to reform monastic life. The term 'christian socratism' has also been applied to his teaching. We could likewise call it a moral teaching on conversion or holiness, or an eschatological doctrine. Actually, what it means is the Gospel lived in a radical way. Abelard's moral teaching, by contrast, lacked this dimension. It is very significant that after Saint Bernard's most sublime mystical experience, the one at least about which he spoke a bit clearly, he said 'I understood that the Word was in me by certain motions of my heart: the desire to correct my faults and curb my physical appetites. I realized the effectiveness of his presence.'[87]

The monastic search for God is particularly situated in the moral order: 'practice', as the ancient monks called it. The journey has been mapped out in the Beatitudes, which on several occasions serve

---

[85] SC 8.6 (SBOp 1:39).

[86] W. Williams, 'L'aspect éthique du mysticisme de saint Bernard', in *Saint Bernard et son temps* (Dijon, 1925) 308–318. The contemporary religious thinker who comes closest to Saint Bernard on this point is Emmanuel Lévinas, for whom moral philosophy is the principal philosophy. He has said: 'Ethics is a view of the divine'. Quoted by L. Crommelinck, 'Dieu dans la pensée de Lévinas', *La foi et le temps* 24 (1994) 404–405. Did Saint Bernard not also say that love is likeness and, by it, comes vision? Cf. SC 82.8 (SBOp 2:297).

[87] SC 74.6 (SBOp 2:243). Cf. SC 52.4 (SBOp 2:92).

as a foundation for Saint Bernard's teaching on conversion. Two other considerations concerning this ethical aspect of his doctrine could be added. The first has to do with the social world in which Bernard lived. Régine Pernoud has pointed out:

> A purely intellectual type of person was almost nonexistent in the twelfth century. People did not believe in 'disinterested' knowledge. They were concerned only about what led in one way or another to transformation of the human condition, having to do either with the practical aspects of life or—above all—with the interior life. It was a technological rather than scientific period; its aim was spiritual development, to which intellectual activity was invited to contribute. One would seek in vain for art for art's sake or knowledge for the sake of knowledge. Just as, after all, in our own day the title 'pure intellectual' scarcely seems something to crave.'[88]

Because of his influence, Saint Bernard could not do otherwise than intensify the spirit of his time. And did he not also influence the french moralists? In fact, he was the first of them. We cannot help but be impressed by the similarity between his thought and the following lines written by a perspicacious french literary critic:

> From Montaigne to André Gide, knowledge of self (and beyond self, of others) has been explored by the essayist, novelist or poet with clairvoyance and rigor which have never failed when they were faced with their discoveries . . . Knowledge of the human being is difficult. It begins necessarily with knowledge of self, and its starting point is the edge of our interior being, towards which each of us can advance so as then to go forth to others.[89]

As for love, another literary critic tells us how important it is in french ethical thought: 'French literature is a continuous discourse on the human being . . . What makes its greatness is its knowledge

---

[88] Régine Pernoud, *Héloïse et Abélard* (Paris: Albin Michel, 1970) 284. [New York: Stein and Day, 1973]

[89] G. Bauer, (of *l'Académie Goncourt*) *Les moralistes français* (Paris: Albin Michel, 1962) 9–10.

of the human heart . . . Nowhere are analysis and experience of love so closely bound together as in french society.'[90]

Saint Bernard's synthesis of spiritual and monastic theology is founded above all on the unity he achieved between the analysis and the experience of the love which is in the heart of every human person. In a society in which troubadour poetry was on the rise, his poetic and even lyrical style was a means he utilized in his zeal as an apostle preaching conversion. The style is the man, and Christine Mohrmann has well described his style:

> The abundance of images and comparisons, the play on words and figures of speech, the richness of his almost spectacular, resounding language should not make us forget that this great mystic, for whom the visible world was a source of inspiration, remained capable of translating his loftiest experiences into a sober and bare language which marvelously brings out the most exquisite nuances of union with God.[91]

His influence spread beyond the borders of Burgundy and France to all of european culture, because in an open Europe the language in which he wrote knew no boundaries. Beyond the twelfth century, right up until our own time and in all cultures, what he taught about the human heart seeking God remains classic.[92]

Today Saint Bernard is still God's fisherman, just as he so ardently was in his own day. The cistercian cloister was for him the place for the conversion of the freedom of the spiritual creature renewing its bond with its Creator. When freedom is saved, intelligence can again clearly see its truth and dignity as the image of God. Love rediscovers the one object that can alone allay its desire. But a person who has become alienated from God is in a situation which makes him or her incapable of conversion, that is, of return. Only a Saviour can rescue such a person from the unhappy plight into which

---

[90] E.-R. Curtius, *Essai sur la France*. Translated from the German by J. Benoist-Méchin (Paris: Grasset, 1932) 199–201.

[91] Christine Mohrmann, *La langue et le style de saint Bernard*. Introduction to *S. Bernardi Opera* (SBOp 2:xxxi).

[92] Charles Dumont ocso, 'Pourquoi le *Miroir de la Charité* a-t-il été publié? 1. Des classiques cisterciens', Coll 55 (1993) 15–16.

he or she has erred in the distant region of unlikeness. God's love was so humble that he came and sought his human creature where it is: where it seeks him from far off, in his tarnished yet nevertheless imprinted image. The creature will be able to recognize its likeness to God in Christ, the One who is the perfect image.

Christ's work will be described in Chapters III (The Mediation of the Incarnate Word) and IV (Going Beyond Self by Love of Christ). Freedom's conversion through liberating obedience will be described in Chapter V, in the context of cistercian observances. The last step on the pathway of peace will conclude, in Chapter VI, this synthesis of Saint Bernard's teaching, which will have converted us by the wisdom of love.

III

CHRIST, THE SACRAMENT OF ENCOUNTER, THE MEDIATION OF THE INCARNATE WORD

1. FREEDOM REGAINS ITS FORM

*T*HE MUTUAL SEARCH of the creating Spirit and its spiritual creature would be fruitless apart from the divine initiative of Love, who comes to meet the heart which is seeking this love just as it is seeking peace. Like spontaneously seeks like; it readily recognizes and loves like. As the eye is made to see light, so the gaze of faith spontaneously recognizes the One it seeks because it is created in his likeness. Simple acceptance of truth saves the spiritual creature from the hopeless situation in which it finds itself after its refusal of God when freedom chose to be autonomous and independent. Salvation lies in freedom's conversion, because freedom is at once the center of our being and the surest vestige of the divine image. Hemmed in by unhappiness, says Saint Bernard, the human creature's whole merit lies in putting all its hope in the One who saves the whole human being.[1] Encounter between the Saviour and the saved is situated within the context of Saint Bernard's doctrine on the Image, who is the Christ in whose image humanity has been created and in

---

[1] QH 15.5 (SBOp 4:479).

whose image it will be re-created. Speaking of the mystery of the Incarnation, he says:

> Then he appeared, whereas until then he had remained hidden. He took on human form, assuming it in his own likeness, as he had created it in the beginning. No, it was not unworthy of God to manifest himself in his image to those who could not know him in his (divine) substance. And so, he who made the human creature in his image and likeness revealed himself to humans by becoming human.[2]

The clearest and most evident characteristic of the divine likeness in the human soul is freedom. Loss of the soul's likeness resulted from wrong use of this gift when the soul arrogantly misappropriated it for self. As we have seen, in the alienation in which the soul finds itself, it is unable to give God what is his due. Consequently, it has lost awareness of its dignity as a free being. It has also lost its love for the God who in his absolute freedom made the soul worthy to participate in his freedom. The image has become unrecognizable, disfigured and ugly—primarily in its own sight. So the Creator came to meet his spiritual creature to restore its original beauty and make us once more aware of it. Nowhere has Saint Bernard spoken more eloquently about the abasement and magnificence of the human spirit than when he dealt specifically with the theme of free choice and grace. First he analyzes at length how the state of free choice, which, because it is the ineradicable and unreserved divine core of our being, by its very nature evades all constraint, whether exterior or interior. Then he shows how our use of free choice has been fettered by the bonds of sin as well as by the limitations and weakness of our human condition on earth. By the interaction between this natural free choice and divine freedom through which those who are born of God can live with new life, are produced two effects in a human conscience: irruption of grace and consent of will.

We have described above this interaction of grace and freedom (Chapter I.3). Let us now listen as Saint Bernard tells us how this

---

[2] Adv 3.1(SBOp 4:175).

meeting takes place, thanks to the Mediator. Because Christ, the only Saviour, as the perfect image of God is the only One completely free from sin and misery, he alone could restore the divine likeness in humankind. Bernard uses the parable of the lost drachma to connote the Redemption. Likeness would have been lost if the woman mentioned in the Gospel had not lit her lamp (that is to say, if Wisdom had not appeared in the flesh), swept her house clean (of faults) and searched for the lost coin, Wisdom's own image soiled and hidden in the dust. Once it was found, she cleaned and restored it from unlikeness to its pristine beauty by making it conform to Wisdom, whose effigy remained imprinted on it. Christ alone could restore divine likeness to the human image—Christ who is the *radiant light and image of the Father's substance* (Heb 1:3).[3] Then comes the beautiful phrase where the word 'form', by being repeated, is given special force:

> It came then, this form to which free choice was to be conformed, because to regain its original form it had to be reformed according to that form, yes, to that form according to which it had also been formed. The form is wisdom. 'Conformation' means that the image does in the body what form does is the world.[4]

The relationship between image and body may surprise us, but a better grasp of what Saint Bernard means by form will help us better understand this essential point. Form is an extremely important aspect of his spirituality. He uses the word *forma* no less than one hundred thirty times, but the force and thrust of this expression elude us. In a way comparable to the contemporary psychology of forms,[5] the concept of form goes back to greek philosophy. With the rise of scholasticism, the meaning of the word changed and

---

[3] Gra 10.32 (SBOp 3:188–189).
[4] Gra 10.33 (SBOp 3:189).
[5] The reader will find a development of the medieval concept of 'form' in C. Dumont OCSO, *Sagesse ardente*. Pain de Cîteaux 8. 3rd Series (Oka, Qc: Abbaye N.-D.-du-Lac, 1995). Chapter XII: 'Formation cistercienne'. On *Gestalt* philosophy, see p. 209; on Régine Pernoud's application of the principle of form to cistercian architecture, see p.304.

became dissociated from beauty. Yet when we are dealing with the opposition between form and deformation, beauty and ugliness are precisely the issue.. Freedom became deformed when it repudiated its dependence, that is to say, when the image lost all likeness to God's absolute freedom.

In his commentary on the words of the *Song of Songs* (1:4): *I am dark but beautiful*, Saint Bernard uses the symbolism of physical beauty to signify beauty of conscience. Beauty comes from form (*formosa*), which, as he points out to those who may be ignorant of it, is essential to any being; whereas color is accidental, its significance can change. Dark eyes or dark hair may have their own charm, yet other beautiful things are colorless. The form is the *compositio*, the internal unity, of a being—its harmony, what makes it beautiful. In this sense, 'the saints have the certainty that nothing is more pleasing to God than his own image restored to its original beauty'.[6] The fundamental freedom, free choice, will therefore strive to govern the body, that is to say, the whole being, just as Wisdom *governs the universe from one end to the other* (Ws 8:1). It will try to gain mastery over the body's senses and members so as no longer to be a slave to sin. It will free itself to the point of being able to 'reclaim its dignity when it will be clothed anew with the likeness worthy of the divine image which is in it; better still, when it will have regained its pristine beauty'.[7]

Because it was by an act of free will that the human spirit turned away from God to be its own master, and because it has been incapable by its own strength of freeing itself from this new situation, the work of salvation is expressly a matter of freedom's liberation by Christ.

> First *created in Christ* (Eph 2:10) unto freedom of will, we are secondly reformed by Christ unto the spirit of freedom, to attain lastly with Christ consummate perfection in the state which will be ours in eternity.[8]

---

6 SC 25.3 and 7 (SBOp 1:165 and 167).
7 Gra 10.34 (SBOp 3:190).
8 Gra 14.49 (SBOp 3:201).

Human freedom regains form and beauty when the splendor of divine freedom permeates it and conforms it to the divine image and likeness. Then all that remains for it to do is to consent right up to the point of cleaving totally and permanently to God. Is there any moral beauty greater than the beauty of a free human person?

2. TRUTH REGAINED BY CHRIST'S HUMILITY

At the beginning of his treatise on the *Steps of Humility and Pride*, Saint Bernard provides a brilliantly enriching prelude in which he comments on Jesus' words: *I am the Way, the Truth and the Life* (Jn 14:16). The way is humility—which leads to truth as the fruit of its toil. Someone will probably object, he remarks, that Christ did not specifically say that humility is the way, but said it only in a general way. His answer to this objection highlights the place which the person of Christ holds as the example and form of every conversion. Did Jesus himself not say even more clearly: *Learn from me, for I am gentle and humble of heart* (Mt 11:29)?

> If you imitate him, *you will not be walking in the dark, but you will have the light of life* (Cf. Jn 8:12). What is this light of life but the truth which *enlightens every human being who comes into this world* (Jn 1:9), and shows where true life is to be found?[9]

It has been very properly pointed out that Saint Bernard's entire teaching could ultimately be given the title: Jesus, Sacrament of Encounter with God.[10] This encounter, however, occurs in utmost lowliness, where God chose to assume our human condition at its humblest, in its misery, in its real state. Without grace, the conversion described by the three steps of truth: truth about oneself (humility), truth about others (compassion), and truth in itself (contemplation) could not happen. So God sought out his spiritual creature. He looked down from the top of Jacob's ladder to see if anyone was seeking him. To those he saw straying far from his truth, God offered the law of humility. When a monk has climbed the

---

[9] Hum 1.1 (SBOp 3:17).
[10] Van Hecke, *Le désir dans l'expérience religieuse*, 168.

twelve steps described by Saint Benedict, he reaches charity, which is truth itself: Christ.[11] But just as compassion with one's neighbor is an extension of truth about oneself, so, too, God, because of his desire to be close to his human creature, wished to participate in our human condition by experience, that is, by becoming a human being so that he might be still more compassionate. The term 'compassion', as Saint Bernard uses it, should be taken in its literal sense: to suffer with (*cum-passio*). It is certainly not 'condescension'.[12] On the contrary, for both God and human beings, compassion is first and foremost a sign of the love which makes equal the persons who love one another. God is incapable of suffering (*impassibilis*), of course, but he is not incapable of 'suffering with' (*incompassibilis*).[13] The apparent contradiction is resolved by the same love which urges Christ to seek his lost hundredth sheep out of love, and we can exult in being sought this way.[14] Only by his concern for total truth in love could God have willed to experience the human condition.

> So it is not absurd to say not that Christ began to know something he did not know before, but that he was with us in heart in our misery (*misericordia*) from all eternity by his divinity, and that he learned to be with us in another way (*aliter*) in time, by means of the flesh.[15]

This concern for truth which led God even so far as to share our lot lies behind the theological daring which Saint Bernard demonstrates in his commentary on the passage in the *Letter to the*

---

11 Hum 2.3 (SBOp 3:18).

12 'There is danger in imagining God's love as a condescending love. God's desire for his creature is such that any portrayal of it would reduce us to dust. That is why he hid this desire in the depths of the gentle suffering heart of Jesus Christ.' Georges Bernanos, *Dernier agenda*. 18 January, 1948, quoted by A. Béguin, in *Bernanos par lui-même*. Collection: Ecrivains de toujours (Paris: Seuil, 1954) 146.

13 SC 26.5 (SBOp 1:173).

14 Adv 1.7 (SBOp 4:166).

15 Hum 3.10 (SBOp 3:23). In other words, 'Not that he did not know mercy before this . . . but what he knew by nature from all eternity he learned by experience'. Hum 3.6 (SBOp 3:21). The same motive for the Incarnation is repeated in SC 56.1 (SBOp 2:114–115).

Hebrews: *He learned obedience by what he suffered* (Heb 5:8).[16] Maurice Blondel, marveling at the boldness of his assertion and fully aware of its importance and implicit ramifications, wrote:

> We have to go that far to see, if not the entire reason and the veritable end, at least the means creating love used in the gratuitous gift of being to others than Being. Without this in view, we will never succeed in establishing the reason for the existence of anything at all . . . [That the mediation] might be total, permanent and voluntary . . . was it perhaps necessary for there to be a Mediator who would endure this reality integrally and who would be like the Amen of the universe?[17]

Such an approach to christian metaphysics may certainly be based on Saint Bernard's daring insight. Teilhard de Chardin may have been referring to it when he wrote about *christogenesis* and the *amorisation* of the universe. For the abbot of Clairvaux, however, the divine initiative was principally intended to permit each of us to rediscover ourselves in truth by God's grace. If God lovingly demeaned himself to our human condition, how much more humbly should his creature recognize this condition and so become able to learn, like God, how to feel close to the misery of others and to regain access to contemplation by charity.[18] Christ is the form of our humility, just as he is the form of our freedom. Our transformation consists therefore in our growing awareness of our own truth in the light of the divine truth within us, in the same way that saint Bernard contrasts knowledge—which knows—to conscience—which savors.[19] The nearness of God who comes to

---

[16] Saint Augustine was not so bold. For him, Christ learned in a certain way in his members what we, his members, learn (*Commentary on the Gospel of Saint John* 21.7).

[17] Maurice Blondel, *L'Action* (1893) (Paris: Presses Universitaires de France, 1973) 460–461. Following Blondel, who quoted Saint Bernard's words as a gleam of light, Xavier Tilliette wrote: 'Christ is thus in his role as Mediator, his knowledge mediates between appearances and reality, phenomena and being. . . . A profound insight, which applies to all Christ's knowledge', *Le Christ de la philosophie* (Paris: Cerf, 1990) 127.

[18] Hum 4.13 (SBOp 3:26).

[19] Conv 13.25 (SBOp 4:99–100); Csi V.13.27 (SBOp 3:490).

meet us in Christ gives Saint Bernard's christology the character of a divine pedagogy. All knowledge is good, but even on the level of knowing we can distinguish between the kind of knowledge which contributes to the transformation of the deepest part of our being in the perspective of our destiny, and another kind which seeks only to acquire tools for action in this world.[20] The monk should obviously give priority to the first kind. In it, knowledge of self is intimately bound up with knowledge of the Saviour, and humility becomes the precondition for all formation, in that it is an attitude of listening and fixing one's attention on the Master, the Creator who came to take an intimate personal interest in the existence of his spiritual creature. When the absolute is a person, Someone present within me, the meeting itself assumes an absolute character which requires immediate and unconditional adherence. This is the primordial experience which should be the monk's point of reference during his or her whole life.

After pointing out that, although the angel greeted Mary as 'full of grace', all of the fullness she kept for herself was humility, Saint Bernard continues:

> Did Christ not speak of humility as being the highest of the virtues and the summit of his teaching? *Learn from me*, he said, not because I am temperate, chaste or prudent, or anything else of that kind, but because *I am meek and humble of heart* (Mt 11:29). And learn it from me! I do not refer you to the teaching of the patriarchs or the books of the prophets, but I offer myself to you as an example, as the form of humility. The angel and the woman envied me my high place near my Father: the angel wanted my power, the woman, my knowledge. As for you, desire better gifts, and learn from me that *I am meek, that I am humble of heart* (Mt 11:29).[21]

---

[20] The distinction between the two ways of knowing is found in the writings of numerous philosophers: Pascal (heart and reason); Bergson (intuition and intelligence); Newman ('real and notional assent'); Heidegger (meditative thought and calculating thought).

[21] Ep 42.17–18 (SBOp 7:114).

The form of our life, and therefore the formation which prepares us for it, is none other than Christ himself. Everything important you need to know, he tells us, learn from me! In another passage Saint Bernard again alludes to the craving of Lucifer and also of Eve, who wanted to know so that she could be like God. But here the soul craves to plead its cause: 'Lord, power of persuasion made me lie. Let truth come forth so that falsehood may be unmasked. I will then *know the truth and the truth will free me* (Jn 8:32).'[22]

The persuasion behind the lie caused loss of simplicity which, to Saint Bernard's mind, is identical with truth. He clearly exposed radical falsehood and universal duplicity when he described simplicity as one of the fundamental characteristics of the image. The serpent pretended to be Eve's friend; it lied to her. Then, once the inhabitants of the earthly paradise had been led astray, they too began to lie.

> From then on, hypocrisy's hereditary poison has progressively infected their whole posterity. Find me just one child of Adam, I won't say who desires, but who can bear to be seen as he or she really is. Yet, in every soul there is a simplicity of nature (*generalis*) which subsists along with hereditary duplicity, and the co-existence of these two increases the soul's confusion.[23]

The converse of truth, then, is not error but lying, hypocrisy, and duplicity, which make the spirit suffer because it still retains its nostalgia for simplicity. It is from this type of falseness— that is, from our falsified and false being—that Christ's truth frees us by reaching the part of us which still yearns for what is true and simple. As with Maurice Blondel, it is when religious

---

[22] Adv 1.5 (SBOp 4:165).

[23] SC 82.3 (SBOp 2:293–294). The fear of truth referred to here was recognized by Pascal: 'So human life is but a perpetual illusion. People do nothing but deceive and flatter one another . . . Humans are nothing but disguise, falseness and hypocrisy, both within themselves and with regard to others. They do not want to be told the truth and avoid telling it to others. All these tendencies, so remote from justice and reason, have a natural root in the heart'. (*Pensées* 100, Brunschvicq's edition).

experience is based on an unremitting ethical option that it attains the transcendent.[24]

We may be astonished to see that, when it comes to conversion, Saint Bernard attributes greater importance to the will's decision than to thought and reflection.[25] Like the existentialist philosophers, especially Kierkegaard, he knew that the speculative intellect can dally in meditation on everything in the range of possibility—that is its function—but never reach the decision by which alone we can consent to being saved.[26]

On 27 January 1950, Thomas Merton wrote in his *Journal*:

> The more I read saint Bernard and the cistercian Fathers the more I like them . . . There was a time when I was tempted not to like Saint Bernard at all . . . I think that now, after eight years and more, I am really beginning to discover the depth of Saint Bernard. This is because I have realized that the foundation of his whole doctrine, which is expressed as clearly as anywhere in *Letter 18*, is that God is Truth and Christ is Truth Incarnate and that Salvation and sanctity for us mean being true to ourselves and true to Christ and true to God. It is only when this emphasis on truth is forgotten that Saint Bernard begins to seem sentimental.[27]

Saint Bernard's *Letter 18*, addressed to a cardinal who took an interest in his writings and teaching, is very explicit about how he saw the nature of truth. He begins by deriding the falseness of human flattery and then goes on to speak of the more serious falseness of

---

24 Cf. P. Henrici, 'Expérience et transcendance selon Maurice Blondel', *Gregorianum* 58 (1977) 557–560.

25 For example, concerning the first two reasons why the soul seeks the Word, SC 85.1–2 (SBOp 2:307–308), or the precedence of will over reason, Gra 2.3–4 (SBOp 3:168).

26 Cf. C. Dumont OCSO, 'Une phénoménologie de l'humilité. L'humilité chez saint Bernard et Gabriel Marcel', in *Sagesse ardente*, Ch. 10, 229–239. [English translation: 'A Phenomenological Approach to Humility: Chapter VII of the *Rule of Saint Benedict*', CSQ 20 (1985) 283–302. See 'Humility-Truth for Saint Bernard and Gabriel Marcel', 292–297].

27 Thomas Merton, *The Sign of Jonas* (New York: Harcourt Brace and Company, 1953) 271–272.

knowledge which is out of touch with real life. He contrasts Christ's truth to the senselessness and vanity of all notions which do not recognize it. Then he shows that this truth can be embraced only by the two arms of faith and desire: faith reaching out towards vision; desire yearning for God *like a doe longing for springs of living water* (Ps 41:2).[28] For Saint Bernard, it seems, the intellect is unable to reach God precisely because of the extreme simplicity of divine unity; the summit of the spirit will be equal to grasping this God—too simple for it—only when it ceases being splintered in dialectical speculation.[29] Love, which by its very nature simplifies and unifies, on the other hand, can conform us to absolute truth and lead us to it quite simply by the grace of humility. Humility, like love, promises what cannot be taught in any language and enables us to grasp what cannot be learned. Why? Not because anyone deserves it, but because it has pleased God that is should be so.[30] An image of Saint Benedict taken from one of Saint Bernard's sermons reminds us that humility is at the root of our growth in the monastic life.

Saint Benedict is a great tree bearing fruit: he is *the tree planted by the bank of the river of living water* (Ps 1:3). Where do rivers flow from? Who does not know that torrents cascade down from the mountain tops into the valleys? *God resists the proud and gives his grace to the humble* (Jas 4:6). It is for us to imitate him, because it was to give us form that he came.'[31]

3. LOVE FREED BY CHRIST'S CHARITY

As we have traced the order by which Saint Bernard presents his spiritual anthropology, with its dynamic of return to God by restoration of his image in us, it has become evident that freedom's conversion is the initial and the decisive step. As soon as free choice recognizes and recovers its radical dependence on its Creator's absolute freedom, it opens itself to grace, which puts it back on the

---

[28] Ep 18 (SBOp 7:66–69).
[29] Csi V.13.27 (SBOp 3:490).
[30] SC 85.14 (SBOp 2:316).
[31] Ben 4 and 8 (SBOp 5:3 and 8).

way of truth. When, for its part, intelligence humbly recognizes God's gift, its seeking is going to pursue its course in love, and freedom will work ever more closely with grace. It is like the bride in the *Song of Songs*, who seeks *the one her heart loves* (Sg 3:1) so she may become conformed to him and be one with him by the attachment of all her being.

In speaking about created will's return by renouncing its autonomy from its Creator, Saint Bernard remarked that this is a perfectly logical act and one which is imperative for all intelligent beings; but at the same time it is extremely difficult and even impossible for our nature when left to its own powers.[32] He continues:

> The faithful, on the contrary, know perfectly well their absolute need for *Jesus, and Jesus crucified* (1 Cor 2:2). In him, they admire and embrace *charity which is beyond all knowledge* (Eph 3:19), and they are ashamed not to give at least the little they are in return for such great love and esteem. Those who know that they are loved more easily love more. . . . [33]

The surge of love called up in us by the mystery of creation and the redeeming Incarnation is perfectly expressed in these few lines. It is a love totally permeated with recognition, in both senses of the word: we recognize God's charity which surpasses any knowledge we can have of it by our understanding; and responding to this love by the gift of ourselves appears easy to us. The whole evolution of our religious life should continue to be marked by this initial sense of gratitude. We shall see that religious sensitivity loses its fervor and even dies just as soon as thankfulness dwindles and dies.[34] In his treatise *On Loving God*, Saint Bernard does nothing if not develop the reasons for loving God with grateful love—first on the human and then on the supernatural level, because God first created and then re-created me.

> In his first work he gave me myself, in his second he gave himself, and by giving himself he gave me back myself. Given, therefore,

---

[32] Dil 2.3–5 (SBOp 3:121–123), commented on above, Chapter I.3, note 45.

[33] Dil 3.7 (SBOp 3:124).

[34] See below. Chapter VI.3.

and then given back, I owe myself in return for myself, and I owe myself twice. And yet, what could I give to God for himself?[35]

It is easy to see in this passage the essential feature of the teaching on the Image: by giving himself to me, God gave me to myself as he created me, that is to say, in his image and likeness. Union with God in love begins here, with God's gift of himself. This is how he seeks and finds us, and we do not seek and find him any other way. The total dependence of freedom on grace and, in a way, the dependence of grace on freedom, grow out of the mystery of love.

And yet, there are different ways of recognizing God's gifts. Saint Bernard mentions three of them when he compares the dependence of a slave, a mercenary, and a son. The first two seek their own interest, out of fear or greed. 'Only the charity of a son does not seek self-interest' (Cf. 1 Cor 13:.4–5). Saint Bernard then describes the basic intentionality of a slave and mercenary, each of whom in his own way lacks freedom, because each is set on pursuing self-interest. He concludes with a phrase which is very important because it defines both the entire process of conversion and the intention which should quicken it. Mark this phrase, which comes at the end of the comparison of the three kinds of relationships: unlike fear and self-interest, 'charity converts souls and makes them free.'[36] Our translation may appear a little too free. It is intended to bring out the parity among will, freedom, and love in Saint Bernard's vocabulary. Will, which lies at the root of the soul and determines the quality of each of its actions, is—according to the etymology of the latin word in the whole christian tradition—the capacity to love.[37] In Saint Bernard, as has been pointed out, will is most often identical to affectivity and desire.[38] When looked at this way, will

---

[35] Dil 5.15 (SBOp 3:132).

[36] Dil 12.34 9 (SBOp 3:149): '*Caritas vero convertit animas, quas facit et voluntarias*'. The same development is found in Div 3.9 (SBOp 6/1:92–93).

[37] A. Demoustier, 'Le sens du mot "volonté" dans la tradition chrétienne', *Christus* n⁰ 144 (October 1989) 439.

[38] For example, with regard to a person's willing choice of humility in imitation of the example of Jesus, humble of heart, Bernard said: '*Cordis affectu, id est voluntate*', that is to say, by will and humility inspired by affection of the heart, and not one which is forced upon us by evident reality, SC 42.7 (SBOp 2:37).

does not give the impression of being a kind of coercion which
opposes desire, as we too often think of it. Instead, it is a matter
of a conversion of desire enlightened by intelligence. The supple
and free interaction of the two leads both to conviction and to free,
fervent decision-making, 'the direct opposite of tense and repressive
willfulness which in reality can only lead to routine or pride.'[39] For
Saint Bernard, love is at one and the same time extremely sober and
unsentimental, but in no way voluntarist. A faulty understanding
of his use of words has sometimes caused misunderstanding on this
point. The whole accent is on love's disinterestedness. Thirty-seven
times he quotes: *All seek their own interests* (Ph 2:21) and thirty-nine
times: *Charity does not seek its own interests* (1 Cor 13:5). Gratuitous by
nature and therefore free, love enlivens a person's whole existence.
With respect to the monastic vocation and its demands, it confers
the gratuitousness which alone gives them their evangelical value.
In the four steps of love, transition from one step to the next
is always brought about by greater disinterestedness, until at the
fourth degree, the soul is totally incapable of turning back to self-
centeredness. Progress from the second step of love to the third
will result from the practice of ascesis, which makes us better able
to love God in a disinterested way.[40]

Finally, at the end of his commentary on the *Song of Songs*,
when with perfect confidence he leaves us a description of the
principal characteristics of love, Saint Bernard insists once more on
its absolute gratuitousness.

It outstrips even the love of a son hoping for his inheritance,
because it seeks something other than itself; it is fragile, because
it still depends on hope. In comparison with the love of the bride,
whose only fortune and only hope is to love, it is impure. 'Love's
only fruit is to exist. I love because I love, to love.' But love is pure
only when it depends on infinite love. Without a bond with grace,
it falls back into its own limits and endless pursuit of objects which
can only disappoint it. Saint Bernard continues by reminding us

---

[39] P.-Y. Emery, Introduction to *Saint Bernard. Sermons pour l'année* (Turnhout-
Taizé: Brepols, 1990) 13.
[40] Dil 15.39 (SBOp 3:152–153).

that all true love is bonded to transcendent love, which guarantees its authenticity. 'Love is a great reality, provided it returns to its source. . . .'[41]

Christ's charity alone was able to break the circle imprisoning love. He has restored its capacity for God who is charity. The Wisdom of love is none other than Christ, who enables us to escape from the grueling and sterile cycle of our all-too-human and never-to-be-satisfied desires. He leads us by a saving shortcut to the very Origin of this infinite desire within us and also its true Object, the only One who can grant it fulfillment.[42]

4. INCARNATE WISDOM, MEDIATOR OF ENCOUNTER

Always seeking his spiritual creature and wanting its love, the Creator,[43] being pure spirit, desired to take on human flesh. And since, according to Saint Bernard, the Creator's search for the soul follows the way of wisdom, which for him means the monastic life, it is not surprising that he uses the expression 'incarnate Wisdom' seven times to signify the mystery of the Incarnation.[44] This wisdom is hidden and veiled, but it is the wisdom of a God inebriated with the wine of charity, who lets himself be seen in his humanity, especially his tenderness.

> His tenderness (*benignitas*) could not have manifested itself more fully, could not have expressed itself more generously, could not have won us over more convincingly.[45]

Commenting on a verse of *Psalm 18*, *Day to day announces the Word*, Saint Bernard distinguished three kinds of words: the word of

---

[41] SC 83.5 and 4 (SBOp 2:301 and 300).

[42] Dil 7.21 (SBOp 3:136–137).

[43] 'The reason for loving God is God . . . It is he who provides the opportunity, he who creates attachment, he who brings desire to its fulfillment. He makes himself loved; or rather, he became human in order to be loved.' Dil 7.22 (SBOp 3:137).

[44] SC 6.7 (SBOp 1:29); Miss 2.13 (SBOp 4:30); Nat 3.2 (SBOp 4:259); Asc 6.10 (SBOp 5:155); Div 29.3 (SBOp 6/1:212); Div 49 (SBOp 6/1:270); Div 57.1 (SBOp 6/1:286).

[45] Div 29.3 (SBOp 6/1:212).

visible realities by which we can know God; the word of the Law; and finally, the word that is living because it is uttered in the flesh. This final word has the taste and savour of the substance and fullness of the one who communicates it to us, Incarnate Wisdom, who also gives us a taste for God and will incite us to conversion.[46]

In Chapter VI, we will develop wisdom's role more fully. Here let us simply point out the character of savour and taste, which Saint Bernard likes to recognize in wisdom, and notice that he has it returning to its origin: divine Wisdom. He does this to show us that by becoming incarnate, Wisdom has been put within our reach. Certain images of the Word are therefore dear to him: the Word unable to speak, the infant-God (*verbum infans*),[47] the abridged Word (*Verbum abbreviatum*).[48] Saint Bernard's whole teaching is centered on Christ who, to make himself loved by human beings, became human. His two natures are viewed as complementary to one another in our salvation. This is a kind of divine pedagogy, where Jesus' human nature sensitizes our heart and draws it beyond the level of the senses to reach his divine nature in the same Person of the Word. Saint Bernard clearly expresses this thought in *Sermon 20 on the Song of Songs*:

> Notice that in a way the heart's love is according to the flesh, because it makes the human heart more sensitive to Christ's flesh and to what Christ did or commanded in his body of flesh. Whoever is filled with this love is easily touched by anything said about these things. He or she listens to nothing more willingly, reads nothing more attentively, ruminates nothing more frequently, meditates nothing more agreeably . . . At prayer, the sacred image of the God-Man is always present before one's eyes: at his birth, teaching, ascending to heaven, or anything else of this type which comes to mind.

Eternal Wisdom willed that we fix our attention on the gospel mysteries of God's manifestation in time. For Saint Bernard, the

---

[46] Div 49 (SBOp 6/1:270).

[47] Nat 3.2 (SBOp 4:259); Nat 5.1 (SBOp 4:266); Miss 2.9 (SBOp 4:27); Epi 2.4 (SBOp 4:303).

[48] V Nat 1.1. (SBOp 4:197); Nat 1.1 (SBOp 4:244); Circ 2.1 (SBOp 4:277).

most evident reason for the Incarnation (a much debated topic in his time) was quite simply that, in order to make himself loved, God had to become man. It is rare that he gives us a written definition of a truth—that is not his style—but here he does so in an almost solemn way when he continues:

> As for me, I think that the principal reason why the invisible God wanted to be seen in the flesh and to live among human beings was first to draw all the affections of fleshly human beings (who could love only in this way) to the saving love of his own flesh, and by so doing lead them gradually to spiritual love.[49]

If, as Blondel came to understand, Christ is in a way the metaphysical mediator between sensorily perceived objects (phenomena) and Being, how much more is he mediator in the realm of the spirit, between human and divine love. So there is a wisdom of love in the sense that love gives us understanding and a taste for God, its origin and ultimate end. The symbol Saint Bernard uses most frequently to signify the mystery of the Incarnation is the two-fold motion of descent and ascent: God lowering himself to his creature, and the creature rising right up to God; humanization and deification.[50] On one of the rare occasions when Bernard directly cites a text, he restates a patristic tradition to express this admirable exchange: 'Contemplation is the fruit of the merciful descent of God's Word even to our human nature, by grace, and it leads

---

[49] SC 20.6 (SBOp 1:118).

[50] ' "Can a sensible man today still want to become God?" [asks Hans Küng]. I answer. Yes. Rarely has an epoch been so determined to do so. Ernst Bloch made *eritis sicut Deus* (you will be like God) the guiding idea for an interpretation of the biblical heritage turned towards the future, in which its revolutionary leaven comes into play against reactionary powers. By doing so, he was simply formulating the most profound longing of our century hidden behind passion for emancipation. The freedom meant here wants to get rid of the limits of the human condition: nothing can content it except the state of divinity, and it is for this reason that its criticism is radical, even to the point of being nihilist. A Christianity which offers humans less than becoming God is too modest. It will try in vain to guarantee its credibility, but in the struggle for humankind in which we are engaged its reply is insufficient.' Joseph Ratzinger, *Le christianisme sans peine* (Reply to Hans Küng), *Communio* III, n° 5 (1978) 95.

to the elevation of our human nature to the Word himself, by divine love.'[51]

The reason Bernard ranks the Ascension among the greatest feasts of the year—along with the Lord's Nativity and Easter—is that he sees it as the fulfilment of the mystery of the Incarnation. The Ascension is contemplated above all in its relationship to us, to our conversion and salvation, as the consummation of the other mysteries.

Love is the mutual attraction between God and his creature which stirs a reciprocal attentiveness and a desire to meet caused by 'I know not what affinity of nature (*vicinitate naturae*)'. But Saint Bernard goes on immediately to show us the aim of this meeting. It concerns the creature's desire, once he or she is conscious of the divine presence, to be conformed to it and transformed according to God's image.[52] Descending and ascending by the mystery of his Incarnation, the Lord left us the means to follow after him. Just as he has given us a description of the stages of the Incarnate Word's descent and ascent, so too he describes the steps of our ascent after him. Paradoxically, this takes place by means of humility, which counteracts our fall caused by pride.[53]

What attracts Saint Bernard's attention most in the Incarnation is not *how* the union of two natures came about, but *why*. For us

---

[51] Div 87.3 (SBOp 6/1:331). See the french edition of *Sermons divers* by P.-Y. Emery (Paris: Desclée de Brouwer, 1982), where in note 1 bis (page 121) he gives several references to the tradition (Maximus the Confessor, Gregory Nazianzen, Origen) which led to this sentence of John Duns Scotus quoted by Saint Bernard.

[52] SC 69.7 (SBOp 2:206). A. Gesché has raised the question: 'Dieu est-il *capax hominis*', *Revue théologique de Louvain* 24 (1993) 3–37, with reference to the expression *Verbum incarnandum* which Saint Bernard used three times (SC 2.7 (SBOp 1:12); Ep 77.V.18 (SBOp 7:198); Adv. *Sermones varii* (SBOp 6/1:9). 'The Word's destiny, if one may so express it, is to become incarnate' (p.12). Without being determinant, this expression can be significant if we situate it within bernardine christology as a whole, principally by joining the theme of likeness to that of love. The same theologian has also said he would like to see a '*pathétique*' characteristic in theology and cites Saint Bernard as an exception to our contemporary theology which is 'too readily rational and intellectual' (*Le mal* [Paris: Cerf, 1993] 158 and note 47).

[53] Div 60.2–3 (SBOp 6/1:291–292). This theme occurs very frequently in Saint Bernard, notably in his treatise *On the Steps of Humility and Pride*.

and for our salvation God became a human being, Wisdom became incarnate. Bernard's comparisons move along the lines of a God who assumed the form of his spiritual creature, that is to say, who adapted himself to our stature. For example, God's setting aside his majesty to reduce himself to our dimensions he compares to the prophet Elijah's adapting himself to the lifeless body of a little child to breathe life back into it.[54] One of the most striking of these comparisons is the image of a bow. Referring to Jacob's last words to Joseph in giving him the city of Shechem, which he had taken from the Amorites by his sword and bow (Gn 48:22), Saint Bernard comments:

> Your bow, Lord, is your Incarnation. There, in fact, the wood-Wisdom is curved and divinity is bent in a way that is full of loving kindness, whereas the bowstring, the cord of the flesh, is stretched to the very limit, and we know that humanity has thus grown in an ineffable way.[55]

Is this comparison not a strikingly significant expression of the synergy of the divine and human in Christ, the work common to his two natures? Human nature expands, like the bowstring as the wood of the bow bends. As at the Ascension, our human nature is deified because divinity bends down, and all the while the two motions remain mysteriously interdependent. In a reflection which

---

[54] SC 16.2 (SBOp 1:90). Cf. Søren Kierkegaard, 'The more superior a man is to someone he loves, the more he will feel (humanly) tempted to raise that person up to his level; but even more, he will be drawn (divinely) to lower himself to the other. This is the dialectic of love. It is quite astonishing, isn't it, that this is so little recognized in Christianity, where people always speak of Christ becoming human as if by an act of compassion or necessity.' *Journal* IV A 32 (in the french translation [Paris: Gallimard, 1942] this occurs at Vol. 1:.158). He makes a similar remark further on: 'The idea that God is love, in the sense that he is always the same, is so abstract that basically it is equivalent to scepticism.' *Journal* IV A 102; p.171.

[55] Sent 1.13. (SBOp 6/2:11). If God is capable of decrease, the very noble human creature is capable of greatness because it is made in the image of God. Consequently, between God and the creature there is such likeness and kinship of natures (*naturarum tanta cognatio*) that the creature is capable and desirous of a sort of majesty. Cf. SC 80.2 (SBOp 2:277). Also, between the Word and the soul there is 'an evident affinity of natures (*palam affinitas naturarum*).' SC 81.2 (SBOp 2:285).

may appear strange to us, Saint Bernard points out that since Christ was unable to increase because of his divine nature (for there was nothing greater than he), he found the means to become greater in another way, by willing to become incarnate, to suffer and die.[56] Several examples of this type of reasoning, which appears almost contradictory, reveal Saint Bernard's convictions about a very human God. At the same time, he avoids anthropomorphism. For example, he points out that in the *Song of Songs* (2:12) God twice used the expression *Our earth*, and spoke so tenderly of this earth that we could believe we were listening to one of earth's creatures. Is it not astonishing and, if I dare to say so, even a bit unworthy of God, asks Bernard. But it is also very pleasant to hear him speak this way. The reason is that God has very strong bonds with the earth. *On our earth*. These words have overtones, not of supremacy, but of sharing (*consortium*) and familiarity. The Creator is like one of us. This is the language of love, equality, and friendship.[57]

The mystery of the Incarnation is therefore essentially a mystery of love. Its most beautiful symbol is a kiss, and Saint Bernard says so in one of his finest sermons on the *Song of Songs*.

> Listen well to me. The mouth which gives the kiss is the Word assuming our flesh; the lips kissed are the flesh which was assumed. So the kiss in which both share equally is the Person formed by union of the Word and flesh, the Mediator between God and humans: Jesus, man and Christ.[58]

Could we not compare this union of two natures in the Word to the union of grace and freedom as Saint Bernard speaks of it, where all is grace and all is freedom? In it, all is God and all is human. Is this not a way of expressing the mystery defined at Chalcedon: union without confusion, distinction without separation? But we must not engage more in speculation than he does; rather, we must always have in view the fruit the divine intention is pursuing. This kiss, I

---

[56] Asc 2.6 (SBOp 5:130); Asc 4.6 (SBOp 5:142).
[57] SC 59.1 (SBOp 2:135–136). Cf. A Gesché, 'Notre terre, demeure du Logos', *Irenikon* 62 (1989) 451–485.
[58] SC 2.3 (SBOp 1:9–10).

too have received, because Jesus is my brother and my flesh. Never more will he be able to reject me.[59] Bernard repeats:

> God became incarnate *to enrich us by his poverty* (2 Cor 8:9), to raise us up by his humility, to make us greater by his self-abasement, to unite us to God by his Incarnation, and to enable us to begin to *form one single spirit with him* (1 Cor 6:17).[60]

Love's sole purpose is to form a union and—in a phrase of Saint Paul often employed by Saint Bernard—to make us one spirit with God, just as a man and a woman unite to become one flesh. 'The heart of the Bridegroom is the heart of his Father.'[61]

> Read in your heart, human creature, read within yourself what truth's witness says about you. By this ordinary light alone you will judge yourself unworthy. Then read in God's heart the covenant sealed by the Mediator's blood, and you will discover the great distance which separates what you possess in hope from what you have in reality. *What is a human being, to be glorified by you?* (Jb 7:17), it is written. Great, yes, a human being is, but in God. And veritably glorified, but by God.[62]

The meeting of the human creature and God is effectively accomplished by incarnate Wisdom, who came to enlighten our intelligence and give life to our heart, purifying them by restoring their original form to the image of the Image who is Christ.

In *Sermon 20 on the Song of Songs*, in which Saint Bernard clearly declares God's reason for taking on human flesh—to win our love—, he continues by describing the apostles' sadness when Christ disappeared from their sight at the Ascension. Of Christ's words: *It is for your own good that I am going, because unless I go the Advocate will not come to you* (Jn 16:6), he comments that obviously Jesus' presence in no way prevented the Spirit from coming, but by

---

[59] SC 2.6 (SBOp 1:12).
[60] Ann 3.8 (SBOp 5:40).
[61] SC 62.5 (SBOp 2:158).
[62] Ded 5.5 (SBOp 5:391).

speaking in such a way 'he was showing us the road we must walk and the form by which we would be marked'.[63]

The distinction here seems to point out the respective missions of the Son and the Spirit, both of whom lead to the Father. Wisdom is made of intelligence and will. Christ teaches truth; the Holy Spirit energizes the will. Will without intelligence is nothing but voluntarism or foolishness; intelligence without will, that is, without love, is nothing but erudition or intellectualism. In the application of the steps of truth to the Persons of the Trinity, it is the Son to whom, as Master, belongs the role of teaching his disciples the form of truth that is humility; and it is the Spirit to whom, as Friend, falls the task of giving them the charity of compassion. The Son wins disciples; the Spirit wins them over as friends who then become sons of the Father.[64]

The Form is wisdom. It is wisdom which will conform us to the image of God, making it brighter and brighter, by converting our free will to evangelical freedom.[65] This is the entire point of the monastic life, and Wisdom will reach fulfilment in peace.

Yet we have seen that, for us, the Incarnation is only the beginning of this journey which should lead us to become one spirit with God, and that what we possess in hope is far from the reality. Let us conclude this section with a charming and profound allegory taken from the story of Ruth. By using it and faithfully following the biblical account, Saint Bernard describes the whole christian and monastic journey. When Ruth turned back the hem of the cloak covering Booz's feet, she sensed Christ's closeness in virtue of the mystery of the Incarnation, and she implored him to protect her with this cloak (see Ruth 3:9). She had not, however, entered into the marriage which would enable her to hear Christ say: *My sister, my spouse* (Sg 4:9). Someone else, the close relative who had a right to her (that is to say, free choice), had to remove his sandal first, that is, give up his right

---

[63] Asc 3. 4 (SBOp 5:133). It is in this sense that the 3rd *Sermon for the Ascension*, as well as the 6th, is entitled: *De intellectu et affectu*.

[64] Hum 7.20 (SBOp 3:31).

[65] Gra 10.33–34 (SBOp 3:189–190).

under the law, and no one can be freed from it save by the grace of Christ.[66]

Progress in seeking God and closer union with him will be dealt with in Chapter IV. For now we have to follow Saint Bernard as he develops his spirituality of the mystery of the Incarnation.

5. MEMORY AND PRESENCE

Desiring his spiritual creature's love, the Creator went out to it. The divine assumed human form, the *Word became flesh* (Jn 1:14), because human beings could not love in any way other than humanly, that is to say, by hearing, touching, and seeing the object of their love. God's intervention in the world, his Incarnation, therefore necessarily took place in time and space, both of which are brief and limited. The mutual seeking by the Creator and his creature and their meeting in Christ, God and man, is at once temporal and eternal because he is one Person in his two natures. This is the mystery Saint Bernard articulates under the theme of 'memory and presence'. That love may endure, it clings to what it remembers. In the spiritual christian order, as Gilson has rightly observed:

> We are and we remain carnal beings, and our sensibility always claims its rights . . . [We need to relate this to] the very important idea that the *memoria*—and by this let us understand the memory, the sensible recollection of the Passion of Christ— is for us the condition and herald of the *praesentia*, that is to say, presence in the full sense of the term, of the beatific vision in the future life, but also already of those visitations of the soul by the Word in this life.[67]

---

[66] Sent 3.51: 'Ruth the Moabite' (SBOp 6/2;92–93).

[67] E. Gilson, *La théologie mystique de saint Bernard* (Paris: Vrin, 1934) 104. [*The Mystical theology of Saint Bernard,* trans. A. H. C. Downes (1940; rpt as Cistercian Studies Series 120: Kalamazoo: Cistercian Publications, 1990) 81–82]. Gilson goes on to mention the hymn *Dulcis Jesu memoria,* which made 'this theme famous in medieval latin poetry', and adds: 'The opposition of *memoria* and *praesentia* has always in fact a technical import in the writings of St. Bernard and of those who appeal to his doctrine', French 105; English 82.. Cf. C. Dumont ocso, 'L'Hymne *Dulcis Jesu memoria*'. Le *Jubilus* serait-il d'Aelred de Rievaulx?', Coll 55 (1993) 233–238.

There is no better way for us to grasp the astonishing dynamic of desire in Saint Bernard's spiritual teaching than to pursue this theme of mindfulness of Christ as it strives utterly towards eschatological presence. Our memory clings to everything manifested in the Lord's life and death so as to advance unceasingly towards the fulfilment in our life, death and destiny of that to which the Gospel mysteries point. The Church, through which we participate in these mysteries, has (in Saint Bernard's beautiful imagery) its eyes fixed on both the remembrance of Christ's passion and equally on the promised happiness already enjoyed by the saints. These two objects of the Church's attention nourish its insatiable desire, because not only does it know what is in store for it, but it already possesses it. As long as this life lasts (*interim*), the soul can repose in this mindfulness which lets it live in heaven already.[68]

Saint Bernard enjoyed using contrasts whenever he was overtaken by strong sentiments. To speak of a place of rest, peace, and joy moves him to tears when he feels himself far from the sweetness of eternity's infinitude.

> I, too, possess the Word, but in the flesh. Truth is offered to me, but in the sacrament. Angels are nourished by the grain of wheat. I, while waiting, must be content with the husk of the sacrament, the coating of the flesh, the chaff of the letter and the veil of the flesh . . . Even in the abundance of the spirit . . . faith does not equal vision, memory is not presence, time is not eternity. The reflection in the mirror is far from being the face itself, the form of a slave is different from the image of God, desire is different from fulfillment.[69]

Let us note the allusion to Christ's two natures—the form of a slave and the image of God—because it is precisely in their union in him as a Person that the sacrament's value and effectiveness reside. Accordingly, it is important clearly to situate meditation on the Gospel mysteries within the context of sacramental remembering:

---

[68] SC 62.1 (SBOp 2:154–155). '*Ambo haec: veluti ante et retro oculata, insatiabili desiderio contuetur.*'
[69] SC 33.3 (SBOp 1:235).

the memorial of the Lord. For Saint Bernard, all the words spoken by him who is God's Wisdom, all his acts and all his suffering, were willed and consequently sacramental (*plena sacramentorum*), and are rich with meaning for our salvation.[70]

The theme 'memory and presence' therefore has its place in Saint Bernard's sacramental theology as a whole. Nowadays, not only has our understanding of symbols become dulled,[71] but the sacramental realism of faith has as well. The Incarnation is the means for the physical beings we are to approach God, but it is God eternal and invisible whom we hear, touch, and see. This is how he saves us. The love for the historical Jesus of which we as Christians are capable is never separated or distinct from the theological virtue by which we can reach God as a person. So there is a distinction between what the imagination can help bring to our minds with the help of Gospel mysteries and the mystery of faith which remains above and beyond all imagining. In one of his *Sermons for the Annunciation*, Saint Bernard demonstrates this very well. The scenes in the narrative of the Incarnation are like flowers in a meadow, pleasing to look at in their great variety. But, he continues:

> In the middle of the meadow I see a terrifyingly deep abyss, an absolutely unfathomable abyss: the mystery of the Lord's Incarnation. Indeed, a truly impenetrable abyss. *The Word became flesh* (Jn 1:14) . . . Who can investigate this, who can reach it, who can grasp it? The well is deep and I have nothing that lets me draw from it.[72]

The practice of remembering, which is the essential trait of bernardine meditation, always takes place through the action of the Spirit and is made effectual by this same Spirit. The form of love in which Creator and spiritual creature meet belongs in the order of the sacred and surpasses what might be due merely to the imagination or the emotions, although it employs these natural capacities in a concrete way by assimilating them to sacramental

---

[70] Asc 4.2 (SBOp 5:138–139).
[71] Cf. P. A. Burton OCSO, 'Pourquoi est-il difficile de lire les Pères cisterciens', Coll 55 (1993) 331–339; 56 (1994) 139–152; 246–260; 57 (1995) 146–162.
[72] Ann 2.1 (SBOp 5:30).

grace. In his *Sermon for the Lord's Supper*, Saint Bernard articulates his teaching on what a sacrament is: a sacred sign or sacred secret denoting an invisible reality in a visible way. Specifically, in so far as the sacrament is divine, attentive 'consideration' must necessarily be given conjointly both to its efficacy due to grace (manifested by the visible sign) and to what is concealed and hidden from our eyes. Meditation on the mysteries is therefore an activity of 'consideration', the activity which, in Saint Bernard's opinion, is at the very heart of the monk's interior life. It is a 'transforming contemplation' which takes place in faith and remains under the influence of grace.[73]

There is real power (*virtus*) in Christ's flesh, but it is in faith's shadow.[74] The practice of remembering, or recalling, by meditation on the words 're-cited' in Scripture and the liturgy, will deepen the mystery to the very presence that it signifies and 'represents'. The liturgy, which itself is entirely remembrance, memorial, is also entirely anticipation and the desire for eschatological fulfillment. Saint Bernard, in his meditation as in his whole life, strained with all his being towards the fulfillment of God's kingdom beyond this world of sense perception, and towards love of God in the Spirit. His mysticism is at the same time dynamic and practical. And it is indeed mysticism, that is, development of faith. On this point he was careful to make a clear distinction between himself and Abelard who, in his opinion, considered the sacraments simply as a recalling of examples. Both developed the practice of dwelling on the remembrance of Gospel mysteries, but for Bernard it concerned the grace of the Redemption, and in this is life.

> It is one thing to follow Jesus, another to hold him, another to eat him. To follow is a salutary aim; to hold and embrace is festive joy; to eat is a blessed life . . . . What are aim or joy without life? Nothing but lifeless paintings. Therefore, neither examples of humility nor signs of charity are anything without the sacrament of the Redemption.[75]

---

[73] 5 HM 1–2 (SBOp 5:67–69).

[74] SC 31.9 (SBOp 1:225).

[75] Ep 190.9.25: 'Abelard's errors' (SBOp 8:38).

Between faith as the way to vision and memory as the way to presence, there is a parallel .[76]

Even if memory counts for little in comparison with presence, if it is mere shadow compared to reality, it is nevertheless already a foretaste of happiness. The practice of remembering, even if it does not measure up to the desire for God our hearts feel, is still the means of making God's word bear fruit for us, because when we call to mind the mysteries of salvation, we return to the source of the grace these mysteries obtain for us, and this allows them to flow in us more abundantly.[77] Consideration, in the sense in which Saint Bernard defines and describes it, is the monk's principal occupation. It is his interior life, his *pietas*, his religion, the activity of his mind in search of truth.[78] Meditative reflection on the Gospel mysteries clearly represents an important part of this consideration.[79] Yet it is only a preparation, a spiritual practice done with a view to contemplating the mystery of God. It is important to remember this, because the great success this new kind of meditation has had in western spirituality has eclipsed the basic reality. It is significant that in Book V of the treatise *On Consideration,* Saint Bernard recalls the doctrine of Christ's mediation but makes no mention of imaginative or sense-linked meditation on Gospel mysteries.[80]

This new 'method'—which, because Bernard put all his poetic and literary art into it, is actually not very methodical at all—had a widespread influence. In his own day he taught it to the Knights Templar, who had the opportunity of meditating on Christ's life, and especially on his death, in the Holy Land, where imagining the setting is fairly easy.

---

[76] Sent 1.12 (SBOp 6/2:10).

[77] Nat BVM 1 and 13 (SBOp 5:275 and 283–284). For memory reinvigorating love by returning to the source of grace, see also SC 51.5–6 (SBOp 2:86–87) and 83.4 (SBOp 2:300).

[78] Csi I.8 (SBOp 3:403–404).

[79] A. Le Bail OCSO, *Saint Bernard, Docteur de la dévotion à N.-S. Jésus-Christ* (Gembloux: 1931). 'La Considération du Dieu-Homme', 7–27.

[80] Practical (*dispensativa*) consideration (knowledge of objects that can be perceived by the senses) is simply a laborious preparation for speculative consideration which, 'recollecting itself . . . , frees itself from what is human to contemplate God' Csi V. 4 (SBOp 3:469).

> Among all the holy places that anyone may desire to visit, in
> a certain way Jesus' sepulchre is the first choice . . . There it
> is easier to visualize the place where he lay when dead. One
> experiences an increase of fervor which I cannot express . . .
> The remembrance of his death, even more than that of his life,
> kindles our love.[81]

In the same exhortation to the Knights Templar there is another
passage on the joy of seeing the Holy Sepulchre with one's own eyes.
It expresses very well Saint Bernard's thought on the 'sacramental'
efficacy of this way of applying the mind by means of attention of
the senses. After a long theological instruction on the redeeming
death of Christ, which must have been a little over the heads of the
knights, he continued:

> Whether by these reflections on this subject or by others of
> the same kind according to each person's inspiration, this is
> what the Sepulchre suggests to the minds of Christians. And
> I think that more fervent emotion is experienced by someone
> who contemplates it with his own eyes. It is not a meager
> advantage to see with one's bodily eyes the resting place of the
> Lord's body. And even if this place is now empty of his sacred
> members, it is nevertheless full of ours, and so becomes like a
> joyful 'sacrament' for us.[82]

In this last sentence, when Saint Bernard refers to our members
being in Christ's tomb, we can see the highly theological way in
which he evokes our burial with Christ in death. He refers to it
expressly in what follows in this passage. Saint Bernard was the
first to describe meditation with the application of the senses,
as if the person meditating had actually been present. By doing
so, he influenced all christian spirituality, particularly ignatian
spirituality.[83] He left it to his disciple, Aelred of Rievaulx, to give
us numerous examples of this sort of meditation. Applying all his

---

[81] Tpl 18 (SBOp 3:229).

[82] Tpl 29 (SBOp 3:236).

[83] Cf. B. De Vrégille, 'De Saint Bernard à saint Ignace', Coll 24 (1990), 238–
244.

educational talent, he passed them on in detail and in sequence in two of his works: *A Rule for a Recluse*[84] and *On Jesus at the Age of twelve*.[85]

As for Saint Bernard himself, it was in his treatise *On Loving God* that he first developed this theme of memory tending towards presence. In Chapter III, after saying that in their unhappy condition as human creatures believers know very well what they owe to the mystery of the Incarnation, he begins (also for the first time) to comment on two verses of the *Song of Songs: Sustain me with flowers, restore me with apples, for I languish with love* (Sg 2:5), and *his left arm is under my head, his right embraces me* (Sg 2:6). This is not the place to explain or even to summarize these pages—so praiseworthy for their fervor and beauty—[86] but we do need to point out that intense eschatological desire underlies all these beautiful, profound reflections. Let us quote a few lines.

> In my opinion, [the soul] realizes that love's strength can become weakened and tepid if it is not unceasingly kindled by such incentives until it is introduced into the chamber and says: *His left arm is under my head, his right embraces me* (Sg 2:6). It will then understand with certainty all the signs of love it received at his first coming . . . The elect to whom complete satisfaction

[84] Aelred of Rievaulx, *Vie de Recluse.* SCh 76 (Paris: Cerf, 1961) 116–145. (See several pages of the Introduction on 'La Méditation: Semences de méditation; mémoire et présence; La dévotion tendre à l'Humanité du Christ', 17–27. [Aelred of Rievaulx, *Treatises* I: *Rule for a Recluse.* Cistercian Fathers Series 2 (Spencer: Cistercian Publications, 1971) 41–102]. On the use of the imagination in meditation, see Mary Ann Mayeski, 'A Twelfth-Century View of the imagination: Aelred of Rievaulx' in *Noble Piety and Reformed Monasticism. Studies in Medieval Cistercian History VII*, edited E. Rozanne Elder. Cistercian Studies Series 65 (Kalamazoo: Cistercian Publications, 1981) 123–129.

[85] Aelred de Rievaulx, *Quand Jesus eut douze ans.* SCh 60 (Paris:Cerf, 1958) [English translation: Aelred of Rievaulx. Treatises,1. *On Jesus at the Age of Twelve.* Cistercian Fathers Series 2 (Spencer: Cistercian Publications, 1971) 1–39].

[86] Dil 3.7–10 (SBOp 3:124–127. Bernard would think of this when commenting on the same passage in *Sermon 51 on the Song of Songs.* There he gives an explanation for the variety of interpretations possible for Scripture, which is like water having various uses. SC 51.3 (SBOp 2:86). Here, his commentary puts the moral interpretation in the foreground, but he does not forget the supportive role of memory which can grow weary while waiting for God.

of full presence has not yet been accorded will not lack the strengthening consolation that comes from memory.[87]

This allusion to remembrance of the first coming leads us to think that memory's activity unfolds in what Saint Bernard describes as an intermediary coming. While we wait, perseverance will, in fact, be sustained by the fruits of the Passion and the flowers of the Resurrection. Saint Bernard's notion of time also corresponds to this dynamic of memory-to-presence (See below, Chapter V. 1 and 4).

In a well known passage Saint Bernard commented on the bouquet of myrrh placed on his heart, that is to say, the remembrance of Jesus' life, and especially the myrrh of his cross and burial. He concludes by saying that as long as he lives he will remember them and that in eternity he will never forget them because it is to them that he owes his life.[88] The name of Jesus will be a source of strength each time a person enunciates it in memory of him. Meditation on this name alone will be a very effective means of making him present in our heart, just as mentioning the name of a beloved person usually does.[89]

To be mindful of God this way, within the mystery of salvation, is therefore the chief occupation of an attentive soul. But, like the desert monks, the monk today will have to struggle to keep memory safe from all the things which can encumber and obscure it. Like intelligence and will, it has lost the pristine vigor it had once, when, in its original simplicity, it remembered God easily. Pressing and absorbing thoughts, not to mention idle thoughts, will be our lot on this earth.[90] Restoration of the soul's simplicity as the image of its Creator also includes the restoration of memory. In Saint Bernard's description of the trinity in the soul which is a likeness of the

---

[87] Dil 3.10 (SBOp 3:126–127).

[88] SC 43.3 (SBOp 2:42–43). Cf. SC 45.4 (SBOp 2:52); Div 22.5 (SBOp 6/1: 173–174).

[89] SC 15.6 (SBOp 1:86).

[90] Div 45.1 (SBOp 6/1:262–263). See below also: 'Pacified Memory' Chapter VI.2.

Blessed Trinity,[91] memory corresponds to the Father. It is placed at the end of the spiritual journey, because it transcends time in 'eternal security, where it will drink at the eternally inexhaustible fountain'.[92] Memory is a function of thought,[93] but thought can rise from consideration to contemplation, from meditation to rapture. Already in his first treatise, when he described the steps of knowledge of God, Saint Bernard attributed restoration of the image in the intellect to the Son, and its restoration in the will to the Holy Spirit, but all the while it is the Father who enlightens the memory. This appears only at the end of his commentary, when memory returns to itself after being transported in God.[94]

Memory seems, therefore, to be the soul's foundation—its 'intentionality' as the existential phenomenologists would say—and also the fruit of recollection and interior unity. In this teaching we can see a correlation with Gabriel Marcel's reflection on the relationship between recollection and memory.

> Recollection is undoubtedly what is least spectacular in the soul. It does not consist in looking at something, it recalls; it is interior reflection, and we have reason to ask ourselves if we should not see in it the ontological foundation of memory, the principle of the interior, affective and unrepresentable unity on which the very possibility of remembering is based. Here, the english expression 'to recollect oneself' is very revealing.[95]

The search for God is essentially the life of the soul's deepest memory craving God's presence.[96] The practice of meditation, in which memory and presence are complementary, will develop quite naturally as it were within the framework of the monk's 'spiritual

---

[91] On the structure of the soul (memory, intellect and will), see Lode Van Hecke's fine development in *Le désir dans l'expérience religieuse*, 54–68.
[92] SC 11.6 (SBOp 1:58).
[93] Div 32.2 (SBOp 6/1:219).
[94] Hum 7.21 (SBOp 3:33).
[95] Cf. Gabriel Marcel, *Positions et Approches concrètes du mystère ontologique* (Louvain: Nauwelaerts, 1949) 64.
[96] Div 4.1 (SBOp 6/1:94). V Nat 4.10 (SBOp 4:227).

practices': *lectio divina*,[97] reflection on this *lectio*, lifting up the heart, and the various experiences of contemplation to which these practices lead. (See below, Chapter V.2).

Memory tending towards presence permeates the entire liturgy. On Christmas Eve, after the monks had just heard in the chapter room the proclamation: 'Jesus, Son of God, is born in Bethlehem of Judaea', Saint Bernard told them that that which makes spirits new is always new and can never grow old. We do not say that Jesus was born, but that he is born. Just as, in some way, he is immolated each day when we proclaim his death, so too he is born when by our memory we are present at his birth.[98]

Saint Bernard liked to call to mind God's blessings in connection with the fragrance of the perfume mentioned in the *Song of Songs* (1:2). This remembering, this *recordatio*, that which etymologically one 'takes to heart'(*cor*), is the opposite of remembering one's sins—and far better.[99]

These various references to the theme 'memory-presence' make it very clear that for Saint Bernard it betokens the reality of the Christian, who belongs to two worlds, but this is because God by his Incarnation also belongs to both. 'The *Word became flesh and dwelt among us* (Jn 1:14). He really and truly dwells in our hearts by faith, he dwells in our memory, he dwells in our thoughts, and he has descended even into our imagination.[100]

---

[97] On the role of memory in reading Scripture, the following reflection is very enlightening: 'Basically, memory is not a passive or "past" (*passéiste*) faculty; a memory is not a photograph or a pure recording of what is remembered. In memory's action there is always a slow operation of sorting out and modeling. When I learn a text "by heart", not only do I change my "heart" by making this text my own, but by some mysterious alchemy the text is transformed as I gradually appropriate it. New meanings appear in it; it reveals unheard of harmonies and gives a glimpse of new depths. The text and reader are mutually metamorphosed and unite in this kind of communion which is meditation: active reading which, by the memory, nourishes our own substance by the substance of a text.' D. Poirel, 'La *lectio divina*, vie spirituelle', *Communio* 19 (1994/3) 45.

[98] V Nat 6.6 (SBOp 4:239).

[99] Sc 12.8 and 10 (SBOp 1:65 and 66); Div 87.6 (SBOp 6/1:332–333); Sent 2.169 (SBOp 6/2:56).

[100] Nat BVM 10 (SBOp 5:282). Quoted by J. De Finance sj, who commented on this passage as follows: 'Scripture's message is not exhausted by what the intellect

For Saint Bernard, the principal reason behind the mystery of the Incarnation was, as we know, God's desire to be loved, to encounter his creature and join with it by love. Mindfulness of the blessings of Christ's mediation is therefore an expression of love responding to love. It is the desire to be more present to the mind and heart of the loved one, while awaiting the joy of total presence and eternal beatitude.

Let us quote one last passage which will also serve as an introduction to the next section of this chapter:

> It is commonly said: 'Far from sight, far from heart.' My eye is my memory. To think about the saints is, in a way, to see them. This is our lot in the land of the living, a lot far from mediocre, if our affection is joined to our memory as it should be. Yes, I repeat, our existence in heaven, even if it differs from that of the saints, is like this: they are there in reality, we, by desire; they are there by their presence, we, by memory. When will we be in their presence by our very being?[101]

6. TYPES OF MEDIATION IN THE BODY OF CHRIST

The Creator's encounter with the spiritual creature whom he has been seeking takes place through the mediation of Christ, in love. Saint Bernard's entire doctrine is centered on the mystery of the Incarnation and the intention he saw in it: God's desire to be loved and in this way to save humanity, which had become separated from God by its perverse will to be autonomous and by its refusal of love. The mediation of Christ, the God-Man, is therefore unique and primordial. It casts its light on the whole work of salvation.

---

can draw from it. It is addressed to the whole human person, it concerns all one's human powers, it presents a challenge on all levels *even to the place where the soul is divided from the spirit* (He 4.12), to this median region of imagination and sensible affectivity which is the privilege of an incarnate spirit. That is why spiritual masters like Ignatius Loyola recommend that we be present to the 'mysteries'-let us understand by that: events-we are contemplating, not as simple spectators but, in a certain way as actors. A lived, existential reading which alone permits us truly to understand.' *Gregorianum* 65 (1984) 680.

[101] OS 5.5 (SBO 5:364–365).

But this mediation is diffused in derived mediations,[102] because that is how Saint Bernard understood the communion of saints. 'No one was more zealous than he', wrote Vacandard, 'to bring out the importance of the dogma of the communion of saints.'[103]

The Church

Mediation derived from Christ's mediation can exist only within his Body, which is the Church. The Church is the mediatrix because it is united as a bride to Christ. Every other mediation receives its grace and mission from the Church. Saint Bernard expressed this mystery by the way he used the symbol of the bride of Christ: sometimes with reference to the Church and at other times to the soul united with God in the Church. 'Each of us who together are the Church', he said, in an expression which sounds very modern.[104] Again: 'The bride is ourselves, if that does not seem unbelievable to you. Yes, all together we form one single bride, and the souls of all of us are each like individual brides.'[105]

Let us look at another text, because this doctrine is important:

> Even if none of us can be so presumptuous as to call his [or her] soul the bride of the Lord, still, since all together we make up the Church . . . we possess fully and integrally what it possesses, and there is no contradiction in saying that each one of us participates in it individually. Thanks be to you, Lord Jesus, who have deigned to gather us together in your Church, so dear to you, not only as your faithful but that we may embrace you as a bride does.[106]

---

[102] 'The unique mediation of the Redeemer does not exclude but rather gives rise among creatures to a manifold cooperation which is but a sharing in this unique source.' *The Documents of Vatican II. Dogmatic Constitution on the Church* VIII.62, edited by W. M. Abbot and J. Gallagher (New York: Guild Press, 1966) 92. Cf. G. Barauna, 'La très sainte Vierge Marie au service de l'économie du salut', in *L'Eglise du Vatican II*, tome III. Collection: *Unam Sanctam* 51c (Paris: Cerf, 1966) 1227–1230 and 1238.

[103] E. Vacandard, *Saint Bernard* (Paris:Gabalda, 1904) 234.

[104] SC 57.3 (SBOp 2:121).

[105] O Epi 2.2 (SBOp 4:320).

[106] SC 12.11 (SBOp 1:67). Cf. SC 61.2: *Ecclesia nomine non una anima, sed multarum unitas vel potius unanimitas designatur*: (SBOp 2:149).

Notice the distinction Saint Bernard makes in the last phrase between believers and the possibility of their attaining a greater intimacy with Christ. This distinction, which we will study in the next chapter, is more important to him than the (today even more accentuated) distinction between the hierarchy and the people of God. His flows from the intensely spiritual idea he had of the Church. Right now, however, we cannot even think about summarizing Saint Bernard's ecclesiology.[107]

Let us simply call to mind the original and figurative way he had of explaining the birth of the Church. He gives an allegorical interpretation of the first verses of chapter 3 of the *Song of Songs*: *I sought him whom my heart loves . . . I will go through the city; in the streets and in the squares . . . I sought him but did not find him. The watchmen came upon me. I was found. 'Have you seen him whom my heart loves?' I asked them. Scarcely had I passed them, when I found him whom my heart loves. I held him fast, and I would not let him go.*

If *predestination* preceded the birth of the Church, comments Saint Bernard, and *creation* was simply the beginning of time, then for the Church to be revealed in time *inspiration* was necessary. The Spirt of the Bridegroom was breathed into human spirits to prepare the way of the Lord. So when the bride says that she was found by the guardians of the city, it should be clear that she was received with kindness, but not chosen by them; recognized, but not converted; it is God alone who converts, inspires, and prepares souls to be found. The Apostles, the ministers of the Church, gave her in a few words the creed of faith in the language of love which she understood. Then, scarcely had she gone past them when she found the one her heart loved.[108]

The scene describes in a very precise, though purely figurative, way Saint Bernard's understanding of the Church as a soul called by God. He was not unaware of the visible and social dimensions of the Church, nor did he lack an active interest in them (even to the point

---

[107] This topic was presented in a masterful way at the Congress on Saint Bernard at Dijon in 1953: Yves Congar op, 'L'écclésiologie de saint Bernard', *Saint Bernard théologien* ASOC/AC 9 (1953) 137–190.
[108] SC 78 and 79 (SBOp 2:266–276).

of being far more involved in them than some people would have liked), but for him the Church was first and foremost spiritual. Also, as Yves Congar has tactfully remarked, it was necessary that the bride be found by the watchmen. This concept of the Church influenced the way the abbot of Clairvaux viewed the role of authority: not as power but as service (*non dominium sed servitium*). The following passage, one among many, shows quite clearly the freedom a spiritual person enjoys in the Church:

> The *Song* shows us that when the bride found the watchmen-
> or rather, when she was found by them, because it was not
> they whom she was seeking-, she did not stop as if she could
> be satisfied with finding them. She inquired in haste about her
> Beloved, so she might fly to him as quickly as possible. Her
> heart did not belong to the watchmen. It was in the Lord that
> she had placed all her trust.[109]

The Church was born of Christ's sleep of love on the cross, because *God is love* (1 Jn 4:16).[110] Love makes it a Church. Love calls it into being, calls it together, and maintains it in charity. And the wisdom of love ought to dwell in the hearts of those who have been invested with authority. Speaking about Jesus' words to Peter: *Do you love me* (Jn 21:15)?, Saint Bernard uses this beautiful phrase: 'How, in fact, could he confide such beloved sheep to someone who does not love?'[111]

Mary

Mary's mediation holds an important place in Saint Bernard's teaching. No one has spoken more fervently or more eloquently about it than he did. The terminology he daringly used in his lyrical style have sometimes disturbed theologians. Here we cannot develop Saint Bernard's mariology any more than we did his ecclesiology.[112] From

---

[109] QH 15.3 (SBOp 4:477).

[110] Sept 2.1 (SBOp 4:349–350).

[111] '*Quando enim sic amatas oves committeret non amanti?*', Conv 19.32 (SBOp 4:109).

[112] This also was presented at the Congress on Saint Bernard at Dijon in 1953, by H. Barré: 'Saint Bernard, Docteur marial', *Saint Bernard théologien*, 92–113.

the point of view we are taking in this synthesis of his spirituality, Mary was for Bernard the person who found what she was seeking, what no one before her had been able to find. *She found grace in God's sight.*[113] What grace? On the feast of the Assumption, Saint Bernard began his sermon by saying:

> It is high time to say to the whole world that Mary, the Mother of the Incarnate Word, has been taken up to heaven, and that no mortal human being can ever cease singing her praise, because by the Virgin, unique in all creation, human nature has been raised above even the immortal spirits.[114]

For Saint Bernard, Mary's unequaled privilege lay in being the Mother of the Incarnate Word, and consequently mediatrix and cooperatrix in the Redemption. Pope John Paul II's encyclical on the Virgin Mary (where Saint Bernard is quoted some ten times, especially in texts on her mediation of grace) well conveys the meaning of this mediation by relating it fundamentally to the primordial grace of divine maternity.[115]

Even though Bernard said, in his familiar way of speaking, that we can approach Mary more easily than Jesus because she is a woman and a mother, and because she is not God, we must never forget that this is the same Bernard who has shown us that the Son of God is infinitely close to us, even one of us![116] Mary comes to our aid first of all by her prayer:

See C. Dumont OCSO, 'Saint Bernard, moine poète mystique de Notre Dame', *Une éducation du coeur*, Pain de Cîteaux 10. 3rd Series (Oka: Abbaye Notre-Dame-du-Lac, 1996) 153–189.

[113] Miss 3.10 (SBOp 4:43).

[114] Asspt 4.1 (SBOp 5:244).

[115] Pope John Paul II, *Redemptoris Mater* (Washington, D.C.: U.S. Catholic Conference, 1987).

[116] 'We are far from the notion of an inaccessible Mediator (Hum 3.6) requiring a mediatrix at his side, as some expressions used by Bernard would lead us to think (Nat BVM 7). Let us say rather that it is the compassion of Mary, who desires to give us salvation, which taught him (Bernard) what Jesus' compassion could be, a fully human compassion while remaining that of a God: a human way of being God.' J. Regnard OCSO, 'La voie théologale de saint Bernard', *La Vie Spirituelle* 145 (1991) 56.

Let your loving-kindness take upon itself to make known to the world this grace you have found with God, obtaining by your holy prayers pardon for the guilty, healing for the sick, courage for the fainthearted, consolation for the afflicted, help and liberation for those in danger.[117]

In a prayer to Mary which Dante put on Saint Bernard's lips: *Vergine madre, figlia del tuo figlio* ('Virgin Mother, daughter of your Son'—does this not sum up the whole mystery of Mary's mediation?), he says that our asking for God's grace without having recourse to Mary would be like a bird wanting to fly without wings.[118]

According to Saint Bernard's undeviating teaching, Mary is the model for the moral life of a monk. The virtues which made her pleasing to God—humility above all, obedience, purity, and mercy—are the graces her mediation offers us.[119] Mary is Wisdom's dwelling-place, where the seven columns of the theological and cardinal virtues have been constructed.[120]

When the angel said to Mary: *The Lord is with you* (Lk 1:28), it was the entire Trinity who was with her: not only the Son whom she clothed with her flesh, but the Holy Spirit by whom she conceived, and the Father who made his Son her son as well.[121] 'To be with' signifies the willing agreement of the divine Persons, to which the Virgin's consent was a response.[122] Mary is with us by the tenderness of infinite compassion, for 'she suffered more keenly because she loved him more tenderly'.[123] Her mediation is therefore compassion for the Body of her Son, and it was of her that Saint Bernard was primarily thinking when he said:

---

[117] Asspt 4.9 (SBOp 5:250).

[118] Dante, *The Divine Comedy: Paradiso* 33.14–15.

[119] Miss 1.5–9 (SBOp 4:17–21); Asspt 4.5–8 (SBOp 5:247–250).

[120] Div 52.2–4 (SBOp 6/1:275–277).

[121] Miss 3.4 (SBOp 4:38).

[122] Miss 4.8–9 (SBOp. 4:53–55). In the second sermon on the *Song of Songs*, where Christ's mediation is spoken of as a kiss: union of God and man, Mary is not mentioned.

[123] Sent 3.87 (SBOp 6/2:128).

Tenderness (*unctio pietatis*) which is compassionate, and makes us suffer with those who suffer, is poured out upon the entire Body of Jesus Christ like an ointment. And when I say the Body of Jesus, I am not speaking about the one which was crucified, but the one acquired by his sufferings.[124]

For Saint Bernard, Mary's universal mediation within the whole Body of Christ signifies that she is the mother of charity (*caritatis mater*). He gave voice to his thought on this when he spoke about the arrow which pierced her whole soul, the arrow of choice, which is love of Christ, which left in her nothing but love. This happened so that this same love might reach us and that she might become the mother of charity, just as God-who-is-Love is its Father.[125]

Angels

The angels' mediation unfurls in an atmosphere of friendship. If Christ became our servant, there can be nothing astonishing about the fact that, because of him, the angels also serve us. They love us, in fact, because Christ has loved us. And Saint Bernard quotes a well-known proverb: ' "Love me, love my dog." Are we not the puppies you love so affectionately?'[126] He invites us to place our loving confidence in the ministry of the angels whom God has ordered to watch over us.[127] They protect us from the ways of obstinacy, greed, and presumption.[128] Pure spirits, they enter into the economy of salvation by inspiring in our minds material images that help us bear the splendor of greater spiritual graces.[129] We ought to love them, even if we would prefer to have direct contact

---

[124] SC 12.10 (SBOp 1:67).

[125] SC 29.8 (SBOp 1:208).

[126] Mich 1.3 (SBOp 5:295–296).

[127] QH 12.1–10 (SBOp 4:457–463).

[128] QH 11.10 (SBOp 4:455).

[129] SC 41.3 (SBOp 2:30). The new distinguishing feature Saint Bernard added to devotion to the angels is human warmth, as though he wanted to humanize them, too. We find in his writings something which ' is most exquisite on devotion to the angels whom we should love tenderly. One can feel the beating of the heart which prompted these pages. This persuasive eloquence enlightens, moves and attracts.' See J. Duhr's article: 'Anges' in the *Dictionnaire de Spiritualité* 1:600–601.

with the Lord whose simple messengers they are.[130] We have seen Saint Bernard expressing the same idea in speaking about church ministers; he mentions it again in connection with the support he finds in friendship.

Saint Joseph

Only a few words are needed to describe Saint Joseph's participation in the mystery of the Incarnation. He was 'the only person on earth chosen by God to be his perfectly faithful helper in his great plan.'[131]

The Saints

The mediation of Saints Peter and Paul is likewise due to the fact that they are Christ's friends and, as such, introduce us into Christ's presence. 'Let us pray to them, so that they may win for us the favor of their friend, who is our Judge'.[132] The terms Saint Bernard uses to describe their mediation are the same as those he employs in speaking of Mary: 'Thanks to their mediation, I will be able to ascend to this Mediator who came to make peace by his blood between what is on earth and what is in heaven.'[133]

Not only did Bernard cherish *all* the saints who are waiting for us, and love their feast day in a special way, but there are a great many individual saints who were dear to him: John the Baptist, Martin, Clement, Andrew, Victor (the saint from Champagne for whose feast he composed the Office) and above all, Saint Benedict. 'His spiritual fatherhood consists chiefly in having given the 'form' (*forma*) of our life.'[134] Christ, divine Wisdom, came to show us the way, to give us the form, to re-form us and restore to us original form which has become deformed. By his *Rule,* Saint Benedict was his mediator and, as an abbot, Bernard was very conscious of being in his turn a mediator of the same evangelical form for his monks. He was fully convinced of his role in the school of charity.

---

130 QH 15.2 (SBOp 4:476).
131 Miss 2.16 (SBOp 4:33).
132 V PP 4 (SBOp 5:187).
133 PP 1.1 (SBOp 5:188))
134 Ben 8 (SBOp 5:7–8).

In the school of Christ where we are, a two-fold teaching is given, one by the single and true Master, the other by his servants. Fear is inculcated in us by his servants, and by Jesus himself, love.[135]

In this distinction we see again the fundamental role of divine love and its appeal to conscience. Apart from the miracle at Cana— that is, if the water of observances is not changed into the wine of love—no one is a true disciple of Christ.

Friends

For Saint Bernard, the mediation of friendship was obvious. He spoke of his own need for it. In weariness or sadness, repugnance or drowsiness, the mere sight of a friend, the sound of his or her voice, or merely the thought of a friend cheered him. He eagerly and gratefully welcomed the gift of friendship. But he asked himself a question: would it not be better to receive this gift directly from God? He came to the conclusion that such mediations are useful and gave three reasons for them: humility, charity, and the awakening of desire.[136] The last seems to me to be the most accurate in his case. In his experience of spiritual friendship his desire for God and for the love which is perfect was enlarged. There are any number of his letters to his friends we could quote. To Robert of Bruges, who had to leave Clairvaux to become abbot of the monastery of Dunes, in Flanders, he wrote:

> I got to know you very late, and very soon you were taken from me! What consoles me is that I suffer only from your bodily absence; by your spirit you are always with me. And yet, I would not have the courage to endure even your bodily absence if it were not for God, and for him alone! The day will come when we will meet again! When each of us will wholly rejoice in his own being and in that of the other, when we will be present to each other in soul and body, never to be separated again! God himself, who today is the reason for our relative separation,

---

[135] Div 121.1 (SBO 6/1:398).
[136] SC 14.6 (SBOp 1:79–80).

will then be the power which will re-unite us perfectly. He will be present to us forever; he will keep us present to each other forever.[137]

In this letter we find once again eschatological tension and desire for presence. In almost passionate terms, he expressed to Peter the Venerable his desire to see him, but it was so that he might recognize Christ in his friend and see holiness mirrored in him.[138]

The Saints' Communication in God

All these types of mediation in the Church, the Body of Christ, were vibrantly alive for Saint Bernard. He did not know the expression 'Mystical Body', but he had an extraordinarily realistic and highly spiritual conception of the current of life that exists in the communion of saints, in which all communicate together. In this respect, Dante is Saint Bernard's best successor, for in his *Divine Comedy* we find the same movement of life in its passage from earth to heaven. Dante's encounter with various persons finds justification in Saint Bernard's spiritual realism. He spoke of Saint Victor, for example, with a confidence which was perhaps naïve, but also vigorous and very human:

> Henceforth free from care about himself, he now does nothing but take care of us . . . Heaven is not a region of forgetfulness . . . It does not harden hearts but expands them . . . and intensifies their affections . . . A saint knows even better than the angels what we need; a saint has learned it by experience.[139]

When Dante has Saint Bernard pray for him, he puts on his lips words which perfectly express the intercessory prayer which is the prayer of every monk as mediator: 'And I [Bernard], who have never desired this vision so much [for myself] as since I desire it for him [Dante], I offer you (Mary) all my prayer. Oh! may it not seem trivial to you![140]

---

[137] Ep 324 (SBOp 8:261).
[138] Ep 265 (SBOp 8:174).
[139] Vict 2.3 *Sermones varii* (SBOp 6/1:34–35).
[140] *The Divine Comedy*: *Paradiso* 33.28–30.

IV

GOING BEYOND SELF BY LOVE OF CHRIST: FROM THE WORD-FLESH TO THE WORD-HOLINESS

1. FROM MERELY HUMAN LOVE TO SPIRITUAL LOVE

*T*HE CREATOR HAS SOUGHT his spiritual creature and they have met in Christ. In the Person of the Word made flesh, the broken link between humanity and the One who created it in his image has been mended. By the grace of the Incarnation human freedom, truth, and love have been saved from their alienation, error, and indifference. In the Person of Christ, by virtue of his two natures, we are sacramentally united to God by faith. We have already seen that for Saint Bernard the most important reason for the Incarnation was God's desire to be loved. A spirit united to a body can, in fact, love only what it can see, touch, and hear, and thus understand. But this initiative by which God approached his creature as closely as was possible does not end with love on the level of the senses. Unfortunately, Saint Bernard has been misunderstood on this point. Some people have seen in his teaching no more than tender devotion to the humanity of Christ. By the very fact that it is spiritual, a spiritual creature has to go beyond this attachment—which Saint Bernard calls merely human (*carnalis*)—and gradually become free of what is sensible in order to attain the divine nature in the same Person of Christ. This doctrine, which Saint Bernard sets forth in *Sermon 20 on the Song of Songs*, he succinctly restates in another passage:

> So that human beings, who knew how to love only by their body (*carnem*), in a merely human way (*carnaliter*), might progress to loving God in the spirit, *the Word became flesh* (Jn 1:14).[1]

Saint Bernard often speaks of passing from the flesh to the spirit. It offers him an opportunity to invite those who seek God to progress constantly in their desire to go further or higher in their quest.[2] Indeed it was on the feast of the mystery of the Ascension that he developed this doctrine of going beyond what is visible and perceptible by the senses, because for the Apostles the Ascension was a critical moment. When Jesus withdrew his physical presence from them they were overwhelmed with sadness because their affection was still of a physical nature and very human. Then, when Christ showed them a higher degree of love, they began to know and love him differently.[3] Saint Bernard's entire spiritual and monastic teaching is intricately interlaced with references to Holy Scripture. His approach to biblical theology is not the same as ours today, but it is not unprofitable for us to have an understanding of it. As for the subject we are dealing with here, going beyond the flesh to the spirit, he uses three key quotations which he feels express this doctrine.[4] They are: *It is the spirit that gives life, the flesh has nothing to offer* (Jn 6:63); *Even if we did once know Christ in the flesh, that is not how we know him now* (2 Cor 5:16); and *The Lord 's Anointed is spirit before our face* (Lam 4:20). This third

---

[1] Div 101 (SBOp 6/1:368).

[2] SC 6.3–5 (SBOp 1:27–28); SC 33.3 (SBOp 1:235); Hum 8.23 (SBOp 3:34); Nat 3.3 (SBOp 4:259); Tpl 6.12 (SBOp 3:224–225).

[3] Asc 3.3–4 (SBOp 5:132–133); Asc 6.12 (SBOp 5:157); SC 20.5 (SBOp 1:117–118).

[4] The three texts are well combined as Saint Bernard develops them in *Sermon 48.7 On the Song of Songs* (SBOp 2:71–72). The first two are sometimes thought to contradict 1 Cor 2:2: '*I wanted to know nothing but Christ, and the crucified Christ*', but this is only an apparent contradiction. For example: P Epi 2.1 (SBOp 4:319–320). On Lam 4.20, see J. Daniélou, 'Saint Bernard et les Pères grecs', in *Saint Bernard théologien*, 48–51, also H.de Lubac sj, *Exégèse médiévale* I (Paris: Aubier, 1959) 232. [*Medieval Exegesis* (Grand Rapids, Michigan: W. B. Erdmans, 1998)].

verse is based on an ancient latin version which, to Saint Bernard, well expressed our going-beyond by following Christ-Spirit, for in the second part of the verse—*In his shadow we shall live among the nations*—the shadow is Christ's flesh, which permits us to see him according to the flesh as long as we are still incapable of spiritual things (1 Cor 2:14).

The soul is truly united to God when it clings to Christ's human nature by prayer or sacrament, and this can come about only through the Holy Spirit. It is a gift of the Spirit.[5] But there is a more intense, still higher, union which Saint Bernard clearly differentiates when he speaks about the fullness of the Spirit.[6] Love of Christ which is no longer in-the-flesh but in-the-spirit has a very pronounced moral character. It is love no longer of the Word-flesh but of the Word-holiness, wisdom, truth, and fortitude. Christ is all of these, says Bernard, *he who by God's doing has become for us wisdom, justice, and sanctification* (1 Cor 1:30). God made him this *for us,* and our holiness is his holiness in us; any progress we make in union with God will therefore consist in conforming ourselves to this Word-holiness. Saint Bernard then compares these two ways of loving God: physical/sensible (*carnalis*) and spiritual. Sensible devotion is good, but it differs from and is inferior to the devotion of someone who has 'constant zeal for justice, loves truth wherever it is found, burns with desire for wisdom, and has holiness of life as a friend'. This kind of love has a stronger, surer character; it is less fragile and more stable than sensible love. What we need to see in this distinction is that spiritual progress is by nature ethical and not intellectual. It remains on the level of the will and consequently of affectivity, but now there is a firmer and more absolute commitment. The expression 'to have holiness as a friend' carries an important meaning here.[7] Holiness of life is the way to union with God. It is essentially conformity of life, spirit, and heart

---

[5] It is important to remember that this knowledge of Christ 'according to the flesh'(*carnalis*) is knowledge in faith and not only historical knowledge, as it might be interpreted today.

[6] SC 20.7 (SBOp 1:119). Cf. Div 29.5: *Virtus ex alto* (SBOp 6/1:213–214) and Div 96.6 (SBOp 6/1:360).

[7] SC 20.8 (SBOp 1:120): '*cui amica sanctitas vitae*'.

in cleaving constantly and faithfully to the Word. Holiness is the wisdom of love.[8]

When Saint Bernard described the pleasantness and delight of an emotive and imaginative attachment to Christ as a human Person, he understood that focusing the spirit on the mystery of the Incarnation this way is extremely beneficial for a soul seeking God, but that the God it is seeking cannot be found in what can be perceived by the senses. The three steps of this love of Christ, which he describes according to the commandment *to love God with all your heart, all your soul, and all your strength* (Dt 6:4–5; Mk 12:30),[9] demonstrate the fundamental distinction between merely human (*carnalis*) and spiritual love.[10] Because love for him is basically will, clearly devotion on the level of the senses, useful though it may be, leaves the heart unstable, and only reason—which should be understood here as right judgment and responsible conduct—will give love the kind of stability and maturity without which the rush of sensible affection will remain ephemeral and risk becoming irrational. Bernard constantly reminded his monks that moments of interior joy are rare, and that to please God one must be utterly determined, fully committed, and well proven in virtue. When the psalmist tells us to *Make the Lord your only joy and he will give you what your heart desires* (Ps 36:4), 'he is not speaking here about what our sensible affection desires, but about a way of life to be put into practice. Sensible desire has happiness in view, but practice has virtue as its goal'.[11]

---

[8] Cf. SC 83.3 (SBOp 2:299–300); SC 85.12 (SBOp 2:315); Csi V.14.30 (SBOp 3:492).

[9] SC 20.4–7 (SBOp 1:116–120); Div 29.1–5 (SBO 6/1:210–214).

[10] Div 101 (SBOp 6/1:368), with the quotation from 2 Cor 5.16.

[11] Quad 5.6–7 (SBOp 4:375). See note 5 on this passage in P.-Y. Emery's translation, *Saint Bernard, Sermons pour l'année* , 271. Also, R. Watkins Williams, 'L'aspect éthique du mysticisme de saint Bernard', in *Saint Bernard et son temps* (Dijon 1929): 'Saint Bernard seems never to forget the ethical aspect necessary for an ideal relationship between the soul and God. The number of times he makes allusion to it is, so to speak, his way of protesting against the custom of depreciating it. The ethical aspect is always evident in his works.' (p. 314) And precisely, with respect to love going beyond itself to spiritual love: 'It is surely here that ethics is very clearly a fundamental principle of his mysticism.' (p. 316).

After the Apostles had received Christ's moral teaching, the Spirit filled their hearts and totally transformed their love by making it spiritual. Their *charity was henceforth as strong as death* (Sg 8:6).[12] In a *Sermon for the Feast of All Saints*, Saint Bernard again glossed the words of the *Song of Songs* as signifying this going beyond in the mystery of Christ:

> Listen once more to the bride in the *Song of Songs*. She confidently and hopefully declares that she is already placed on the altar: *His left hand is under my head and his right embraces me* (Sg 2:6). The blessed soul, in fact, goes above and beyond (*transcendit*) Christ's Incarnation and humanity, which she rightly calls his left hand. Yes, she goes above and beyond it to contemplate from higher up his divinity and glory which she calls, not without reason, his right hand.[13]

If this is the saints' lot, then the left hand which sustains our love during our life on earth is our mindfulness of the benefits of the Incarnation, but it is a mindfulness which is eager for the presence the saints enjoy. Memory's role will be to conform us to Christ's mysteries. Saint Bernard is repeating Origen's doctrine:[14]

> There are some for whom Christ has not yet been born; there are others for whom he has not yet suffered; there are others for whom he is not yet risen from the dead. For others he has not yet ascended to heaven, for still others he has not yet sent his Spirit.[15]

In the *Sermon for Easter* in which he quotes this passage, Saint Bernard applies the Gospel mysteries to reform of moral or spiritual weakness. Those for whom Christ is risen but not yet ascended to heaven are those who have not yet gone beyond the easy paths of sensible joy to the point of accepting Christ's departure and his

---

[12] Asc 6.15 (SBOp 5:159); SC 20.4–5 (SBOp 1:117–118).

[13] OS 4.2 (SBOp 5:356–357).

[14] Origen, *Homélies sur la Génèse* III.7. SCh 7 (Paris: Cerf, 1943) 123.

[15] Pasc 4.1 (SBOp 5:110).

Ascension.[16] They should not believe that they have been forsaken by grace but should wait for greater spiritual gifts, so that they may enter into the highest way of love.[17] Patient waiting, supported by the mindfulness of Jesus' mysteries lived over again in our own life, is the way towards the happiness of divine Presence.

2. THE SPIRITUAL AND THE UNSPIRITUAL (CARNALES)

In his commentary on the verse of the *Song of Songs* which mentions clefts pierced in the rock, Saint Bernard says that those who are perfect dare to pierce the mystery of Christ even so far as to intimacy with the Word, because they have a pure conscience and sharp intelligence; but that others, who are unable to pierce clefts by themselves, ought to be satisfied with contemplating the saints doing it. Finally, there are still others who ought to be satisfied with *Jesus and Jesus crucified* (1 Cor 2:2).[18] At the same time, he often remarked that he himself knew nothing but Jesus crucified.[19] When he speaks this way, we always find it disconcerting. A passage in his treatise for the Knights Templar expresses his thought still better and deserves to be quoted in full. When the Knights go to Bethlehem, they are to meditate on the stable, the ox, and the hay:

> The Word, the bread of angels, became food for beasts so that human beings, who had become unused to being nourished interiorly by the bread of the word, might have the hay of

---

[16] Cf. H. De Lubac: 'But, as we are terribly and almost incurably carnal, even the Saviour's Resurrection would risk being misunderstood by us. After the Resurrection comes the Ascension, meant to show us its meaning and to oblige us to look upwards, to go beyond our earthly horizon and everything which has to do with the natural human condition. Thus, the lesson of the Ascension does not contradict the lesson of the Incarnation; it prolongs and deepens it. It does not place us below or alongside human life; it obliges us to bring it to fulfillment in ourselves by making us look beyond it.' *Paradoxes suivis de Nouveaux Paradoxes* (Paris: Seuil, 1958) 45. [*Paradoxes* (San Francisco: Ignatius Press, 1987)].

[17] Pasc 4.2 (SBOp 5:111).

[18] Sc 62.6 (SBOp 2:159).

[19] SC 15.6 (SBOp 1:86); SC 43.4 (SBOp 2:43); SC 45.3 (SBOp 2:51). Cf. Sr Brigitte OCSO, 'Jésus et Jésus crucifié chez saint Bernard', Coll 57 (1995) 219–237.

the flesh to ruminate until they are restored to their original dignity and may say with Paul: *Even if we did once know Christ in the flesh, that is not how we know him now* (2 Cor 5:16). This is certainly something no one can say with complete truthfulness except a person who, like Peter, has heard it from the mouth of Truth: *The words I have spoken to you are spirit and life, but the flesh is of no avail* (Jn 6:63) . . . He was speaking about the *wisdom of God* (1 Cor 2:7), but only for those who were perfect, *teaching spiritual realities to spiritual people* (1 Cor 2:13). As for children and beasts, he took into account their level of understanding and was careful to teach *nothing but Jesus and Jesus crucified* (1 Cor 2:2). And yet, there is only one same food which comes from the heavenly pastures, and it is indeed with pleasure that it is ruminated by beasts and eaten by humans. It gives strength to those who have reached maturity and nourishes children.[20]

In this passage, let us notice first of all the references to the *First Letter to the Corinthians*, where the terms perfect, spiritual, unspiritual (*carnales*) and little children are all found. These distinctions are being made among believers who already have the eyes of faith. They do not refer to conversion to the faith, as we today might interpret them.[21] Nor is there any hint of putting aside the nourishment of the Word and the sacraments. It is said explicitly that the nourishment which comes from the heavenly pastures is the same for everyone. Knowledge of Christ according to the flesh remains indispensable, but its purpose is to increase the soul's capacity. It is also very important to notice that, for Saint Bernard, 'to go above and beyond' in no way implies some kind of gnosticism for a chosen elite; it is holiness, and above all the holiness of charity, which lets the spirit become more and more perfect.

---

[20] Tpl 6.12 (SBOp 3:225).

[21] For example, as Kierkegaard said about the disciples of Emmaüs: 'Then their eyes were opened and they recognized him, but he disappeared from their sight. Here we have a link between seeing Christ by sense perception and seeing him by faith. They recognized him and he became invisible to them. The second fact is as it were an interpretation of the first.' *Journal* IX A 319. Vol. 2:.353.

Our leveling mentality finds it repugnant to accept such discrimination. But is it discrimination or simply recognition of
the fact that there are different spiritual states? . . . The first
level is offered to us by the Gospel within the context of time,
the second is offered in vision face-to-face. As for what concerns
us here, it is important to notice that the second level is, in a
way, anticipated in the spiritual life. Although we always live by
faith, putting it into practice ought to lead us beyond Christ's
humanity, or rather, ought to make us tend by means of it to an
ever greater comprehension of the divinity.[22]

Father Charles Bernard wrote these lines about Origen, but he
also pointed out that the augustinian tradition on love diminishes
still more any hint of the suspicion of gnostic intellectualism. Saint
Bernard also said, 'Alas! Human beings have lost their dignity. Look
at them! They are like calves feeding on hay! But God had pity on
them . . . to those who knew only the flesh he offered his own flesh
so they might learn to taste spiritual knowledge.'[23]

We can therefore define merely human or unspiritual (*carnalis*)
love as an imaginative and affective attachment to Christ in his
human nature, as the fruit of the grace that comes from Scripture
and the sacraments; and we can define spiritual love as an attachment
to Christ in his divine nature. By its deeper comprehension of
his Mystery, this kind of attachment leads a person to seek to
conform his or her moral and interior life to it until it reaches the
transforming union of holiness. Progress in the spiritual life always
takes place in the context of faith. Father Henri de Lubac pointed this
out in reference to Saint Bernard.[24] Moreover, instruction given to
a community presupposes different spiritual capacities among the

---

[22] Ch. A. Bernard, *Le Dieu des mystiques* (Paris: Cerf, 1994) 119 and 121.

[23] SC 6.3 (SBOp 1:27).

[24] 'If, by the word "faith" we mean first of all only submission to the Word which
resounds outside us, we can say that this faith is a promise of experience, and that
is what Saint Bernard meant when, for example, he spoke in language analogous
to that of Saint Augustine who said that faith is a promise of understanding.
But Saint Bernard knew very well that by his experience he did not in reality
go beyond faith.' H. de Lubac sj, *La mystique et les mystiques* (Paris: Desclée de
Brouwer, 1965) 27.

listeners. In this sense, the abbot of Clairvaux's teaching is very balanced and discreet, just as Saint Augustine's was: 'Little children should not always be given milk as nourishment, so that they will not remain without comprehension of Christ as God. But they should not be deprived of milk either, for fear they may abandon Christ the man.'[25]

In this distinction between the spiritual and the unspiritual, there is no question of making a separation like the one the Cathars made between the 'perfect'—the elect who had received the baptism of the Spirit—and simple believers. Saint Bernard knew this type of heretic, as is plain in an extant letter he wrote to Eberwin, the prior of the Steinfeld Premonstratensians.[26] When Bernard described spiritual and rational love, he pointed out that persons who are really spiritual heed the definitions of faith, have a sense of the Church (*ecclesiastici sensus*), and are not taken in by the wiles of the enemy. In their personal life they do not go beyond the limits of good judgment by superstitious practices, frivolity, or the impetuosity of a too fervent spirit.[27] The desire to be spiritual presupposes growth in humility and a greater awareness of human misery—just the opposite of the errors taught by the Cathars.[28]

3. SHADOW AND LIGHT

In Saint Bernard, the contrast between shadow and light expresses the mystery of our relationship with God in Christ. This theme is parallel to the theme 'memory-presence'. The bride in the *Song of Songs* knows that if she remains faithful in the shadow of memory, she will surely reach the light of presence.[29] The shadow is the flesh of Christ; it is also the shadow of faith. Because we are incapable

---

[25] St Augustine, *Commentary on the Gospel of Saint John*. 98.6. *Corpus Christianorum. Series latina* 36:579–580.

[26] SC 66 (SBOp 2:178–188).

[27] SC 20.9 (SBOp 1:120). Cf. SC 20.4 (SBOp 1:116–117).

[28] The Cathars taught a sort of Manichaeanism, the chief error of which was that those who were 'pure' escaped from the principle of evil, whereas simple believers were subject to it without any possibility of resisting.

[29] Nat BVM 13 (SBOp 5:284).

of contemplating the Divine, which would dazzle us, God became flesh. By doing so, he veiled the brilliance of his divinity but at the same time permitted us to reach him in the Person of the Word who became one of us. We are *in the shadow*, Bernard says, repeating the text of *Lamentations* 4:20, so long as *we live among the peoples*, that is to say, in the context of time. But *Christ the Lord is spirit before our face*, and leads us to an understanding of faith, that is to say, to the vision towards which we are tending. Piercing the shadow, we will experience *that the flesh is of no avail; it is the Spirit who gives life* (Jn 6:63). Just as the body of Jesus veiled the splendor of his divinity for his mother Mary, for me, says Bernard, it is faith in the same incarnate God which veils it. We must first approach the shadow and then go beyond it, because if you do not believe you will not see. Saint Bernard comments on the verse of the *Song of Songs, I am seated in the shadow of the one I long for* (Sg 2:3), that it is one thing to live in faith and another to stay seated in it; and he repeats yet again the distinction between the active and contemplative life, both of which are founded on faith in the Beloved, the Incarnate Word.[30]

When we say that we live in the shadow of Christ, we are comparing the ways we contemplate him. But Christ is not a shadow. In him we attain God truly, corporally.[31]

In a *Sermon for the Ascension*, Saint Bernard comes back to this comparison between shadow and light, using different images:

> The disciples were fleshly beings and God is Spirit; and because flesh and Spirit do not easily go together, he veiled himself under the shadow of his body, so that gazing upon his life-giving flesh they would see in this flesh the Word, in the cloud the sun, in the earthenware lamp a light, and in the lantern a lighted candle.[32]

In connection with the Ascension, Saint Bernard also speaks about a gradual progression in faith from understanding to love. He raises the question of why the Spirit had to wait until the Lord had

---

30 SC 48.6–8 (SBOp 2:70–73). Cf. SC 20.7 (SBOp 1:119).
31 SC 31.8 (SBOp 1:224–225); 4 HM 2: God is present in him, *non umbratice sed corporaliter.* (SBOp 5:57).
32 Asc 3.3 (SBOp 5:132); Asc 6.11 (SBOp 5:156).

departed to enlighten the Apostles and says that obviously Christ's presence did not prevent the Spirit from coming, but that Jesus spoke this way to the Apostles

> because even though their understanding had been enlightened, the impulse of their desire (*affectus*) had not been purified . . . It was to show us the path we would have to take and to set before us the form which would be imprinted on us . . . So their intelligence was enlightened by Christ and their will was purified by the Spirit, that they might know what was good and also will it. In this alone consists perfect religion and religious perfection. [33]

In some way, shadow and light go together because the shadow is the promise of light, but we should not imprudently wish to see the truth, and still less speak about it, prematurely. To see the divine light we must be transparent and pure, as this light is. Otherwise, struck blind by its brilliance, to which we are not accustomed, we would fall back into the shadow, not the shadow of Christ, but the shadow of our own unlikeness. We must wait for dawn. Dawn is purity and the love which does not seek its own interests. Truth, which conceals itself from pride, reveals itself to a pure heart. [34]

Union of the Word and reason engenders humility; union of the Spirit and the will begets charity. [35] In Saint Bernard's teaching we progress towards total truth, without being able to distinguish the will from the soul's consciousness of it:

> But that still takes place in shadow, that is to say, like *a dim reflection in a mirror* (1 Cor 13:12). The time will come when the shadows will fade away as light increases; they will finally vanish completely and give way to vision, which will imperceptibly become totally transparent and henceforth eternal. [36]

---

[33] Asc 3.4 (SBOp 5:133); Pent 3.2 (SBOp 5:172); Hum 8.23 (SBOp 3:34). Cf. L. Brésard OCSO, 'L'Ascension pour Bernard', Coll 57 (1995) 238–248. (Purification of intelligence and *affectus*, 243–248).

[34] SC 62.7–8 (SBOp 2:159–160).

[35] Hum 7.21 (SBOp 3:32).

[36] SC 48.8 SBOp 2:72).

4. LOVE, THE AGREEMENT OF TWO WILLS

What is the way to this progress in faith, this going-beyond to a more totally spiritual life permeated with the Spirit of divine love? When Saint Bernard began his treatise *On the Steps of Humility* he referred spontaneously to these words of the Gospel: *I am the Way, the Truth and the Life* (Jn 14.6). His commentary on this passage brings us back to the spiritual anthropology we described in Chapter I: loss of divine likeness is the consequence of the estrangement of the soul, the image of God, from its divine Prototype. The first step in this loss of likeness was claiming autonomy by a freedom which then became rebellious and nearly incapable of depending on its Creator. By this very fact the soul became ignorant of the truth about itself and at the same time unable to love the real Object of its desire. So the soul must retrace its steps and return by the pathway of humility, which is the recognition of truth, in order to rediscover the life which is love. The way is austere, but its fruit has the sweet taste of charity.[37] Union with God is a union of love, which for Saint Bernard means the agreement of two wills. Here we must bear in mind the ancient meaning of the word 'will': the faculty of loving.[38] Conversion of affectivity consists first of all in this step of humility, which makes the soul recognize its dependence quite simply; yet all love already includes this interior attitude of dependence. Bossuet expressed it perfectly:

> What do we mean by the term 'love' if not a sovereign power, a compelling force in us which draws us out of ourselves, a something which tames and captivates our hearts under the power of another and makes us depend on someone else and love our dependence?[39]

The way is indeed humility, then, and Saint Bernard provides a description of the transition from the painful kind of humility which comes from the truth about oneself to the kind which inclines us towards heartfelt affection.[40] As has been pointed out, for him,

---

[37] Hum 1.1 & 2.3 (SBOp 3:16–17 & 18).

[38] See above, Chapter III, note 37 (Demoustier).

[39] Bossuet, *Sermon pour la fête de l'Assomption*, 1663.

[40] SC 42.7 (SBOp 2:37).

it is not anthropology which is the foundation of humility, but humility of anthropology. This gives the word 'anthropology' a nuance: no longer does it apply to knowledge of a human being by exterior observation, but to knowledge of a human being by a human being: knowledge of self. No longer is it a matter of knowing what a human being is but rather who a human being is.[41]

So we have here a question of existential anthropology, and this implies a humble vision of self and the world and, above all, of God. Once consciousness is in the right relationship, in absolute dependence on God, the form this dependence assumes is love, which springs naturally from humility. In the context of the experience of monastic life, seeking God is identical to communion with his will in loving consent. The acquiescence of the human will, its agreement with the divine will, is for Saint Bernard the very definition of love and, we might add, the foundation and the dynamic of an entire life of obedience. From this perspective, he commented on the bride's words in the *Song of Songs* (Sg 3:4): *I held him fast!*:

What is stronger than this bond (*copula*) affirmed so forcefully by the will common to both? *I held him fast!*, she said, but in return she is held just as fast by the one she is holding, to whom she says: *You have held my right hand* (Ps 72:24).[42]

Saint Bernard understood love as the common will of the Creator and his spiritual creature, as a radical conformity and agreement between the two; as the activation of the will, which in antiquity was principally understood as the divine and human faculty of love. He clearly expressed this teaching on union with God in his comments on the following verse of the *Song of Songs*: *My beloved is mine and I am his; he feeds among the lilies* (Sg 2:16). Here Saint Bernard takes the verb 'to feed' (*pascitur*) to mean also 'to be fed': to nourish and be nourished. 'He strengthens us with his spiritual joy, and at the same time he finds joy in our spiritual

---

[41] R. Brague, 'L'anthropologie de l'humilité', in *Saint Bernard et la philosophie* (Paris: Presses Universitaires de France, 1993) 136.
[42] SC 79.5 (SBOp 2:275).

progress.' Saint Bernard then goes on to develop the image of union in terms suggested to him by nutrition:

> I am chewed when I am accused, swallowed when I am instructed, digested when I am changed, assimilated when I am transformed, united when I am conformed (*unior cum conformor*).[43]

'May your goodness appear, O Lord', he says in a sermon for Christmas, 'the goodness to which a human being created in your image can be conformed.'[44]

To help us better understand in what transforming love consists, Saint Bernard uses an inverted analogy to show how the union of the Father and the Son both resembles and differs from our union with God. 'The Father and the Son are two in one, they *are* one (Jn 10:30)', he says; 'whereas I, who am nothing but dust and yet rely on the authority of Scripture, am *one same spirit* with God (1 Co 6:17).'[45]

Saint Bernard often quotes this pauline phrase (forty-seven times). It gives him assurance of the reality of the union with God possible to the human will which cleaves to the divine will. In God union is consubstantial, and although it is not possible for spiritual creatures to experience this kind of union,[46] it is however possible for them to be united to him by consent of the will. God and the soul adhere, or 'inhere', to each other by the 'conglutination' of love (*glutino amoris inhaerent*). This union results less from a cohesion of natures than from a 'connivance' of wills.[47] The word

---

[43] SC 71.5 (SBOp 2:217). Cf. SC 62.5: '*Transformamur cum conformamur*' (SBOp 2:158). In this last passage the distinction between union in contemplating God's glory and union consisting simply in humble submission of our will to his appears very clearly.

[44] Nat 1.2 (SBOp 4:245–246).

[45] SC 71.6 (SBOp 2:218).

[46] Saint Bernard distinguished different types of unity. Union by adhesion is called 'votive'; it is 'union of a soul attached to God by all its desires (its vows), and who is *now one spirit with him* (1 Cor 6:17).' Csi V.8.18 (SBOp 3:482–483). This definition could be applied to the vows of religion.

[47] SC 71.7 (SBOp 2:220). Cf. 1 Nov 5.2 (SBOp 5:318–319). '*Conglutinari*', in this sense: Hum 7.21 (SBOp 3:32); Div 4.3 (SBOp 6/1:96). Saint Bernard also

'conglutinated' may not appear in any dictionary, but we find it in Claudel, who speaks of 'Someone to be with my soul, to be conglutinated to me by means of my heart and to pluck it from me.'[48] Claudel was speaking about human love; he expresses the radical nature and happiness of the profound union of one being with another. He also knew how difficult, as well as how irresistible, is this way towards the Other:

My beloved, you have conquered me ! . . .
I fled in vain: everywhere I found the Law again.
One must finally surrender! O portal, you must let
The guest in; trembling heart, you must submit to the master,
Someone who in me is more myself than I am.[49]

For Saint Bernard this is a matter of two wills freely consenting to each other, and in the process finding the joy of loving. It is a 'consensus', an identical sense of life as a whole, of its dynamism and its goal.[50]

In the Middle Ages, being 'one spirit by loving consent' brought to mind a 'kiss', and Saint Bernard used this symbol freely in commenting on the first phrase of the *Song of Songs: Let him kiss me with the kiss of his mouth* (Sg 1:2). A kiss is, as it were, the union of two breaths, two 'spirits' (*spiritus* means breath).[51] Christ bestows God's kiss on the soul, because 'if by marriage according to the flesh two beings become one flesh, still more does spiritual union

---

wrote to Peter the Venerable that his soul was 'conglutinated' to his, Ep 387 (SBOp 8:355).

[48] P. Claudel, *Partage du midi* ('Cantique de Mesa'), 1948 version. Oeuvres complètes XI (Paris: Gallimard, 1957) 190.

[49] P. Claudel, *Vers d'exil*, VII, Oeuvres complètes I, 38. Bernanos expressed this in a paradoxical way: 'It is not a question of conforming our will to his, because his will is ours; when we rebel it is only at the price of uprooting our whole interior being, of monstrous dispersion of ourselves. Our will has been united to his since the beginning of the world . . . How soothing it is to think that even when we offend him, in the deepest sanctuary of the soul we never cease to desire what he desires.' (*Dernier agenda:* January 23, 1948), in A. Béguin, *Bernanos par lui-même* (Paris: Seuil, 1959) 146–147.

[50] SC 71.10 (SBOp 2:221–222).

[51] Cf. Y. Carré, *Le Baiser sur la Bouche au Moyen Âge. Rites, symboles, mentalités à travers les textes et les images, XIe-XVe siècles* (Paris: Le Léopard d'Or, 1992).

join them as one spirit. In fact, a person who cleaves to the Lord becomes one spirit with him (cf. 1 Cor 6:17)'.[52]

In the fourth and highest degree of love, which can be achieved on earth only rarely, fleetingly, and for an instant, a spiritual being no longer loves itself except for God's sake. This means that someday the spiritual creature will be in complete conformity and total agreement with its Maker (*conformet et concordet*—*con-forma* and *con-corda*). We must therefore get to the point of willing everything we will entirely for him, so that his will, and not ours, may be done absolutely. That is how it is with the saints; their affections and their wills all come together in an inexpressible way and flow into the unique divine will. To experience this state is to be deified.[53] Dante was surely translating Saint Bernard when he wrote these beautiful lines:

> Our peace is in his will,
> It is this sea into which all things flow,
> All that it creates and all that nature brings forth.[54]

By the profound and unswerving agreement of two wills—the will of God and the will of the spiritual creature who obeys him—there is established a harmony between what the divine and what the human will desire. This is the space of peace, as well as the end of the spiritual journey mapped out by Saint Bernard. In Chapter VI we will try to show this.

The love song that is *The Song of Songs* has no other theme than the celebration of mystical union; and it is a song of thanksgiving for the grace of knowing love. At the end of his first sermon on the *Song*, Saint Bernard declares that

> anyone who has experienced love will easily recognize the meaning of this poem . . . because it is not about music but about the heart's exaltation; it is a harmony, not of voices, but of wills . . . From beginning to end it is a marriage song

52 SC 8.9 (SBOp 1:41–42).
53 Dil 10.28 (SBOp 3:143).
54 Dante, *The Divine Comedy*: *Paradiso* 3.85–87.

telling of . . . harmony of life and the charity which comes from mutually consenting affections.[55]

> By some affinity of nature . . . the soul is drawn by such great love that with no delay she is conformed to [God] and transformed into his very image. God then appears to you as you have appeared to God: *you will be holy with the holy, blameless with the blameless* (Ps 17:26). Why not also loving with someone who loves, approachable to someone approaching him, attentive to someone attentive to him, and caring toward someone who cares about him?[56]

At the end of his commentary, Saint Bernard insists again on the perfect accord of wills which constitutes mystical marriage. He means a tacit agreement to will or not will the same things. This total union of spirits is like an embrace; the harmony between the two wills makes them equals in love and drives away all fear. Nothing in this world procures greater happiness than this conformity of a human will with the will of God's Word. Love alone allows a creature to use the same language as its Creator and to reply to him as an equal, or at least as like to like,[57] because when God loves, he wants nothing but to be loved in return.[58] Although God is present throughout the universe, although reason can reach out to him, it is love alone that understands him. He is present to those who love him by harmony of wills. It is not unworthy of God that He wills what they will, because they are never in disharmony with his will. They are thus spiritually espoused to God[59]

Cardinal Henri de Lubac thoroughly understood the character and value of bernardine mysticism:

> More than once Saint Bernard commented on this *unus spiritus* which results from the union of love which is the unity of wills. If both Saint Bernard and all those who, like him, expound mysticism of the will are incorrectly understood, it is due to a

---

[55] SC 1.11 (SBOp 1:7–8).
[56] SC 69.7 (SBOp 2:206).
[57] On the language of the soul, see SC 45.7 (SBOp 2:54).
[58] SC 83.3–4 (SBOp 2:229–301).
[59] Miss 3.4 (SBOp 4:38). Cf. V Nat 2.3 (SBOp 4:206–207).

lack of awareness that for them the will is not simply a 'faculty' but the most profound constituent of the soul[60]

Because it is love which unites us to God most truly, it falls to the Spirit of love to dispose our hearts by an outpouring of charity, which is nothing but good will.[61] The Spirit bends our will—or rather, says Bernard—straightens it up and orientates it increasingly towards the Spirit's own will.[62] This will has nothing in common with Schopenhauer's voluntarism or Nietzsche's 'will for power'. Paradoxically, we could speak of a will of powerlessness, in that it depends entirely on grace. It is also clear that a monk's 'self-will' shows a deep-rooted discord with the divine will. On the other hand, a will in accord with God's will provides the foundation for fraternal charity, in which different persons will and reject the same things, and where one person understands another because he or she wills to love that person. Spiritual friendship likewise draws its strength and confidence from a will in harmony with God's.

In his book *L'idole et la distance*, the theologian Jean-Luc Marion knowledgeably quotes Saint Bernard in commenting on the following verses of the poet Hölderlin:

> Yet I know, the fault
> Is mine alone!
> Because too ardent a fervor
> Binds me to you, O Christ.

Marion writes:

> Such fervor is not wrong, except that this love does not attain the height of what it ought to love: the distance itself, where

---

[60] H. de Lubac sj, 'Mystique et mystère', in *Théologies d'occasion* (Paris: Desclée de Brouwer, 1984) 67; augmented edition of *La mystique et les mystiques* (Paris: Desclée de Brouwer, 1965) 31–32. About the will which 'is not a simple "faculty,"' only a few words have been added. This is not the place to bring up again that, for Bernard, intelligence, memory and will most often *are* the soul. In a note supporting his remark, de Lubac cites the four steps of love in the treatise *On Loving God* 15.39 (SBOp 3:152–153). He also cites G. Fessard sj, *La Dialectique des Exercices spirituels de Saint Ignace de Loyola* (Aubier: 1956), tome.1, 207–214.
[61] Pent 1.5 (SBOp 5:164). On the equivalence of love and will, see also SC 57.9 (SBOp 2:124).
[62] Pent 2.8 (SBOp 5:170).

the Father's remoteness makes the Son stand out . . . Hölderlin was following this tradition, but he radicalized it and renewed its theological point, the same point which Saint Bernard, for example, formulated with precision when he said that the disciples' attachment to Christ's immediate physical presence remained a 'carnal love' which attempts to possess with the frantic infantilism of tense, frenzied, and powerless desire. By approaching Christ this way, 'carnal love' does away with the distance.

Marion goes on to quote Saint Bernard's *Sermon 28.8 on the Song of Songs* and comments very much to the point of this passage:

> Attachment to the body of Christ is not 'carnal' here, as if corporeal reality were marked with infamy (Christ sanctified it by assuming it), but because in the immediacy of close familiarity the body becomes so banal that the divine which is manifested through it goes unnoticed.[63]

This modern discussion of spiritually 'going beyond' in the love of Christ provides a good translation, in new terms, of Saint Bernard's thought. But what a surprise it is, ten pages further on, to see reflections which clarify what we have just said about the importance of the will for union with God. Jean-Luc Marion, commenting this time, not on Saint Bernard, but still on the poet Hölderlin, shows that in its remoteness, the divine 'by its will remains intimately close to everything'. Divine presence is brought to fulfilment in fatherly withdrawal, wherein a will is enough to activate the will of a son who 'dwells' at a distance. 'These two wills alone can subsist in the distance they measure, endure and consume . . . These two wills alone can bridge the distance.'[64]

---

[63] J.-L. Marion, *L'Idole et la Distance* (Paris: Grasset, 1977) 151–152.

[64] Marion, *L'Idole et la Distance*, 162. In an article entitled 'L'image de la liberté', J.-L. Marion shows very well how in Saint Bernard free choice is an almost divine absolute, and he quotes Heidegger to say that Bernard (whom he does not quote) in a way anticipated his thought in that 'the human being is defined less by the understanding capable of representing than by the decision of a will absolutely free in its choice', *Saint Bernard et la philosophie* (Paris: Presses Universitaires de France, 1993) 71–72.

When Saint Bernard says that charity converts souls because it makes them willing—that is to say, free[65]—isn't this precisely because it is the will that forms the point of entry for divine charity, the charity which transforms love and conforms it to God who is Love ? 'Truly, charity is at the same time God and gift of God. Charity therefore gives charity.'[66]

Love alone, if one does not make an idol of it, can span infinite distance.

5. THE EXPÉRIENCE OF LOVE AS PROGRESS IN FAITH

Faith, although it remains obscure during our entire journey, is nevertheless by its very nature a promise of clarity, as remembrance tends toward presence and the dim hues of dawn precede daybreak's burst of light. The eyes of faith hope for the happiness of vision, but, for Saint Bernard, this vision is identical to transforming love. For him, spiritual experience is the experience of stronger and more constant union with God. At the beginning of his first sermon on the *Song of Songs*, where he summarizes the life of a monk, he says—directly following Origen[67]—that reading this love song presupposes that a monk has already read the two books of the Bible which immediately precede the *Song: Proverbs (Parables)* and *Ecclesiastes*. From *Proverbs* the monks will have learned how to live according to trustworthy doctrine and to renounce self-love; and from *Ecclesiastes,* how vain is the sort of knowledge which leads only to love of the world. Saint Bernard tells his monks to reflect on their own experience. Was it not after they had abandoned the spirit of the world and the woeful swamps of sin, and after they had sung the Psalms and the Canticles 'of the Steps' that they arrived at the summit of the *Song of Songs*?[68] The goal of the whole cistercian school is therefore to prepare the spirit for contemplation, which is nothing but a loving union with God. This, above all, is what makes it a school

---

65 Dil 12.34 (SBOp 3:149).

66 Dil 12.35 (SBOp 3:149).

67 Cf. L. Brésard OCSO, 'Bernard et Origène commentent le Cantique', in Coll 44 (1982) 183–193. Re-edited by *Cisterciensia* (Forges: Scourmont, 1983) 29–39.

68 SC 1.2 & 9–10 (SBOp 1:3–4 & 6–7).

of charity. As in every school, there are lower and higher levels. We go up or down ; we make gradual progress towards the perfection of knowledge, or still better, the perfection of the spiritual art. After the first two books mentioned by Bernard, the monk is ready to begin the third, the 'theoretical course on the sacred',[69] and by the adjective 'theoretical', of greek origin, he means the contemplative life. The same adjective is used two other times to designate the king's chamber, the goal of the whole spiritual journey described in *Sermon 23 on the Song.* The journey leads from the garden (in the literal sense: salvation history); to the three storerooms (in the moral sense: discipline, social love, fervent charity); and finally to admission to the king's chamber (contemplation, that is to say, union in love and total agreement of wills).[70]

In this sermon, after mentioning 'theoretical' contemplation and describing the journey which leads up to it, Bernard makes a distinction between fear and wisdom in the King's ante-chamber, where God is both master and judge. Fear draws us closer to wisdom than does knowledge, which risks puffing us up, because this type of fear is already wisdom, that is to say, a taste for God. It is the wisdom of love, which lets us enter into peace.[71] There, God no longer appears as a judge or as a master, but as a Father who loves and placates our desire by fulfilling it. 'God, calm, calms all things, and so to contemplate him is to be at peace.'[72] We should notice in this passage that it is in the king's chamber where we receive proof of his love, that is to say, of his good, kind, and perfect will towards anyone who loves him and wants to be united with him.

Saint Bernard declares that a soul who has passed through the various cellars is perfect.[73] As for the chamber, the Bride (the Church) has of course entered into it, but the differences among souls who penetrate that far are very great. He always said that he had not had this experience, but this was so that he could speak

---

[69] '*acceditur ad hunc sacrum theoricumque sermonem*', SC 1.3 (SBOp 1:4).

[70] SC 23.4–9 (SBOp 1:140–145).

[71] SC 23.14 (SBOp 2:147–148).

[72] SC 23.16 (SBOp 1:149).

[73] SC 23.8 (SBOp 1:144).

about it in a vague way and show that such experiences can vary greatly in degree and intensity.[74]

A reader familiar with later mystical literature may find it rather difficult to get a precise idea of what kind of mystical graces Bernard means: ordinary, extraordinary, or those he experienced himself. Although he says that he has not entered the king's chamber, he also says that he has received the Word's visit, several times, in fact. This passage in *Sermon 74 on the Song of Songs* is both well-known and much esteemed. Its very sobriety accentuates the truthful nature of his confidential disclosure.[75] He says that anyone who has had such an experience can think of nothing but repeating the experience, and is unceasingly mindful of the Word. So when, precisely in the context of his comments on the word '*Return!*' in the *Song* (2:17), he introduces the account of his rapture, this is because he vividly remembered it. But he also wanted to explain the brief, fleeting, and rare character of such an experience.[76] When he treats of God's mysteries, mysteries which touch the life of the soul, they usually raise in Saint Bernard's mind the question 'why' rather than 'how'. In *Sermon 69 on the Song* he refers again to one of the special graces which result from the Word's visitation, but he does so to explain how such fullness increases his humility and love.[77] Such moments of the fullness of the Spirit are very rare and very brief, and perhaps we have here another example of his surprise when he found himself faced with contrasts which made him reflect and suffer at the same time.[78] The vicissitudes of the spiritual life, that is to say, the mysterious and unpredictable alternation of absence and presence, strongly affected his passionate character. As he said:

> Our created spirit sometimes rises toward the creating Spirit, attaching itself to him *to form one single spirit with him* (1 Cor 6:17). But this contemplation is very fleeting, because our spirit

---

[74] SC 23.9–10 (SBOp 1:144–145).

[75] SC 74.5–6 (SBOp 2:242–243).

[76] SC 74.1–4 (SBOp 2:239–242).

[77] SC 69.6 (SBOp 2:205–206).

[78] Dil 10.27 (SBOp 3:142); SC 23.15 (SBOp 1:148–149); SC 85, 13 (SBOp 2:315–316); Csi V.14.32 (SBOp 3:493).

enclosed within the walls of the body unceasingly sinks back into anxiety about the flesh, and whereas it is highest in the creature, we immediately find it lower than the most worthless things. As for the creating Spirit . . . sometimes he comes to us without our realizing it and sometimes he leaves us without our being aware of it . . . Generally, the more persistently a person seeks him, the more rapidly he withdraws . . . But the Spirit can also come unexpectedly when we are not seeking him and can flee when we are seeking him. So it is that the *Song of Songs* shows us the bride seeking without finding, then finding without seeking.[79]

Here, once again, nearly at the end of the journey, we have the same quest which Saint Bernard placed at the starting point (See above, Chapter I.1). From beginning to end, the mystical life is a search for God. It takes place in daily life, gratuitously on the part of the divine Spirit, but not unless the spiritual creature believes in it and waits for it in hope.[80]

In teaching his monks, Saint Bernard spoke in a very understated way about these mystical graces. He told them:

Everyone to whom this experience may have been granted has because of it a personal comprehension of sublime and delicate insights concerning the special gift of the Bridegroom's ointments. As for me, I tell the community what I have received from common sources.[81]

The common source, 'the fountain of life', is obviously Scripture, because almost immediately Saint Bernard goes on to quote Saint Paul and Job, whose words flow from this fountain. When he speaks about the lover coming near and being seen by the loving

---

[79] Div 41.11 (SBOp 6/1:252). See also SC 17.2 (SBOp 1:99); SC 32.2–3 (SBOp 1:227–228).

[80] See two studies by Dom J. Leclercq osb: 'L'expérience mystique d'après S. Bernard de Clairvaux' and 'Une mystique pratique dans les sermons de S. Bernard à ses moines', in *Studia Missionalia* 26 (1977) 59–71 and 73–86. These articles were reprintend in *Recueil d'études sur saint Bernard et ses écrits* (Rome: Ed. di Storia e letteratura, 1992), Ch. X, 403- 414 and Ch. XI, 415–428.

[81] SC 22.4 (SBOp 1:131).

soul, he says that he himself would prefer to hear explanations from someone more experienced in these matters than himself, but that since those who have acquired this knowledge generally prefer to 'remain silent about what they have learned in silence', he will speak because it is his responsibility to do so. He will, however, say only what he has gained from his own experience and the experience of others.[82]

Experience! But what experience does he mean? The experience of the will's true and free accord with the divine will. Is this not also the experience of freedom's consent to grace? Maurice Blondel was well aware of the importance of this doctrine of Saint Bernard, where in some way grace and freedom unceasingly seek each other, not easily of course, but like two people who cannot live without each other. Linking this to his own philosophy, Blondel wrote the following lines which are well worth rereading:

> Too often, in the meanderings of our quest and in conforming to our usual way of speaking about appearances, we have spoken and reasoned as if we possessed what we have received, as if it were our own completely and in a definitive way, or—and this is a still subtler temptation—as if we could use it in an independent way without needing the constant support or help of grace . . . We are never, even for an instant, utterly alone and completely our own . . . Saint Bernard intimated this with profundity in a remarkably clear and nuanced passage in his treaty *On Grace and Free Choice* (Gra 14.47).[83]

Blondel could also have quoted what Saint Bernard said at the beginning of the same treatise:

> Created as our own, in a way, to enjoy free will, we become God's property as it were by good will. Moreover, he who created our will free makes it good. He makes it good *so that we may be a kind of first-fruits of all that he has created* (Jas 1:18),

---

[82] SC 57.5 (SBOp 2:122).

[83] M. Blondel, *L'Être et les Êtres* (Paris: Alcan, 1935) 319–320.

because surely it would be better for us never to have existed than to remain our own.[84]

The mystical life is an intensification of the life of faith by which a pardoned creature belongs to God. The natural affinity between the soul and the Word makes it always capable, despite the worst kind of reprobation and despair, not only of returning to grace 'but even to aspiring to marriage with the Word'—provided that the soul conforms its will to God's will and 'that it takes its place alongside the King of the angels under the yoke of love. What could it not safely dare with the one whose glorious image it is, and whose likeness it bears so nobly'.[85] In this passage people have detected a hint of the universal call to mystical contemplation.[86] In a mysticism of the will, when the human will is yoked in love with the will of its Lord—as Bernard so beautifully expresses it—it is united to him by the least little act, if its intention is pure. According to the ancient theological notion of mysticism, as Dom Anselm Stolz explained it: 'Ascesis is not only a prelude to the mystical life, but an essential element of that life: it is the progressive death of the body's life of sin. Ascesis and mysticism are therefore two elements of one single supernatural process.'[87]

The unity of the entire composite human being enters into the movement of transforming and conforming grace. From the moment he wrote the *Apology* Saint Bernard affirmed this, accentuating the importance of balance in the cistercian life. While maintaining the superiority of the exercises of the spiritual life, he affirms equally that it is next to impossible—if not impossible—to enter into or continue a spiritual life without the help of physical practices. The

---

[84] Gra 6.18 (SBOp 3:179).

[85] SC 83.1 (SBOp 2:298–299).

[86] Cf. 'If we say, for example, that it (mystical contemplation) is the actualization of the gift of wisdom and that it could not be refused to a simple christian in the state of grace, the reply is that the gift of wisdom is possessed in very different degrees according to the fervor of one's love, and it is this fervor which permits believers who have it to an eminent degree to enter into the mystical life in the full sense of the term. And for this, it is not necessary to submit to lengthy speculation,' C. A. Bernard, *Le Dieu des mystiques*, (Paris: Cerf, 1994) 418.

[87] A. Stolz osb, *Théologie de la mystique* (Chevetogne, Belgique: 1947) 222.

person who best observes the Rule will be the one who puts to use both spiritual and physical practices with moderation and in a suitable way.[88] But on the subject of this synthesis formed by ascesis and mysticism in the christian order, Kierkegaard was quite right when he remarked that when the goal is the eternal, the means are identical to the end, and just as important. 'Eternity is not impatient or curious about results, as temporality is, because the means have exactly the same importance as the end.'[89] As soon as an intention is formed in the heart, union with the divine will already exists. Maximus the Confessor, whose writings Saint Bernard no doubt knew in John Duns Scotus' translation, had long before clearly defined this mysticism of the will. Jean-Luc Marion also noticed this, when he spoke of Maximus as parallel to Bernard. For Maximus the Monk, in mystical union and deification the human will is under the influence of guiding grace. The will desires conformity with God's nature, because its own origin stems from this Will. As he explains:

> I do not say that it loses its free choice, but grace sets it in agreement with Nature, firm and unchangeable. There is a voluntary going beyond self, that is to say, we desire that motion should come whence being comes to us, just as the image passes into the archetype. Neither of the two, being or motion, has or can be drawn anywhere else.[90]

It is perhaps in his teaching on the third Coming, that is, the advent of God intermediary between his coming in history and coming in eternity, that Saint Bernard best expressed his moral and monastic mysticism. Although the Church—or the soul—has eyes to reflect on the past and on the future, it is in the present that God's infinite grace intervenes each day in the hidden life of consciousness.

---

[88] Apo 7.14 (SBOp 3:93–94). Cf. C. Dumont ocso, 'Saint Bernard, mystique selon la *Règle de saint Benoît*', *Lettre de Liguÿé* n° 206 (1981) 34–46. Republished in *Sagesse ardente*, 83- 100. ['Saint Bernard: a mystic according to the Rule of Saint Benedict'. CSQ 16 (1981) 154–167].

[89] S. Kierkegaard, 'Un discours de circonstance', in *Discours édifiants à divers points de vue* (1847). Oeuvres complètes, tome XIII (Paris: L'Orante, 1966) 137.

[90] Maximus the Confessor, *First Ambigua*, PG 91:1076. Cf. R. E. Asher, 'The Mystical Theology of St. Maximus the Confessor', ABR 29 (1978) 93.

In his Fifth Sermon for Advent, he ably demonstrates that to love means to observe the word. To keep the word (*ob-servare*) is to keep the commandments, but in the same way as a person assimilates food. In this way is born the New Human Being, freed from the desires of the flesh which are supplanted in the heart by love of charity and humility. Saint Bernard concludes this sermon with a sentence from the *Letter to the Romans* which he often quotes because it sums up what accord between body and spirit means: *The word is very near you; it is on your lips and in your heart* (Rm 10:8; Cf. Dt 30:14). Eternity descends into time, and the sign of this is the expectation and unfailing hope which exists in the loving soul. Thus the wisdom of love teaches us obedience of faith by patient living. Father Lode Van Hecke expressed this perfectly:

> He [Bernard] prefers to speak about contemplation, a term which he interprets more broadly than the term 'mysticism' and which actually includes the whole christian life. We have seen that a humble effort to accomplish God's will already constitutes the first degree of contemplation. Simple faith, as well as rapture, is a form of contemplation . . . Union with God is the normal expectation and choicest fruit of the christian life. The accomplishment of God's will and the gratuitousness of love are the two themes Bernard develops most.[91]

The basic attitude of conscience, therefore, is a firm resolution to love and to will intentionally what God wills. This intentionality will endure in the midst of temptations and wandering thoughts, even through carelessness or negligence, which are only human. We must protect our determination of spirit like we do our life; only a willful and deliberate fault can shatter it. And if the will does succumb, we should not despair. It may seem, of course, that all our interior strength and our liking for what is good have been lost; when that happens, only intention can bring the spirit back to reason.[92]

---

[91] L. Van Hecke ocso, *Le désir dans l'expérience religieuse*, 194. Cf. C. Dumont ocso, 'Contemplative Action: Time in Eternity according to Saint Bernard', 145–159.

[92] Div 6.1–3 (SBOp 6/1:105–107).

For Saint Bernard, intention—in the strict sense of the word *intentio*—corresponds to what is now called the basic option, but he was not unaware that this can be interpreted in the wrong way, because he says: 'Woe to anyone who sins by abusing hope'.[93]

The essential intention of the spirit ought to be understood in the perspective of the restoration of the divine image, which is fundamentally intact in every spiritual creature. The return to health is progressive and follows the order Saint Bernard gives in speaking of freeing freedom. Free choice separates itself gradually from sin, and with the freedom of the children of God it can tend towards total freedom, yet without ever being able to claim that it has achieved it. Not only does intention thenceforth limit itself to what is permitted, but it begins to do what pleases it, because more and more this is also what pleases God. But even though the three liberations—from necessity, from sin, and from our human condition—reflect the image of divine freedom, likeness has been restored only by Wisdom: Christ, who came into the world. After receiving strength and wisdom, the soul has regained its pristine beauty, its native form, its former comeliness.[94] There is in Saint Bernard a theology of aesthetics, as we have already hinted. His spirituality, like cistercian formation, is completely centered on the form of the Creator which has been imprinted on his creature. The same line of thought is found in *Sermon 85 on the Song*. The soul receives strength and wisdom from the Word, and once it has been adorned with these virtues, its beauty charms the king, who, as the psalm says, *will fall in love with your beauty* (Ps 44:12). Saint Bernard speaks daringly about God's desire to see his Bride (the Church or a soul) adorned with the same beauty as his Image, Christ. This beauty is moral beauty, but in some way it affects the body and its behavior: gestures, words, glances, way of walking, laughter.[95] Over and above strength (power) and wisdom (knowledge) there is

---

[93] QH 2.3 (SBOp 4:391).

[94] Gra 10.32–34 (SBOp 3:188–190).

[95] SC 85.10–11 (SBOp 2:313–315). Cf. C. Dumont ocso, 'Une Phénoméno-logie de l'humilité' Coll 45 (1983) 265–271. Re-published in *Sagesse ardente*, 213–222.['A Phenomenological Approach to Humility : Chapter VII of the Rule of Saint Benedict', in CSQ 20 (1985) 283–302].

beauty, the synthesis of both, so to speak, perfection of form and in this sense conformity; a being's perfect likeness to the divine Image that is Christ, and consequently, union in love and fruitfulness.[96]

Each time beauty is mentioned in the *Song of Songs*, Saint Bernard lingers over the passage, and the poetic form his style assumes corresponds to the moral or spiritual form of his thought. At the words *I am dark but beautiful* (Sg 1:5), he presents a little lesson on aesthetics, first the distinction between form and color, then interior and exterior beauty.[97]

> Union takes place in the spirit, because God is spirit and is enamored (*concupiscit*) with the beauty of a soul whom he sees advancing in the ways of the spirit.[98] . . . How, while you are not entirely beautiful, could you believe that you are capable of contemplating absolute beauty? . . . I will appear to you the day when you will be perfectly beautiful, as I myself am, and when you will be like me you will see me as I am. Then you will hear: *You are perfectly beautiful, my beloved* (Sg 4:7). . . .[99]

Bernard has Jesus say to Mary Magdalen in the garden after the Resurrection: 'Why do you want to touch me when I lack my true form (*deformem*)? Wait until I am beautiful to touch me . . . Become beautiful and then touch me; live by faith and you will be beautiful'[100]

In the intention, which is the soul's face, there are two indispensable factors: the object and the motive. By these two, which are like two cheeks, the beauty or disfigurement of the soul is to be judged.[101] *How beautiful you are, my beloved, how beautiful you are!* (Sg 1:14). This cry of admiration is repeated, because 'this is a rare bird on earth: to see humility that is not caused by loss of holiness but is linked with holiness . . . Now I know that you are incomparably

---

[96] SC 85.12–13 (SBOp 2:315–316).
[97] SC 25.1–9 (SBOp 1:163–169).
[98] SC 31.6 (SBOp 1.223).
[99] SC 38.5 (SBOp 2:17).
[100] SC 28.10 (SBOp 1:198–199).
[101] SC 40.2 (SBOp 2:25).

and boundlessly beautiful, my beloved, . . . not only because of
your love for me, but simply by your humility.'[102]

We have already (in Chapter II.7) seen the danger of losing
our beauty entirely by appropriating it for ourself and refusing to
depend on our Creator for it.

> You have lost wisdom by your beauty (Ezk 28:17). Lucifer
> possessed not only wisdom's form but also its beauty. By
> wanting to appropriate it for himself, he lost it, so to say that
> he lost wisdom by his own beauty or by his own wisdom is the
> same thing. Appropriation caused this.[103]

As for Eve, she saw that the tree was beautiful, but a different
kind of beauty was intended for her: eternal beauty, which has
its source in eternity. Why did she let her soul take on a form,
or rather a deformity, which was alien to it? She was only going
to be afraid of losing it, and her freedom was going to become
unrecognizable.[104] A mystical teaching on moral holiness not only
underlies Saint Bernard's spirituality, then, but it takes the form of
a theology of beauty, of spiritual aesthetics.

Before concluding this chapter on a note of beauty, let us briefly
call to mind the steps of the journey we have been following: the
development of faith by going beyond self spiritually; the distinction
between those who are 'unspiritual'(*carnales*) and those who are
'spiritual'; the contrast between shadow and light. These steps have
led us to an understanding of what Saint Bernard meant by love:
union of wills. If spiritual experience is progress in faith, it remains
true that its essential trait is transforming love, which is simply
accord of the human will with the divine will: these are the wills
which bridge distance.

The next Chapter (V) will obviously be based firmly on this
foundation because obedience, the governing principle of monastic
observances, can have no meaning (just as Jesus' obedience could
have no meaning) apart from love of the Father. It should come as

---

[102] SC 45.3 (SBOp 2:51–52).

[103] SC 74.10 (SBOp 2:245).

[104] SC 82.4 (SBOp 2:294–295).

no surprise that we pass from mysticism to practice. As Cardinal de Lubac admirably remarked: 'Mystical aspiration is not a luxury. Without it, a person's moral life would risk being simply repression, ascesis sheer aridity, docility sleep, religious practices mere routine, ostentation or fear.'[105]

---

[105] H. de Lubac SJ, *Sur les chemins de Dieu* (Paris: Aubier, 1956) 189–190. [*The Discovery of God* (Grand Rapids, Michigan: W. B. Erdmans, 1996)].

V

OBEDIENCE AND OBSERVANCES AS SPACE FOR ENCOUNTERING GOD

1. AGREEMENT OF WILLS BY OBEDIENCE, IN PRACTICE

*T*HE SPIRIT OF GOD seeks his creature's spirit, but the creature's spirit exists in the flesh. To enter into contact with us, God became incarnate and since then we do our seeking through Christ. Our desire for the conformity which gives rise to love is set in the context of the world, that is to say, in a human body and consequently in time and space. A little later, we will see what the body and time meant for Saint Bernard, but more concretely we will set our encounter with God, in Christ, in those spaces where our will becomes united and conformed to his, because 'only wills can cross distance'. Following the example of Jesus, who learned obedience by suffering, the monk also learns it by practicing the observances of a life according to a rule. Like a test of faith, they provide the monk with means of giving evidence of his or her longing search for God.

Etienne Gilson very astutely wrote about Saint Bernard:

He borrows [from tradition]; but all that he borrows is ordered in such a way as to prepare the solution of his own particular problem, namely: to give a coherent doctrinal interpretation and a complete theological justification of the cistercian life. . . .'[1]

The synthesis created by Saint Bernard in his monastic and cistercian teaching, which we are attempting to explain, is solidly founded on a very firm spiritual anthropology and a christological teaching which very concretely corresponds to it. The four chapters which have preceded this one are not only a preparation for it but are also an interpretation of the whole cistercian regular observance and a justification for it. If our intention is not directed at conversion and restoration of God's image, any observance is vanity and whistling down the wind, just as freedom without grace is vain and useless. Beginning with this long 'consideration' was necessary. We could say that, by analyzing the spiritual creature's fallen condition and the work of its salvation, we have accomplished an act of 'piety', in the sense that Saint Bernard understood this term. For him, piety was (as we have seen) the practice of consideration. To say that piety is the worship of God is the same thing, because consideration is the religious act by which a person actively and consciously seeks God. As we venture to describe the cistercian life, both exterior and interior, let us listen to what Saint Bernard said, not only to Pope Eugene III, but to himself as well:

> First of all, it is certain that consideration purifies its source, that is, the mind where it originates. It also brings sentiments under control, guides one's actions, corrects excesses, improves

---

[1] E. Gilson, *La théologie mystique de saint Bernard* (Paris: Vrin 1934) 64. Translated by A. H. C. Downes, *The Mystical Theology of Saint Bernard*, Cistercian Studies Series 120 (1940, rpt Kalamazoo: Cistercian Publications, 1990) 46. This should be completed by the following remark: 'Saint Bernard addressed his teaching especially to the monks of his abbey, to his friends—most of whom were monks— and to the whole Order which owed its development to him. His doctrine embodies a profound kinship with the cistercian life. But the cistercian life is an authentic form of life in the Church, and by this right, its riches belong to all the members of the Church. That is why Saint Bernard, while remaining a doctor of monastic life, and because he is first of all that, is also a doctor of the Church.' Jean. Leclercq OSB, *L'Amour des lettres et le désir de Dieu* (Paris: Cerf 1957). Translated into English by Catherine Misrahi as *The Love of Learning and the Desire for God* (New York: Fordham University Press, 1961).

behaviour, puts good order and honesty into a person's life, and lastly, imparts knowledge of both what is divine and human.[2]

When earnestness disappears from the religious spirit, the meaning of monastic life becomes blurred, even unintelligible. Everything that is sought outside this ultimate consideration is, for a monk, secondary and superfluous. When speaking to his monks about the banquets people prepare for Christmas, the abbot of Clairvaux tells them that in what concerns them they cannot excuse themselves because of ignorance. They know God, and if they say they do not know him, they lie, because who, after all, has led them to the monastery? How could anyone persuade them spontaneously to renounce the affections of those dear to them, the pleasures of the flesh, and worldly vanities? Yes, he repeats, who could persuade you to do that, if you did not know that God is good to those who call upon him. This knowledge of God is interior and personal. Then, quoting Saint John: *If anyone loves me he will keep my word and my Father will love him, and we shall come to him* (Jn 14:23),[3] he develops his beautiful teaching on the second—the spiritual and hidden—coming. Clearly, the justification of cistercian discipline is related here to faith and love. The vocation to this kind of austere life is attributed to Christ's interior coming, his presence within us, and to our response which in concrete terms means reform of our life by the practice of obedience and the observances. The intermediary coming, between Christ's coming in history and his final return, takes on a moral character, but it is totally penetrated both with the grace that has already been received and with anticipated glory. It is 'the way' by which we pass from the first coming to the last.[4] It often seems, in Saint Bernard's sermons for Advent, as if the intermediary coming signifies the moral (or tropological) sense, that between the allegorical and the anagogical (eschatological) senses. It is within the context of time, as we shall see (Chapter V.4), that

---

[2] Csi 1.8 (SBOp 3:403–404).
[3] Adv 3, 2–4 (SBOp 4:176–177).
[4] Adv 5.1 (SBOp 4:188–189).

this dynamic of the spiritual life develops, but in a humble, hidden way, amid suffering.[5]

In commenting on the kiss of the mouth in the *Song of Songs*, Saint Bernard has it preceded by two other kisses: of the feet and of the hands. These two stages and experiences are necessary, because a person does not arrive at the summit all at once, but little by little (*paulatim*).[6] One must experience this progression in one's life from conversion until perfect union, because the kiss of the hands signifies at one and the same time doing what is right in an amended life and being grateful for the grace which enables one to do so. The increase of confidence and peace resulting from this threefold progressive experience (*tres affectus sive profectus*) makes us aspire to a more intense presence of Christ within us.[7] In an interview, Emmanuel Lévinas once said: 'Vision of God does not mean seeing God, but seeing what we ought to do'.[8] And what we ought to do is love. There is no greater love than the love we find in the pascal mystery. It is a matter of renouncing self-will and resolving to pursue holiness.

Saint Bernard's sermons for Easter are centered principally on conversion of the will which, as the basis of freedom and love, is the depth of the soul and the source of its moral dynamism. We strip the feast of Easter of its meaning if it is not a real 'Pasch' for us, a real passage, and if, after our lenten reflection and desire to do better, we turn back instead of going beyond. By entering into communion with Christ's sufferings, we have been transplanted in him anew by this baptism of sorts, which consists in tears, penance, and confession. We have been advancing along a road on which God shows us salvation; we are transmigrating; we must not look back if we do not want to be unworthy of his Kingdom.[9] Christ lives in us

---

[5] Adv 1.10 (SBOp 4:168–169); 3.4–5 (SBOp 4:177–179); 4.2–7 (SBOp 4:183–187); 5.1–3 (SBOp 4:188–190). Cf. C. Stercal, 'Il *"Medius Adventus"*. Saggio di lettura degli scritti di Bernardo di Clairvaux' (Roma: Editiones Cistercienses, 1992).

[6] SC 3.4 (SBOp 1:16).

[7] SC 4.1 (SBOp 1:18–19).

[8] Quoted by P. Miquel in *Lettre de Ligugé* (1991), n° 257, 57.

[9] Pasc 1.15 (SBOp 5:92).

by faith; so he lives in us as long as our faith remains alive. If it dies, Christ dies in us, too. Works confirm that faith is alive, just as the movements of a body prove it is alive, and faith without works is dead. But if the life of the body is the soul, then the life of faith is love; and if love grows cold faith dies, just as the body dies when the soul leaves it. God has made the life of faith dwell in love.[10] The beginning of his *Second Sermon for Easter*, which we have summarized, without giving the scriptural quotations, wonderfully expresses the spirit in which Saint Bernard understood the practice of monastic works, which are bound to faith by love and consequently animated and justified. In a way, the primacy of the wisdom of love resolves the problem which can result from an exaggeration of the opposition between faith and works.

The opposite of love is really self-will, which is exactly contrary to having a common will with God and with our neighbor in whom we love God. Saint Bernard speaks out in harsh terms against a twofold leprosy, that is to say, the sickness of self-will and private judgment (*proprium consilium*). He means a will that is in disagreement with God and other human beings, a will that is ours alone. When we spoke of freedom, we saw that it destroyed itself by wanting to become autonomous vis-à-vis its Creator. The action of refusal by way of liberty darkens the intelligence and makes love of God impossible. Hardness of heart and obstinacy of mind come, not from meditating on God's law, but from concentrating on our self-will alone.[11] Self-will is the enemy of God's will, and therefore of love. Saint Bernard expressed this forcefully and clearly in the following passage:

> Being its exact opposite, [self-will] sets itself dead against the love which is God (cf. 1 Jn 4:8). It is inimical to it and wars relentlessly against it. What, in fact, can God hate more and punish more severely than self-will? If it were to cease to exist, hell would disappear. Whom would its fires ravage, if there were no longer any self-will? Even here and now, when we suffer from cold and hunger or some other similar evil, what

---

10 Pasc 2.1–2 (SBOp 5:95–96).
11 Quad 2.5 (SBOp 4:363).

within us feels wounded, if not our self-will? On the other hand, if we endure these things willingly, our will has already become common [will] . . . Here, will is defined by what we consent to, what our free choice inclines towards. The desires and concupiscences which dominate us *against* our will are therefore not our will, but its corruption. [In so far as it is a corrupted will, self-will] snatches at and appropriates for itself, as much as it can, what belongs to God. What limits, in fact, would human covetousness set for itself?[12]

This passage sums up Saint Bernard's whole spiritual teaching. It corresponds very well to the existential description of the divine image which has been not destroyed but damaged. The will remains good by nature, but it has been corrupted by its desires. Free choice is truly free when it yields, whereas disordered love remains insatiable and grasping. As for reliance on our own judgment, that is pride and a crime of idolatry. Those who obstinately hold to self-will divide and disturb the life of the community, by their senseless zeal they are full of self-complacency. Where can this twofold leprosy be cleansed? In the Jordan, like the leprosy of Naaman, who prefigured Jesus' descent and the humility of his life. After he replied to his mother that he had to be about his Father's business, the Word modified his idea of what he was going to do (*consilium*) and from the time he was twelve until he was thirty, he submitted in silence and obedience to his human parents.[13] 'In my life,' Saint Bernard has Christ say, 'you will come to recognize your life: and so, just as I have unfailingly kept to the paths of poverty and obedience, humility and patience, love and mercy, you in turn will follow my steps.'[14]

Obedience is the form love takes in the life of a monk. It is nothing other than the obedience of the Incarnate Word communicated to the monk by his grace. In Elisha's raising of a dead child (2 Kgs 4:35), Saint Bernard saw Christ spiritually raising each one of us from the dead each day. The prophet's hands on the child's hands signify that Jesus places his hands on mine to give me

---

12 Pasc 3.3 (SBOp 5:105–106).
13 Pasc 3.4 (SBOp 5:106–107).
14 Pent 2.5 (SBOp 5:168).

his life as an example and as the form it should take: the 'form' of obedience.[15] Obedience is the form, which according to the ancient sense of the word means the fundamental intention in our life which gives value to all our desires and all our actions. More essentially, it is the practical expression of a will which goes straight to what is good. Saint Bernard describes four steps of good will. As is the case with other series of gradations frequent in his writings as well as in those of other contemporary authors, we must be careful not to reduce these steps to static or chronologically successive states. Quoting Job (14:2), he points out that a human being can never remain in the same state, because he or she will either regress or progress. Ideally, one ought to go forward, and for anyone who has set out on the way, 'ascensions'—as Psalm 83 tells us—are in the heart, that is to say, in the will. In the first stage, the soul accepts God's law with its mind. The will is *upright*, but it exists in weak flesh; it fails to do the good it desires and it commits the evil it detests (cf. Rm 7:15). In the second stage, the soul is *vigorous*. It withdraws from evil and has the strength to accomplish the good it wants to do, but not without some ponderousness. In the third stage, the soul is completely *consecrated* to God. It runs along the way of the commandments with a free heart and takes pleasure in doing good. Finally, in the fourth stage, where the angels abide, it accomplishes good the way they do: with the kind of *ease* which makes them always will it. The fourth stage of the will's progress is very much like the fourth step of the love of God: the soul can desire it, of course, but because it is a stable perfection, the soul cannot attain it as long as it is in the body, and the body weighs it down (Ws 9:15).[16] The highest step of love, like that of obedience, is therefore this peace which can come only from perfect accord between my will and God's. As long as we live in our body—which signals our limitations—the holiness of this peace remains our aim, our patiently and deliberately pursued aim in spite of all our weaknesses and deviations.[17]

---

[15] SC 16.2 (SBOp 1:90–91).

[16] Div 124.1–2 (SBOp 6/1:402–403).

[17] *In labore messis* 1.2 (SBOp 5:218).

When, in his sermons for Easter, Saint Bernard speaks so insistently about renunciation of self–will, and therefore about obedience, our very astonishment ought to make us understand that for him it is there, in the moral conscience, that the pascal mystery leads. Die to self to live for God. Saint Bernard's whole teaching on ascesis rests solely on this free but arduous act of will, the unconditional acceptance of the ethical reality of the spiritual life. In the face of suffering, which is inherent in all existence and requires the constant effort of interior consent on the part of the will, Saint Bernard distinguished three ways of taking up one's cross: patiently, willingly, and ardently. Without ever reducing them to a system, he posits in this progress of a soul coping with pain or suffering three successive stages of love for Christ: it is like a long apprenticeship.[18] A person begins by submitting patiently to the cross without rebelling, then accepts it willingly (*libenter*) in hope, so as finally to embrace it lovingly in charity.[19]

> Consequently, all of us, whoever we are who follow our Head . . . let us not cease to do penance, let us not cease to carry our cross perseveringly, as he himself persevered on the cross, until the Spirit tells us to rest from our labors. Whether *it comes from flesh and blood* (Mt 16:17) or from some spirit, brothers, let us not listen to any persuasion to come down from our cross. Let us persist in remaining on the cross, let us die on the cross: let us be taken down from it by the hands of others, and not brought down by our fickleness.[20]

With the realism of the sacramental sign which we have already mentioned (cf. Chapter III. 5: *Memory and Presence*), Saint Bernard

---

[18] Cf. H. de Lubac SJ: 'It is not always good to take refuge too quickly in God's embrace. This escape can hide secret pride or an avid seeking for an anesthetic. A person who suffers has the best opportunity to accomplish the law of the christian life: let him or her not be ashamed to resemble the Man of Sorrows and have recourse to him.' *Nouveau Paradoxes,* 75.

[19] And 1.5 (SBOp 5:430). Dom Vital Lehodey OCSO, *Holy Abandon* (Dublin: McGill & Son, Ltd, 1951), after referring to modern authors' comments on this passage of Saint Bernard, says that 'none has been happier than he either in distinguishing the degrees or assigning their respective motives,' p. 26.

[20] Pasch 1.8 (SBOp 5:83–84).

presented in dramatic form the Apostles' reply: *'This is intolerable language'* (Jn 6:60), when the question came up of sharing in Christ's suffering in the sacrament of the Eucharist and concretely imitating his way of living. Yet on the other hand, when the sacramental bread penetrates our being by faith, it is really he who dwells in our hearts, and: *whoever abides in love abides in God and God in him* (1 Jn 4:16).[21] Here again we find Saint Bernard's moral mysticism. It reminds us, as we begin to reflect on monastic observances, that for him they have no other value than the value which comes from a fundamental intention to seek union with God through obedience. This is the form a monk's life takes; that is, this is what confers its meaning, its value, and also its beauty.

On the occasion of the consecration of the abbey church, Saint Bernard expressed very explicitly the relationship between the hardness of the cross and the gentleness of grace, connecting them with the ritual of blessing the crosses on the walls with holy oil:

> The ointment of spiritual grace must come to help our weakness by assuaging the burdensome cross of monastic observances and all types of penance by the grace of interior acquiescence. Because to follow Christ without the cross . . . that is not possible! Yet, who could bear the hardness of the cross without this ointment ? The reason why many people are terrified by the cross and flee penance is that they see the cross, yes, but not the ointment.[22]

This can never be repeated too often, because even when this doctrine is toned down, it is still demanding and indisputable; it is also very little heeded in a society won over by hedonism. Saint Bernard's teaching embodies the total radicality of the Gospel and the Beatitudes. The perfect joy of divine union presupposes humility, poverty and suffering with patient, free—even ardent—consent. In a word, it is the obedience of Christ even to the cross. If we endure hardship and pain in the consecrated life we do so freely, willingly, in the image of the Son of God. Because we have left everything for

---

[21] QH 3.3 (SBOp 4:394–395). Cf. Ben 12 (SBOp 5:11–12); Dil 4.11 (SBOp 3:127–129).
[22] Ded 1.5 (SBOp 5:373). Cf. SC 21.11 (SBOp 1:128).

the One who left everything for our sake, we can meet him in our daily acts, both interior and exterior, which are consecrated by an obedience motivated by love.[23] It is there, by seeking God in what is most temporal in our life, by our acts, that we can expect and even desire the happiness of finding him.

> The Lord Jesus embraced us by taking upon himself our labor and sorrow. Let us also cleave to him by embraces in response to his; yes, let us cleave to justice, his justice, by directing our acts towards this justice and bearing our sufferings because of this justice. And let us say with the bride: *I held him fast, I will not let him go* (Sg 3:4). Let us say also, with the patriarch: *I will not let you go unless you bless me* (Gn 32:27). In fact, what remains for us to expect but a blessing? After being embraced, what more remains for us to desire but a kiss ? United with God to this point, how could I not desire to cry out: *Let him kiss me with a kiss of his mouth* (Sg 1:2).[24]

The encounter of Creator and spiritual creature will be perfect only in the contemplation in heaven, but the way which leads there, the way of obedience, is already resplendent with the light of the divine on the cross. While showing the unity there is in progress, Saint Bernard very often brings out at the same time the contrast inherent in seeking and in this wisdom of love which already possesses what it will never be able to cease to desire.[25]

2. SPIRITUAL AND PHYSICAL PRACTICES IN THE SCHOOL OF CHARITY

Like every art, the spiritual art requires an apprenticeship, a time of formation, of theoretical and practical exercises. So we have

---

23 Cf. St Mechtild: 'It would be monstrous folly to aspire to reach Jesus Christ simply by extenuating efforts and inhuman works, while still having an unloving heart. Those who would have such presumption certainly lack the true humility which alone can lead to God's heart. Rather, they prove that their holiness is false; their self-will dominates the heart' IV, c.25. [*Revelations* (London: Longmans, Green & Co., 1953).]

24 4HM 14 (SBOp 5:66–67).

25 Cf. Div 41 (SBOp 6/1:243–254: The seven degrees of obedience and contemplation.

here a school, but a school whose curriculum is oriented toward the acquisition of charity, which is the form—that is to say (let us repeat once more) the meaning and the value—of the christian life and particularly the monastic life. If we do not keep this fundamental motivation in mind, all our activities can become futile and dangerous to the goal our way of life sets before us. So we should consider all the practices of interior as well as exterior ascesis to be so many proofs of our search for God. Our life then becomes a test of our desire for conversion. As we have already seen, charity alone converts souls by making them willing, and consequently free, to conform themselves to the divine and be united to God in love.[26]

Saint Bernard calls the cistercian school of charity 'the school of the Holy Spirit'. In a letter, he told his friend Malachy, an irish archbishop, that he was going to keep the young men whom Malachy had sent to Clairvaux with a view to making a foundation, a while longer, to let Christ be formed in them more fully, and to let them learn thoroughly about spiritual combat. Then, once they have had their rough edges smoothed (*eruditi*) and they have greater spiritual sensitivity in the school of the Holy Spirit, they will be able to return to their own country, clothed with strength from on high.[27] Saint Bernard described progress in this apprenticeship of God's love by four steps. It is a matter of tearing oneself away from exclusive love of self to lose oneself finally in God.[28] A clear idea of how the significant transition from the second to the third step of love and progressive disinterestedness takes place is very important to have:

---

[26] See above, Chapter IV.4, notes 64 and 65. See also Sent 3.21 (SBOp 6/2:78).

[27] Ep 341 (SBOp 8:282–283).

[28] Like his entire century, Bernard was a platonist. Cf. J.-M. Déchanet, 'Aux sources de la pensée philosophique de S. Bernard', *Saint Bernard théologien* 56–77. G. Lardreau, 'Amour philosophique et amour spirituel', *Saint Bernard et la philosophie* (Paris: Presses Universitaires de France, 1993) 27–48. As concerns us here, let us simply mention what is evident when we read Plato: that the principal dynamic of the soul is love, which is a divine force; that ascension towards the Ideal is brought about by the passion of love, as in the *Symposium;* and that this force ought to be orientated towards spiritual Good, whereas it is attracted by sensuality and Evil. As Plato described it: a winged chariot drawn by two horses, one noble and one vicious, in the *Phaedrus* 246–247 and 253–256.

So in the second step of love, a human being loves God for his own sake and not for God's sake. When, because of his own needs, this person begins to honor God and to be attentive to him in meditation, *lectio*, prayer and obedience, familiarity develops between them. Little by little and gradually (*paulatim sensimque*) God reveals himself and then shows his tenderness. And so, because this person *has tasted how good the Lord is* (Ps 33:9), he passes on to the third step of love, in which he now loves God not because of himself but because of God.[29]

Real experience of the feebleness of our love, centered as it still is on self-will, and constant testing of our desire for God through the practices of our daily life animated by obedience, characterize the slow progressive way beyond our control, by which our heart is purified of its egocentric aspirations and finds itself—quite naturally, as it were—drawn by God's tenderness. By its assiduous attention to God, it comes to know him.[30]

Staying close to God pertains, then, to will, desire, and love, which operate in an ordered activity. Commenting on Saint Paul's words at the time of his conversion, *What do you want me to do?* (Ac 9:6), Saint Bernard cried out:

Look at this expression of perfect conversion, brothers . . . Only a few words, certainly, but they are rife with meaning— living, effective and worthy of being accepted unconditionally. Very few people with this kind of perfect obedience can be found, persons who renounce their self-will to the point of no longer possessing even their own heart.

Saint Bernard goes on to add (not without a touch of humor) that, on the contrary, superiors are often obliged to ask their monks what Jesus asked the blind man: *What do you want me to do for you?* (Mk 10:51). For heaven's sake, Saint Bernard continues, let them make some progress in this matter and stop being forever children who have to be asked what they want. Then Bernard comments on Christ's reply:

---

29 Dil 15.39 (SBOp 3:152–153). Cf. Div 5.5 (SBOp 6/1:103–104).
30 Dil 9.26 (SBOp 3:141).

Go into the city, and you will be told what you have to do (Ac 9:6). *O Wisdom, who orders all things for good* (Wis 8:1). When you speak to someone, you send that person to another human being to learn your will, to show the value of community life.[31]

Here we can see that Saint Bernard understood monastic life as an act of response to God by means of the community's mediations. It is therefore an action enlivened by contemplation, so to speak, because love, the basic intention behind our acts, cleaves to divine love and becomes one with it.[32] If the monk is dead to the world, it is a happy death which permits Christ to live in him as he did in Saint Paul. The monk can then say with joy: 'I am dead to everything else . . . but whatever comes from Christ finds me alive and available'.[33]

Available, prompt, generously open to life, without being a conformist, without worrying about a kind of fidelity which would be routine or lazy; for God the monk applies himself or herself to the activities of a life completely oriented toward the Other and to others. Availability, an aspect of obedience, essentially characterizes the human person, said Gabriel Marcel, in the sense 'that the knowledge of an individual being is inseparable from the act of love or charity by which this being is anchored in what constitutes it as a unique creature or, if you prefer, as an image of God'.[34] This availability is not the kind that is purely empty or thoughtless activism, which often amounts to the same thing; it is above all the state of belonging interiorly to God and one's neighbor by self-renunciation. This is why the people who are the most available, Marcel adds, are also the most consecrated.[35] Heartfelt availability

---

[31] Pl 6–7 (SBOp 4:331–333). Cf. Pre 10.23 (SBOp 3:269–270).

[32] Cf. C. Dumont OCSO, 'L'action contemplative, le temps dans l'éternité d'après saint Bernard', Coll 54 (1992) 269–283. Re-published in *Une éducation du coeur*, 57–77. ['Contemplative Action: Time in Eternity according to Saint Bernard', CSQ 28 (1993) 145–159].

[33] Quad 6.2 (SBOp 4:378).

[34] G. Marcel, *Homo Viator* (Paris: Aubier, 1944) 28–29. [*Homo Viator* (Chicago: Henry Regnery, 1951)].

[35] G. Marcel, *Être et avoir* (Paris: Aubier, 1935) 179. [*Being and Having* (Boston: Beacon Press, 1951)].

or sulky unavailability make all the difference in the daily activities and community relationships of a monk's life. Everyone receives the same instruction and yet, remarks Saint Bernard, evident signs show that this teaching bears fruit in some and not in others. Often incentive (*affectus*) is lacking. Not everyone has the same willing resolve. Monastic observances either contribute to spiritual progress or, on the contrary, become an obstacle to it.[36] So it is we find people in community who have no moral energy. Their joy is short-lived, their thoughts are only of this world, their whole being remains tepid; they obey without conviction, speak without restraint, pray without heart, and their reading bears no fruit in them personally (*lectio sine aedificatione*). They see what they ought to do, but do not do it, and nothing can make them change: what a bitter contradiction![37] We must face the cross courageously and keep it before our eyes, put it in front of us, like the bouquet of myrrh in the *Song*, and not just over our shoulder; otherwise we feel only its weight. But when Christ's sufferings are in our thoughts, we will understand the meaning of our own. They are real and inevitable, but then they can be loved.[38]

Within the context of regular discipline and a simple and austere way of life, we move ahead, we might say, freely taking on those things which in every human existence require an effort and balanced organization of time. The three monastic occupations of prayer, spiritual reading and work were harmoniously adapted in the cistercian reform in a way which, from a humanist point of view, worked well.[39]

Saint Bernard's anthropology strongly accentuates the interaction between body and soul. Their practices are respectively called physical or spiritual, exterior or interior. The primacy of the spiritual was clearly affirmed, even though the cistercian reform

---

[36] Asc 3.6 (SBOp 5:134–135).

[37] Asc 6.6–7 (SBOp 5:153–154).

[38] SC 43.5 (SBOp 2:43–44).

[39] Cf. C. Dumont OCSO, 'Humanism and Rusticity : Aim and Practice of the Early Cistercians', CSQ 17 (1982) 65–81. 'L'équilibre humain de la vie cistercienne d'après le Bienheureux Aelred de Rievaulx', *Sagesse ardente*, 15–32. ['Saint Aelred: The Balanced Life of the Monk', *Monastic Studies* 1 (1963) 25–38.

was characterized by a return to manual work. Saint Bernard says
this openly in his *Apology*. He begins by insisting on the primacy of
the spiritual, quoting Saint Paul: *Physical exercises are of little worth;
piety, on the other hand, is of unlimited use* (1 Tm 4:8), and we know
that for him piety is the constant activity of consideration. After
saying once again that the holiest monk is the one who is the most
humble, not the most tired, he nonetheless affirms the necessity of
physical ascesis:

> I do not want to say that we should neglect exterior works or that
> someone can simply omit them and become a spiritual person.
> On the contrary, one can scarcely arrive at spiritual practices,
> even though they are better, and keep to them, without the aid
> of physical practices . . . The monk who is better is the one
> who practices both in a discerning and appropriate way (*discrete
> et congrue*).[40]

After stressing again that the interior life is what is most
important, he says (in speaking about fasting) that even conversion
of the body is not to be underestimated, because it sustains the
spirit's conversion in a not insignificant way.[41] Both these kinds of
activity, interior and exterior, are indispensable in the monastic life,
and Saint Bernard liked to see in the image of Mary and Martha
living together under the same roof the condition for receiving
Christ.[42]

Saint Bernard spelled out several times what he meant by
physical practices. They are silence, psalmody, vigils, fasting, manual
work, chastity of the body, and voluntary poverty.[43] Each time he
lists them, he concludes by saying that they have no other goal than
the acquisition and exercise of charity. In a commentary on the

---

[40] Apo 7.13–14 (SBOp 3:93–94).
[41] Quad 2.4 (SBOp 4:361–362). Cf. Jean Leclercq osb: 'The means grace
employs to reform the human being are ascetical practices, occasions for ex-
ercising voluntary consent to everything that God has done, and does, for the
salvation of the world.' *Bernard de Clairvaux*. Collection: Bibliothèque d'Histoire
du Christianisme 13 (Paris: Desclée, 1989) 108.
[42] Asspt 3.3 and 6–7 (SBOp 5:240 and 242–243).
[43] Div 55.1–4 (SBOp 6/1:280–283); P Epi 2.7 (SBOp 4:324–325); Ep 142.1
(SBOp 7:340).

marriage feast of Cana, Saint Bernard compares these observances to the stone jars which contained only water. The works of physical ascesis must be transformed into wine, and this wine is charity. Our actions should be neither servile or self-centered, but animated by filial love. He comes back to the three kinds of obedience: a slave's, a mercenary's and a son's. Fear is changed into love.[44] The water of ascesis becomes mystical wine in the sense that action itself becomes contemplation; for when action is energized by the fervor of love, then by the agreement of the will which set the action in motion, union with God results. There is a metamorphosis, that is to say, a change of form, a re-form, a conversion. In the observance of discipline, the transition from fear to love is brought about by a kind of differentiated pedagogy. God's servants, those who have authority in the community, inculcate in us a concern with obeying God. They fill the urns with water, whereas Christ himself, the true and only Master, changes this cold water into wine.

> We are in the school of Christ (*schola Christi*) . . . He says, in fact: *This is my commandment: Love one another* (Jn 15:12). It is as if he were saying, 'By my servants, I set down many commandments to you; but as to the commandment of love, it is I, very particularly and directly, who give it to you'[45]

This distinction seems to me very important in bringing out the role of religious authority and also the monk's responsibility to reply to the commandment to love, a reply which cannot be anything but personal and intimately addressed to Christ as a person.

Spiritual practices concern the interior life, and Saint Bernard frequently makes allusion to them.[46] The term 'spiritual exercises', used later in modern spirituality, usually refers to applying onself to reading, meditation, and prayer as they were practised by monks

---

[44] P Epi 2.8–9 (SBOp 4:325–326); Div 56.2 (SBOp 6/1:285–286).
[45] Div 121 (SBOp 6/1:398).
[46] Circ 3.11 (SBOp 4:290); P Epi 2.5 (SBOp 4:323); Sept 1.5 (SBOp 4:348); QH 5.2 (SBOp 4:403); Pasc 1.18 (SBOp 5:94); Asc 6.8 (SBOp 5:154); PP 3.7 (SBOp 5:196); *De altitudine et bassitudine cordis* 2 (SBOp 5:215); Asspt 2.6 (SBOp 5:236); And 2.6 (SBOp 5:438); SC 21.10 (SBOp 1:128); Conv 6.8 (SBOp 4:80); Div 5.5 (SBOp 6/1:104); Div 16.5 (SBOp 6/1:147).

in their daily life at the time of Saint Bernard.[47] Reading Holy Scripture, to which the benedictine *Rule* devotes a large part of the monk's day, means persistent reading following the four classical senses. Meditation is prayerful reflection on the text being read and applying the senses and the imagination, with the goal of living participation in the gospel mysteries. This meditation will be interrupted by prayers directed personally to God, in the style of Saint Augustine's *Confessions.* Finally, contemplation is when the mind's activity stops to linger for a while on a word or an image which has touched our heart more compellingly. It has been said that, although Saint Bernard rarely spoke specifically about prayer, he spoke of nothing but prayer in the sense that all his sermons, and especially his commentaries on the *Song of Songs,* are nothing but the uninterrupted prayer of a soul eager for freedom, and by it union with God in love. His

> conception of continual prayer is the opposite of the kind of continuous application which engenders lukewarmness. It is supported by an intensity of desire which freely and tirelessly pursues the face-to-face and arrives at unity.[48]

Everything Saint Bernard wrote is prayer, in the sense that it also manifests a sober affectivity to which the factor of receptivity is fundamental. 'In the sphere of religion, this receptive attitude is denoted essentially as prayer.'[49] Further on (Chapter VI.3), we will see that for Bernard the best prayer of all was thanksgiving, precisely because it expresses the gratitude resulting from radical dependence, receptivity, and love, which is always indebted and happy to be so.

Lectio divina, spiritual reading, is at the root of prayer as an activity. In a cistercian monastery it is the principal personal occupation of the monk. A type of personalism which was emerging in the twelfth century assigned a special value to study of the Bible

---

[47] Cf. Guigo II the Carthusian, *The Ladder of Monks* 1–7. Cistercian Studies Series 48 (Kalamazoo: Cistercian Publications, 1981) 67–74.

[48] F. Callerot OCSO, 'Une étude du sermon 25 *De Diversis* de saint Bernard sur la prière' Coll 54 (1992) 66–79 (75).

[49] C. A. Bernard, *Théologie affective* (Paris: Cerf, 1984) 78.

and the great Fathers of the Church who had commented upon it. The masterpieces of spiritual literature written by Saint Bernard and his school, principally the commentaries on the *Song of Songs*, are proof enough of the cultural level at cistercian monasteries. This spiritual knowledge, however, was completely oriented toward conversion and holiness. The theme of how it differed from the kind of knowledge taught in the schools has already been dealt with (above, Chapter II. 5).

In the school of the Spirit, as Saint Bernard says yet again, while they do not scorn philosophical knowledge, the monks seek God in simplicity of heart. At this school they learn goodness, discipline in their daily life, and also knowledge. Not knowledge like the subtle reasoning of Plato or Aristotle, but the kind of knowledge they ask for with the psalmist: *Do not deprive me of your holy spirit; create a clean heart in me* (Ps 50:13).[50]

Purity of heart is the goal of all ascesis and the condition for contemplation. In the parable of the marketplace, where the monk goes to barter beatitudes, his bundle (purity of heart) contains vessels of gold and silver: piety, charity, and joy in the Holy Spirit; and also cloaks which can be unfolded in readings, meditations, prayers and contemplations.[51] The word 'contemplations' is interpreted quite broadly in Saint Bernard and can signify fairly sustained meditations, as it does here in the plural, or, as elsewhere, contemplation in the special sense of exceptional graces. If you are not a contemplative, says Saint Bernard, do not despair: apply yourself to the practices of the monastic life . . . and one day you will arrive at purity of heart.[52] This purity of heart is the beatitude of the vision of God, which for him is union with God by total conformity to his will.

Among spiritual practices, we must insist again on the eminent value of *lectio divina*. Reading Holy Scripture, to which by the *Rule* a monk ought to consecrate a good part of his or her time each day, is part of bernardine consideration, the religious spirit which makes the monk really and truly seek God. The activity of reading

---

50 Pent 3.5 (SBOp 5:173–174).

51 Par VII (SBOp 6/2:297).

52 Av 6 (*Sermones varii*) (SBOp 6/1:15).

or spiritual study takes on a sacred character; it is in continuity with the liturgy and gives the monk's mind a contemplative quality, in the sense that the mind habitually comes back to things of heaven, not only in thought but especially in desire. *Lectio* itself, as a practice, is illustrated in the totality of Saint Bernard's work; it is not difficult to see the mental and affective activity which animates it.

Spiritual reading, according to the patristic meaning of the term, seeks in Scripture the life, the way, and the truth of human existence, as well as its destiny. The monk applies himself to it in this very special way, and comparing it with theological or exegetical study in the modern sense is quite useless. These are two different disciplines which are not really opposed to each other, except when they senselessly exclude one other or become caricatures.[53] In his way of reading Scripture, Saint Bernard continued along the same line as Origen and Saint Augustine, a way which remains perfectly tenable today.[54] In an allegory which provides an example of this, Saint Bernard shows how he understands reading God's Word. It concerns Ruth, the sinful soul, who follows her mother-in-law, the Church, and leaves the region of darkness for the land of faith. There, in Boaz' field, the field of Holy Scripture, she gathers up the ears of corn left by the reapers. This means that she collects small commentaries (*sententiolas*) which the great doctors have not touched upon. Nevertheless, she follows the reapers to avoid going

---

[53] Søren Kierkegaard, ' If we think of the Middle Ages as being monastic and ascetical, we could say that our times are more professorial and scientific. Not everyone can become a professor, but each person receives a varnish of scientific culture which makes him a kind of professor. And just as in the first centuries not everyone became a martyr but took martyrdom as a reference, and as in the Middle Ages not everyone went off to the cloister but considered anyone who did so to be a true Christian, so also today everyone takes the professor as the point of reference for a true christian. And the professor produces knowledge, and knowledge begets doubt, and knowledge and doubt stir up the instructed public who object and quibble. When the 'cloister' is a deviation of christianity, it is necessary to put faith into practice (Luther); when the 'professor' is, it is necessary to practise imitation of Christ (the cloister),' *Jugez vous-mêmes: pour un examen de conscience recommandé aux contemporains* (1846), *Oeuvres complètes*, vol. 18 (Paris: l'Orante, 1966) 238–239.

[54] O. Rousseau, 'Saint Bernard, "Le dernier des Pères' ", *Saint Bernard théologien*, 300–308.

astray in her interpretation of catholic doctrine. The great reapers are Augustine, Jerome, Gregory, and others like them who have bound up great bundles of scriptural explanations, leaving a few glistening ears of grain for us to glean. With them, with what we understand from their [insights], our soul will be able to meditate (*ruminat*); it will be able to live off them. After that, it is not right for us to go to glean other fields, I mean to go and plunge (*immergere*) ourselves into profane studies, once we have dedicated ourselves to christian truth.[55]

Without insisting on the significance of the the inspiration which strengthened the spirit of the sacred author and will also inspire the reader, it is appropriate to stress clearly the character of a monk's reading, which is in its own way sacred and continues in a personal way today the reading of the Fathers and the ancient monks as it works the furrow they laid down.

In the Creator's encounter with his spiritual creature, sacred reading is the best place for an intimate dialogue from the heart. According to the ancient patristic adage: 'When you read, God speaks to you; when you pray, you speak to God'.

In one of Saint Bernard's numerous maps for monastic conversion, he presents an allegory about Elijah's flight to the desert. Elijah arrived at Beersheba, a word which can mean 'the well of satiety' because of the refreshment provided by Holy Scripture. About this satiety, the psalm says: *He has led me to the waters of repose* (Ps 22:2), and in another: *They become inebriated on the abundance of your house* (Ps 35:9). An idea familiar to Saint Bernard follows: 'Such inebriation does not lead to disgust, but by certain desires awakens an insatiable appetite'. Then, quoting Saint Gregory's words, he adds: 'On this river of spiritual reading the lamb walks and the elephant swims; at the table of catholic teaching, in fact, each person finds satisfying portions in keeping with his or her intelligence'.[56]

This passage, among many others, shows very well the essential role reading the Bible plays in the conversion and life of a monk. Of

---

[55] Sent 3.51 (SBOp 6/2:92–93).
[56] Div 94.1–2 (SBOp 6/1:351–352. Cf. Gregory the Great, *Moralia sur Job* I and II. Dedicatory Letter 4. SCh 32 (Paris: Cerf, 1952) 121.

all the observances, *lectio divina* is the one which keeps the monk alert to spiritual realities in an active and personal way. It is there that we meet God in meditation and prayer. It is there that we can be united to God by sustained and affective reflection.

Saint Bernard offered us the example of his brother Gerard in a moving sermon he preached after his death. There is a phrase which expresses neatly what we could call the charism of *lectio divina* Gerard possessed, even though he was the most active member of the entire community of Clairvaux: 'He was not learned in letters, but he had an intuitive understanding, and he also had the Spirit who enlightened him'.[57]

Attentive, affective, intelligent, and reflective listening to the Word of God gives the spirit an attitude of obedience which sheds its light on a person's whole life in the midst of multiple activities, whether interior or external. Agreement of the human will with the divine will finds in spiritual practices, just as in physical practices, the means of growing and deepening. In them, grace and freedom are joined in a love which is always being put to the test, but which passes these tests right up till the end.

3. THE BODY, ON EARTH AND IN HEAVEN

While the Creator, *the Word became flesh* (Jn 1:14) to encounter his spiritual creature, the creature remains spirit and body, which are inseparably bound together in both the earthly and heavenly condition. Saint Bernard is very realistic on this point and his spiritual anthropology takes into consideration both the help the body gives the soul and the heaviness it represents in its earthly condition. The composite human person—body and soul—is destined for blessedness. To understand what Saint Bernard means when he speaks of the body's value, we must take the fulfillment of this human destiny as our starting point. He distinguished three stages in the body's cooperation with the life of the soul.

---

[57] SC 26.7: '*Non cognovit litteraturam, sed habuit litterarum inventorem sensum, habuit et illuminantem Spiritum*' (SBOp 1:175).

For a soul who loves God, the body is of value when it is weak, after its death, and after its resurrection . . . It is with good reason that the soul does not want to seek its perfection in the body; it understands that in each of these stages the body is its servant for doing good. For a spirit which is itself good, the flesh is truly a good and faithful companion. If the flesh is felt to be a weight, it is also a helper. When it stops helping the spirit, it also stops weighing upon it. And finally, it becomes a great help to it without weighing on it.[58]

The intermediate stage presents a problem today because Saint Bernard, like Saint Augustine, was convinced that the souls of the saints are waiting for their bodies in heaven so they may be perfectly happy.[59] If this notion runs counter to the dogma which teaches that the beatific vision is accorded to holy souls immediately after death, it is just as important to remember that Bernard manifested a very strong conviction about the union of the human components in the state of blessedness. Consequently, he often stressed the importance of the body and its senses to the spiritual life. For ultimate blessedness to be possible, sensory experience must previously have existed.[60] Souls need a body and bodily senses; without them they cannot have mutual knowledge of each other and they are unable to accomplish anything.[61] And if Saint Bernard insists so forcefully on the body's participation in heavenly blessedness, this too comes from his strong conviction about the unity of the human being, especially relative to its affectivity, which he considers the center of personality and in which the body shares.[62] In its earthly

---

[58] Dil 11.30–31 (SBOp 3:145).

[59] Cf. B. de Vrégille, 'L'attente des saints d'après saint Bernard', in NRT 70 (1948) 225–244. P.-Y. Emery, note to 'L'attente des saints', in *Saint Bernard, Sermons pour l'année*. Introduction, 30–31.

[60] SC 5.1 (SBOp 1:21–22).

[61] SC 4.5 (SBOp 1:20–21).

[62] Cf. G. Martelet: 'Intimately bound to the mystery of the body, affectivity is in many ways the deepest center of our personality', *Résurrection, Eucharistie et genèse de l'homme* (Paris: Desclée, 1972) 210. A. Vergote: 'The sign of the resurrection . . . includes the idea that the body is the whole person, in solidarity with the other beings with whom it is in relationship. In corporal solidarity with Christ, the corporal human being will be entirely transformed', 'Le corps. Pensée

condition the body helps the soul but is a weight to be borne; in its heavenly condition the body still helps the soul but without being a weight. The continuity of the same body, transfigured, no doubt stems from the mystery of the Incarnation, because it is in Christ's humanity, in his risen body, that soul and body enjoy eternal happiness together.[63]

At the resurrection of the body, no longer will there be any question of giving the breath of life to the body, as at the moment of creation, or the spirit of holiness to an earthly creature, but the Spirit will burst forth with great force, and on that day not only hearts but also bodies will become spiritual and inebriated with happiness in God's house.[64] If during this life we need to pray for what is beneficial to the body, we ought to ask with ardent desire for the blessing of eternal life, because it is there that happiness of body and soul will be totally and perfectly fulfilled.[65]

Happiness of the spirit will be peace; the capacity of our desire will be filled to the brim by the infinite presence of God. The body, our outer person, will also be permeated with God's glory. Saint Bernard tries to explain what the condition of the four component elements of our body will be at the resurrection. *God will live on our earth* (Ps 84:10) so that our earthen body, no longer afraid of returning to dust, will also be freed from its various kinds of slavery. Otherwise there would be another kind of endless death. The liquid element in us will be perfectly free from disturbance, because it is disordered humours which arouse our passions. Our body, made up of air, will be light and agile, like the bodies of the blessed, free of the limits of time and space.

---

contemporaine et catégories bibliques', in *Revue théologique de Louvain* 10 (1979) 163. G. Marcel: 'I perhaps do not feel much need to imagine (the résurrection of the body), but what is sure is that for me it is a sort of extremely deep wish of my being. Something is there which goes beyond the notion of immortality.' Dialogue with Jean Boutang, quoted in *Vocabulaire philosophique de Gabriel Marcel* (Paris: Cerf, 1985) 302. Gabriel Marcel also understood very well that Christ's résurrection was the intermediary between the Incarnation and the resurrection of human bodies, *Vocabulaire philosophique,* 302.

[63] OS 4.2 (SBOp 5:356).
[64] SC 72.6 (SBOp 2:229).
[65] Quad 5.8 (SBOp 4:376).

What will the body still be lacking for perfect blessedness? Only beauty. Destined for access to this utterly perfect beauty, we can reasonably attribute it to the part of us which comes from fire. The Apostle says, in fact: *We are waiting for the Saviour, who will transform our weak, mortal bodies and make them like his own glorious body* (Ph 3:20), *thus showing what was promised*: *The just will shine like the sun in the kingdom of their Father* (Mt 13:43).[66]

Fire is the archetype of an impetuous, passionate character, such as Saint Bernard's. Does he not mean this fire when he speaks of the Word's visit to him?[67] Fire is both heat and light, as he often remarked (*lucet et ardet*), and a certain spiritual beauty already becomes apparent in the bodily mien of a purified and holy soul:

> When the light of this beauty completely fills the depths of the heart with its abundance, it must of necessity glow exteriorly . . . It bursts out and its rays appear in the body which is a reflection of the soul. This beauty spreads to the limbs and sensibility, so that the whole body manifests its splendor.[68]

For both the soul and the body, then, there is real continuity between life on earth and life in heaven, and this is why Saint Bernard, following Origen, made such frequent use of the doctrine of the five spiritual senses. In some mysterious way, they so suggest a particular type of symbolism that we can say with Gabriel Marcel that 'I am my body'. Saint Bernard could say therefore that he heard the word of God and breathed its fragrance, and that there is a taste for God whose sweetness he could scent and whose light he could see. He cried out: 'How long will we smell the fragrance without knowing its taste, how long will we look towards the promised land without entering it?'[69] He described five forms of love according to the five senses of the body.[70]

---

66 OS 4.6 (SBOp 5:359–360).
67 SC 74.7 (SBOp 2:243–244).
68 SC 85.11 (SBOp 2:314).
69 SC 50.8 (SBOp 2:83).
70 Div 10.2–4 (SBOp 6/1:122–124).

If the human creature, the image of God, is a little lower than the angelic creature, even though it is endowed with reason as the angels are, this inferiority is due only to its body.[71] It possesses at the same time an angel's nobility and an animal's weakness.[72] Its earthly condition ought to be evaluated in the light of its eternal destiny. Thirty-seven times Saint Bernard quotes the sentence of the *Book of Wisdom* (9:15): *A perishable body presses down the soul.* But no more than the sacred author intended to do, does Bernard give these words a platonic interpretation. Furthermore, he often points out that it is not the body as such, which by its nature is one with the soul[73] and works with it in a kind of interdependence.[74] The body which weighs down the soul is not simply the body, but the corruptible body; Adam's soul was protected from this weight because it governed an incorruptible body.[75] In its present condition, the body contributes to conversion of the heart. Physical practices have an integral role to making progress in our search for God.

> Conversion of the body alone would be valueless: if conversion is just a formality and never attains truth, it remains ineffective and merely gives the appearance of religious devotion (*pietas*). Someone who is completely focussed on external realities without knowing anything about his interior being is greatly to be pitied. Thinking himself to be something, whereas he is nothing; he deceives himself . . . Yet, even conversion of the body is not to be underestimated, because it provides appreciable support for spiritual conversion.[76]

---

[71] SC 53.8 (SBOp 2:100).

[72] Ep 412.1 (SBOp 8:394).

[73] Csi V.8.18. (SBOp 3:482).

[74] Csi V.5.12 (SBOp 3:476).

[75] Sept 2.2 (SBOp 4:351). Cf. SC 56.3 (SBOp 2:116); Pre 20.59 (SBOp 3:292).

[76] Quad 2.2 and 4 (SBOp 4:360–362). Cf. J. M. de la Torre OCSO: 'In fact, to love God with one's whole heart and soul it is equally necessary to love him with one's whole body. The body also has a right to love's enlightenment. To love God with one's whole body means to love him by means of fasting, vigils and, especially, by manual work which frees a person from so many illusions and maintains the whole person in harmony and humility ', *Un chemin de vie, la vocation cistercienne.* Voix monastiques 1 (Oka: Abbaye N.-D.-du-Lac, 1989) 49.

Here again we find the same doctrine on balanced interdependence of observances which Saint Bernard had already taught in the *Apology*.[77]

The body is not a prison for the soul, but its house. Speaking to the soul, Saint Bernard asks it to respect the guest with whom it has such a personal relationship. When the soul comes into the Lord's presence, it will remember its body and that this body spared nothing for the soul, multiplying its fasts and enduring labor, vigils, hunger, and thirst. The Lord will glorify the body at his second coming, whereas at his first coming he saved souls. Let our soul, says Saint Bernard, take pleasure in meditating on the realities to come and let even our body repose in hope. *My soul thirsts for you, my flesh is longing for you* (Ps 62:2). The prophet's soul, he continues, desired the first coming by which it would be redeemed. But more, much more, did his flesh desire the last coming when it would be glorified. Our desires will then be satisfied and the whole earth will be filled with the Lord's majesty.[78]

Saint Bernard's idea of the body is set in the context of his desire for eschatological fulfillment. In his description of the fourth step of love, at which a human being somehow forgets self entirely and has the rare, brief experience of passing into God, this person is immediately brought back to the reality of life on earth by the heaviness of the body. The nostalgia of the flesh and heart, which fainted away in this moment of joy, turns completely towards the promised plenitude. There, when we have shed all the weakness of the flesh and are no longer limited by the demands of the body, its substance will remain intact but it will henceforth be totally absorbed and transformed in the freedom of the spirit.[79]

4. ETERNALIZING TIME.

The encounter of the eternal Creator with his beloved creature living in time can be realized only at the point where eternity and

---

77 See above, note 40.
78 Adv 6.3–6 (SBOp 4:192–195).
79 Dil 10.27 and 15.39–40 (SBOp 3:142–143 and 152–153).

time come into contact and, as it were, become so like one another as to form one single reality. Several times, in a paradoxical and original way, Saint Bernard situated time between two eternities: the one from which we have come; and the one towards which we are going.[80] First we will quote the passage in which he most clearly states his insight, and then comment on it:

> So then, let anyone who already is approaching the port of salvation by his thoughts and eagerness listen. He has, as it were, cast the anchor of his hope ahead of him and already appears to be resolutely attached to that land which is so desirable. Yes, let him listen every day as long as his present combat lasts, waiting for the moment when he will be transformed. The principal and surest way to approach this port is this: the choice you have made to prepare yourself to leave this world. This preparation consists in your *vocation* and your *justification* by God. A kind of link (*connexio*) has thus been set between one eternity and another, that is to say, between *exaltation* and *predestination* . . . But do not think that this link we have been speaking about—this link established between two eternities—was invented by us. Listen to the Apostle. Does he not say the same thing in clearer words? Those whom God *chose specially long ago*, he says, *he intended to become true images of his Son* (Rm 8:29). How and in what order do you think he will glorify them? Because truly, whatever comes from God is ordered. Do you imagine that you will suddenly jump from predestination to exaltation? No. You must first provide yourself with a bridge between the two, or rather go forward on the bridge already prepared for you. *He called those he intended for this; those whom he called he justified, and with those whom he justified he shared his glory* (Rm 8:30).[81]

---

[80] To consider the briefness of a lifetime against the background of eternity is modestly to avoid the self-sufficiency of making time everything. 'When I consider how short my life is, absorbed in eternity which has preceded and will follow . . . I am fearful, and astonished to see myself here rather than there; because there is no reason why (I am) here rather than there, in the present rather than in the "then,"' B. Pascal, *Pensées* (205, ed. Brunschvicg).

[81] QH 7.6 (SBOp 4:416–417).

The Church which exists from all eternity and is predestined in God entered into time at creation, to be revealed in time in those who are quickened by grace.[82] This grace conforms us to Christ by calling us to conversion and its continuation in holiness of life. Such an existence becomes profoundly dynamic by reason of the eschatological hope that it will be consummated in the fullness of the resurrection. By placing time between two eternities, Saint Bernard clearly puts it within the perspective of infinity in both directions. The time of christian vocation and of a life tending toward holiness is thus plunged into the eternal. A sort of eternalization[83] of time then corresponds to sanctification and signifies that one's whole being is being progressively and gradually transformed into the image of the Son of God, who is simultaneously eternal and temporal. Passing from one eternity to the other is the test of time, and it is only within time that the path linking them is marked out. 'Of your vocation', said the abbot of Clairvaux to his monks, 'yes, and of your justification, I seem to see certain signs in the humility of your kind of life'.[84] A monk does, in fact, use time to become conformed ever more closely to the form which comes from the eternal, by a moral life made up entirely of modesty, gravity, patience, compassion, mildness, and humility.[85]

Our glorification remains secret, but *the Spirit will bear witness that we are children of God* (Rm 8:16). How? By our vocation and our justification, because 'these two acts form a kind of passage (*transitus*) which links eternal predestination to the glorification to

---

82 SC 78.3 (SBOp 2:267–268).

83 The expression is found in F. Rozensweig, *L'étoile de la Rédemption* (Paris: Seuil, 1982) 305. In the same work by this jewish religious philosopher, who was Lévinas' master, when he describes 'the christian act', we find the manner of situating time the same as in Saint Bernard: 'Seen from the shore of eternity, all time is simultaneous: this is something that hardly needs to be explained. But time which leads like an eternal road from eternity to eternity (from Creation to Redemption) also has a simultaneous character. Because it is only to the extent that it is a mid-ground between eternity and eternity that it is possible for humans to meet in it. Someone who sees that he is on the way is at the same point of time, that is to say, at the exact center of time. It is brotherhood which transports human beings to this center. *L'étoile de la Rédemption*, 408.

84 Asc 2.5 (SBOp 5:129).

85 SC 27.7 (SBOp 1:187).

come'.[86] Saint Bernard brings up the theme of two eternities again when he inserts it into his teaching on free choice. Although, in fact, my vocation comes from grace alone, whenever it is a matter of my justification, grace is operative only with my collaboration. Between the two eternities my free choice also has its own worth, but the Lord always reserves for himself the beginning and the end. He is the alpha and omega.[87]

In a letter to Thomas of Beverley, which is an enthusiastic defense of the cistercian spirit, Bernard once again expressed what he thought about life on earth. It is only an *interim*[88]—an interval—between two eternities, during which God's Spirit makes known to us the grace of our divine vocation and sanctification by communicating this grace to us. This transitory knowledge, imperfect though it may be, nevertheless assures us that God loves us and that we can love him, and this fills us with hope and joy.[89]

> The mystery of time is unceasingly present in Saint Bernard's thought and writings, and we know how much his thought and writings are permeated with Scripture. Liturgy is involved in two ways: directly, because it was principally during the liturgy that Bernard lived out his spirituality of time; and indirectly, because it makes up the space *par excellence* in which we read and sing Scripture, which reveals the meaning of time to us and provides the basis for meditation and preaching.[90]

From Advent to All Saints' Day, the liturgical 'memorial' constantly joins the past to the present and future. The Advent sermons celebrate Jesus' intermediate coming in the *interim* between his two advents, past and future, when he lives in us by his Word and sacraments, and gives us his life and wisdom. The intermediate coming gives us in the present, not the meaning of history, but the

---

[86] Ded 5.7 (SBOp 5:393).

[87] 1 Nov 4.4 (SBOp 5:317–318).

[88] During this *interim* mindfulness of the fruits of redemption gives us strength while we are waiting: Dil 3.10 (SBOp 3:127); SC 51.1 (SBOp 2:84).

[89] Ep 107.9–10 (SBOp 7:274).

[90] P.-Y. Emery, 'Liturgie et temps chez saint Bernard', in *Liturgie O.C.S.O.* (1992) n° 82, 217.

meaning of the eternal in time.[91] The present therefore is closer
to the two eternities than are the past or the future. It is the
bridge, the two ends of which disappear from our sight in two
oceans of light, but it joins them by spiritual mediation and the
moral transformation of our being. This bridge is the holiness of
our vocation and our continual conversion. From this perspective,
action becomes contemplation.[92]

The liturgy is thus the daily sign and reminder of our passage
to the eternal.[93] A moral and holy way of living unifies time in our
life: past, present and future. On a verse of Deuteronomy (32:29):
May they be wise and intelligent, and prepare their destiny, Saint Bernard
comments:

> As I see it, these words recommend three realities to us:
> wisdom, intelligence, and foresightedness. I think that these
> can be applied to three periods of time, so that *a certain image of
> eternity* may appear to be restored in us. Yes, we have to manage
> the present with wisdom, judge the past by our intelligence, and
> prepare our final end cautiously. This is, in fact, a summary of
> the whole spiritual effort. This is the rule of a zealous spiritual
> life: to organize our present life with wisdom, reflect on our past
> in the bitterness of our soul, prepare for the future with great
> care. *Let us live in this world soberly, justly and with piety* (Tt 2:12),

---

91 Cf. G. Thibon, *L'ignorance étoilée* (Paris: Fayard, 1974) 122: 'Deliverance
consists in seeking beyond time what men seek beyond the present . . . Because
we have to choose between two conceptions of a human being: one which makes
him a product of the past going toward the future (as progressists do) or one
which sees in him a being who has fallen from eternity and can only attain his
destiny by going back to his origin . . . In the first hypothesis, time is the stuff
of our destiny; in the second, it is only the split—"the eclipsing curse of birth"'.
P. Shelley, *Adonaïs*.

92 Cf. C. Dumont, ocso, 'Contemplative Action; Time in Eternity According
to Saint Bernard', 152–154.

93 In words which surprise us, the philosopher E. Lévinas, in *Humanisme de l'autre
homme* (Paris: Fata Morgana, 1972) 42–43, applies the concept and term 'liturgy'
to signify generous and disinterested action based on ethics, which requires 'a
losing investment', without advance remuneration in time. Its result is assured
only in return for patience and complete domination of *my* time, going beyond
it to the infinite: by sacrifice, this passage is possible towards the Other—in
eternity.

says the Apostle. This presupposes observing sobriety in the present, redeeming by just satisfaction the time which has gone by without bearing fruit of salvation for us and, lastly, opposing the shield of godliness to the dangers that the future holds for us. In fact, only *godliness is valuable for all things* (1 Tm 4:8); in other words, worship given to God with humility and eagerness.[94]

In this 'piety' we recognize bernardine consideration, the 'spiritual effort' which conforms our life to Christ's and thus gives it a certain image of eternity. After this passage, Saint Bernard also mentions the beatitudes of the poor, the meek and those who mourn, which are rehabilitation of time by holiness of life.[95] Elsewhere, he speaks again about these three Beatitudes, repeating that by poverty, meekness, and tears, a certain likeness and *image of eternity* are renewed in the soul.[96]

Perseverance is also an image of the eternal within time. 'Actually, the image of God's eternity is perseverance in our vocation (*conversationis nostrae*) . . . our way in this world of imitating his immutability.'[97]

Time, when mastered, spiritualized, and lived in the holiness of a serious moral life, is not only the expectation of eternity, but by perseverance becomes a symbol of the eternal and already grants it to us. Perseverance is a work of love, and love remains the very image of God:

> Who continues and perseveres in love, if not someone who emulates the eternity of charity? Does perseverance not offer us some image of eternity? Furthermore, it is to perseverance alone that eternity is given. Better yet, it is perseverance that imparts eternity to a human being.[98]

Peace is also a reflection of eternity, because by conforming our will to God's we already have a little foretaste of eternal peace.[99]

---

[94] PP 2.7 (SBOp 5:196).
[95] PP 2.8 (SBOp 5:196–197).
[96] OS 1.14 (SBOp 5:340).
[97] Div 111.7 (SBOp 6/1:389).
[98] Csi V.14.31 (SBOp 3:492–493).
[99] Div 26.4 (SBOp 6/1:196–197).

Those who abide in this spiritual peace, 'by their way of living have already begun to imitate the state of being reserved for them in eternity'.[100]

Equanimity, which the passionate-natured Saint Bernard often spoke of as if it were a difficult moral ideal, is also a sign of eternalization of time in a spirit subject to change:

> The noble creature, made in the image and likeness of him who made himself, shows that it is recovering its pristine dignity . . . when it judges it unworthy of itself to conform to this unstable world and, striving . . . to reform itself by renewal of its spirit, attains the likeness in which it knows it was created.[101]

This then is how Saint Bernard thought of time, the mystery which has intrigued so many great minds. Time is given to the spiritual creature only that it may rediscover its Creator in love. But time consequently takes on new density and an infinite dimension: that of divine Love.[102]

On the other hand, following Saint Paul, Saint Bernard likes to compare time—which is continuous and in which all kinds of suffering flourish—with the weight of promised glory. This two-fold consideration is far from being a comforting assurance of reward. Viewed on the horizon of the eternal, our time of suffering, we know, is insignificant. Lent is the sacrament of time in that it is a period of waiting for the Pasch and ardently hoping for the Resurrection.[103]

This mystery of the eternalization of time is nothing other than the Incarnation, by which Christ, eternity and time, 'has made eternal that which bears the mark of time'.[104]

---

[100] Div 84.2 (SBOp 6/1:326).

[101] SC 21.6 (SBOp 1:125).

[102] Cf. G. Marcel, 'It is possible that each of us will be called upon, during the course of this life, to weave in a certain way the first rows . . . of a different time, perhaps destined to attain fulfillment beyond death, in . . . what I personally would see as the first fruits of eternity . . . Most great spiritual persons have thought of time this way.' *Vocabulaire philosophique de Gabriel Marcel* (Paris: Cerf, 1985) 511.

[103] C. Dumont OCSO, 'Le carême, sacrement du combat spirituel selon saint Bernard', in Coll 24 (1962) 18. Re-published in *Une éducation du coeur*, 79–91.

[104] Div 119 (SBOp 6/1:397).

5. DEATH: PORT AND PORTAL OF LIFE

While the span of our life is given to us so we may seek God and encounter him by progressive conformation to the image of his Son, the end of a life is the moment when the body and time unite in one last test of obedience: death. Death is cessation of motion and change; it is the possibility of eternity. Saint Bernard, passionate contemplative that he was, often interjected this contrast between the Creator and the creature. For example, he said that God does everything he wills by the simple faculty of willing, without agitation and without considering time or place. God judges and disposes all things with calm wisdom. The human creature, however, is unable to free itself either from some degree of mental excitement or from physical or spiritual agitation.[105] The soul, by its immortality, has been made in the image of God, but the image lacks likeness because it is mingled with mortality.

> God alone is immutable by nature . . . True and perfect im-
> mortality does not admit change and does not end because, if I
> may say so, all change is an imitation of death. Everything that
> changes passes from one state to another, and must therefore
> in some way die to what it is in order to begin to be what it is
> not. If there are as many deaths as changes, then what becomes
> of immortality?[106]

Death, the final change, is the end of the crossing, the end of the test, of its vicissitudes and fluctuations. Death is the port of entry and, at the same time, the portal of life. Both images are traditional, but Saint Bernard superposes them twice in discussing the death of his friend Malachy, the irish bishop who died at Clairvaux.[107] The

---

[105] SC 78.2 (SBOp 2:267). See SC 6.1 (SBOp 1.26). Divine immutability prevents the creature, changeable by nature, from grasping God's simplicity: SC 31.1 (SBOp 1:219); 51.7 (SBOp 2:87–88); 80.5 (SBOp 2:280–281). Death is thus a symbol of contemplative rapture: SC 52.5 (SBOp 2:92–93).

[106] SC 81.5 (SBOp 2:286–287). Cf. SC 82.3 (SBOp 2:293–294). Grégoire de Nysse, *La Vie de Moïse* II, 2–3. Sch 1 bis (Paris: Cerf, 1955) 32. [English translation by Everett Ferguson and Abraham Malherbe, *Gregory of Nyssa, The Life of Moses* (Kalamazoo: Cistercian Publications–New York, Paulist Press, 1978)].

[107] '*Mortis portus et porta vitae*', De sancto Malachia 8. *Sermones varii* (SBOp 6/1:55); V Mal 31.75 (SBOp 3:378).

two moments constitute just one single moment, and the portal of eternity opens as soon as one arrives at the port of death. Life is merely a passage, so death—in the full sense of the word—is *the* passage, the *transitus*, as we read in the title of the sermon at Malachy's funeral (where the expression 'portal—*janua*—of life' is also mentioned). It is the ultimate reality of what life is: a paschal mystery.[108] Death is part of life and Saint Bernard, who was highly conscious of the contrast between life and death, also remarked: 'It is absolutely necessary for the end of this present life to be consistent with the beginning of the life to come'. He drew a comparison with a belt that someone would like to lengthen by adding another piece: to be joined, the two ends must fit together. With our eyes fixed on both ends, we have to prepare for our future life by thinking of death, of 'what the spiritual quality of our existence has been'.[109]

All the same, Saint Bernard was very painfully affected by the reality of death. He expressed in violent terms the dread it aroused in him. 'The thought of death, my own and that of those dear to me, fills me with dread', he said when his brother Gerard died.[110] When his prior Humbert, very dear to him, passed away, he cried:

> The insatiable killer has spared neither me nor you, and me even less than you. *Is this the way you separate, bitter death* (1 S 15:32)? Oh, cruel beast! Oh, bitterest of bitterness! Oh, horror and terror of the sons of Adam.[111]

The horror of death can be overcome only by obedience for Christ, as was Saint Martin's,[112] or by love of Christ, as was the case with Saint Clement.[113] Because Saints Peter and Paul were friends of Christ, their death is expressly celebrated, whereas, regarded in a purely human way, nothing inspires greater horror than death.[114] And yet, did Christ not also know the horror of death, and death on

---

[108] Mal 4 (SBOp 5:420).

[109] PP 2.6 (SBOp 5:195–196).

[110] SC 26.9 (SBOp 1:177).

[111] Humb 1 (SBOp 5:441).

[112] Mar 17–18 (SBOp 5:411–412).

[113] Clem 2 (SBOp 5:414).

[114] PP 2.4 (SBOp 5:195).

a cross?[115] Saint Bernard's realism about death is often very striking, as in this passage:

> What sweetness the spirit finds in its full accord with the flesh! Yes, but it is their sad separation which lets it be measured, because the spirit can hardly leave the body it vivifies before the body's corruption becomes absolutely unbearable to it.[116]

The pain of separation from loved ones, however, touched Bernard's heart far more than physical pain. When, as we saw, he quoted the scriptural passage, *Is this the way you separate, bitter death?*, he did it because death cruelly put to an end to a very beautiful and very true friendship. And if grieving could be changed into song and horror into joy, as when his brother Gerard died, this was only because of his faith in his friend's happiness and his hope that the friendship would live on despite separation.[117]

Death can offer us three advantages: rest after life's toil; the joy of newness; and the security of eternity.[118] Although Saint Bernard usually condemns curiosity, he sometimes speaks about a good kind of curiosity, too: a curiosity about the things of God.[119] And it is this latter curiosity which will blossom forth fully in heaven, in the infinite joy of newness. Many artists and poets have dreamed about it:

> O death, old captain, it is time! Weigh anchor!
> This country bores us, Death! let's get underway! . . .
> In the depths of the Unknown, to find something *new*! [120]

Not only will we be surprised by the newness of that other world, but the world of spirits—of angels and God—will have a

---

[115] SC 11.7 (SBOp 1:59).

[116] Sept 2.2 (SBOp 4:351).

[117] Cf. Jean Leclercq , 'La joie de mourir selon saint Bernard de Clairvaux', in *Recueil d'Etudes sur saint Bernard et ses écrits* (Rome: Ed. di Storia e letteratura V, 1992) 435. ['The Joy of Dying According to Saint Bernard', CSQ 25 (1990) 163–174.]

[118] Div 64.2 (SBOp 6/1:298); Sent 3.85 (SBOp 6/2:124).

[119] See above, Chapter II, note 69.

[120] C. Baudelaire, *Les fleurs du mal* CXXVI, viii (Le voyage) (Paris: Garnier-Flammarion, 1964) 155.

surprise, too. Saint Bernard asserts this when he talks about the entry of the saints, as well as himself, into the world of eternity which has not experienced the human adventure.

> To pass from death to life doubles the gift of life. This will be my part in the heavenly feast, and the blessed spirits will not have known it. I even dare to say that the life of beatitude does not know the happiness reserved for me, unless it consents to taste it in me and by love for me. It really seems to me that in this way I will add something to that perfection, something important.[121]

Elsewhere he says that at death the measure will overflow and something will be added to fullness, because a superabundant outpouring of light will also be reflected in bodies.[122]

Fear of death was not unfamiliar to Saint Bernard, and he condemned the nonchalant attitude of hardened sinners. Images illustrating danger serve only to make our conscience more sincere and to remind it that

> the true life of the soul is God . . . Alas! brothers, we can always amuse ourselves with trifles and delight in indulging ourselves in idle pastimes. This does not prevent these twin serpents from hovering nearby, ready to deprive us of our two lives, one of the body and the other of the heart. What is to prevent us from sleeping in peace except the fact that when there is serious danger, negligence indicates not so much security as despair.[123]

For someone who is just, however, someone who has held firm in the midst of temptations and the difficulties of spiritual combat, death will come without inflicting harm. For someone who loves God, it will be like sleep; it will be the 'portal of life'. Such a person will not be tormented by the three forms of affliction which death assumes: dread of leaving this world; the pain of passing away; the shame at standing in the presence of God's glory in all its splendor.[124]

---

[121] SC 68.5 (SBOp 2:199–200).
[122] SC 72.10 (SBOp 2:232).
[123] QH 10.4 (SBOp 4:445–446). Cf. SC 56.5 (SBOp 2:117).
[124] Div 28.5 (SBOp 6/1:207–208). See Tpl 1.2 (SBOp 3:215).

In the life of a monk, is what is most important not union with Christ by conformity of our will with God's will, in obedience until death? Let us quote this beautiful passage from the *First Sermon on Easter*, where Saint Bernard exhorts his monks to wait for the resurrection on the third day:

> And so, let all of us, whoever we are, who follow our Head during the whole of this day on which we were made (Gn 2:7) and then redeemed: let us not stop doing penance, let us not stop carrying our cross with perseverance—as He persevered on the cross—until the Spirit tells us to rest from our labors (Rev 14:13). Brothers, let us not listen to anyone, whether someone of flesh and blood or some spirit, who would try to persuade us to come down from the cross. Let us persist in staying on the cross; let us be taken down by the hands of others, not by our own fickleness.[125]

His last letter, written to a friend, gives us perhaps the best proof that he remained united to Christ on his cross until the very end, just as he had ardently embraced it as a young monk. At the same time, it also reminds us of his realism, his extreme simplicity and his keen mind, all of which make us feel very close to him:

> Sleep has abandoned me, so I do not have the relief from my sufferings that it could give me. I cannot sleep. Almost all my trouble is due to my stomach . . . My legs and feet are swollen like those of someone with dropsy. But in the midst of all that—so that a caring friend may not be unaware of his friend's condition as concerns my 'interior man'—if I dare say so, the spirit is willing in this weakened flesh. Pray for me to the Lord . . . I am writing to you by my own hand so you can see my great affection. But I would have preferred to answer a letter from you.[126]

Faced with death, friendship still makes him look forward to a letter. What could be more human?

---

[125] Pasc 1.8 (SBOp 5:83–84).

[126] Ep 310 (SBOp 8:230), to Arnold of Chartres, the benedictine abbot of Bonneval.

6. THE WISDOM OF SUFFERING FOR LOVE OF CHRIST.

In its earthly state, the spiritual creature can no longer be perfectly happy except at the very rare and brief moments when it regains its entire freedom. It then escapes from what Saint Bernard calls *miseria*, which is its usual condition and in which it is far from being able to enjoy freedom of pleasure (*libertas complaciti*).[127] Being a practical realist, Saint Bernard was no more pessimistic than Sartre, and he could well have assented to the following statement by the philosopher of nothingness: 'The human reality is suffering and perpetually haunted by a totality which it is without being able to be it . . . By nature, therefore, it is unhappy consciousness.'[128]

Saint Bernard describes this deterioration by focussing completely on freedom's original adventure, as does Sartre. The creature wanted to take its autonomy in hand independently of any relationship with its Creator. Blocking out the truth about self (pride) and love's inability to attain its true object (God) are direct consequences of this. (See Saint Bernard's anthropology, Chapter II). Human suffering is therefore not something accidental, as hedonist philosophers may imagine it is, but the very substratum of our existence. Saint Bernard often described the experience of insatiable desire[129] and the unremitting invasion into our life of *miseria*, of 'unhappy consciousness.' The various kinds of physical or moral suffering which overwhelm us to the point that lesser suffering gives us an illusory impression of happiness, are signs of this.[130]

For Saint Bernard, who uses it fifteen times, the biblical expression *labor et dolor* in psalms 9 (vv. 28 and 35) and 89 (v. 10) means this suffering in our life. What he considers important is not so much to seek an explanation for it, but to find the right way of facing up to it. 'Most people endure toil and pain by necessity, and not by free choice. Such people do not reproduce the image of God's Son (cf.

---

[127] Cf. Gra 5.15 (SBOp 3:177); Dil 10.27 (SBOp 3:142–143).
[128] J.-P. Sartre, *L'être et le néant* (Paris: Gallimard, 1943) 134. [*Being and Nothingness* (New York: Philosophical Library, 1956)].
[129] Dil 7.18–20 (SBOp 3:134–136).
[130] Gra 5.13–14 (SBOp 3:175–177).

Rm 8:29).' Obviously, God does not take into account the hardships of those who endure suffering in order to do evil.

> On the contrary, persons of good will who by free christian choice have traded riches for poverty . . . and left everything for Christ, as he left everything for them, are the ones who follow him . . . For me [the abbot says to his monks], such imitation of Christ is the surest proof that the Saviour's passion and his likeness to our humanity are advantageous for me. This is the savor, this is the fruit of toil and pain.[131]

This passage follows an admirable reference to the mystery of the Incarnation.

> He became *like human beings* (Ph 2:7), said the Apostle, and not 'like the human being', because the first human being was not created with sinful flesh or even in the likeness of sinful flesh. Christ immersed himself in what is most opaque and profound in universal human misery.[132]

These passages show Bernard's real attitude towards suffering. It means freely imitating Christ in his poverty and suffering, because he participated in ours by his Incarnation. In this, Bernard concludes, there is a savor and a kind of wisdom which comes as the fruit of suffering which is no longer pointless.

To participate in Christ's sufferings is to participate preeminently in the sufferings of humanity. Twice in commenting on verse 5 of psalm 72, *they do not suffer as other men do*, Bernard explained the spiritual intention which allows someone to suffer wisely, seeing in these words a condemnation of the idleness and egoism of the rich who sleep in comfort on Christmas Eve while the shepherds, who suffer during the night (as poor folk do), hear the voices of angels.

> Let people then be aware of this: those who do not participate in human toil do not deserve to be visited by angels. Yes, we

---

[131] 4HM 12 (SBOp 5:65).
[132] 4HM 10 (SBOp 5:63).

ought to be aware of how pleased the citizens of heaven are when they see toil that has a spiritual intention.'[133]

By this final phrase, esteem for work is clearly linked to a spiritual intention: human solidarity, in Christ, with the toil and suffering of all human beings.

Recalling the eschatological character of monastic life, in which the cares of daily life are generally fewer than for seculars, Saint Bernard insists on the monk's responsibility to remain in peace and see that God is God (cf. Ps 45:11).

Yet to be able to arrive at this some day, you must first apply yourself to seeing who *you* are. As the prophet said: *Let them know that they are only human* (Ps 9:21). It is to this two-fold reflection that your freedom of mind and your time should be devoted, in keeping with the saint's prayer: 'Lord God, that I may know you and know myself!'[134] How can a human being reach self-knowledge if he or she flees toil and suffering?[135]

Knowledge of self, which leads to compassion because it is knowledge of the human condition, is experienced by the monk in obedience and patience. And because these two kinds of nourishment are tasteless, they need to be seasoned with the salt of wisdom. 'What has more taste than wisdom? . . . This is why we call people insipid when we want to imply that they have no wisdom whatever.'[136]

If we are to act and suffer wisely, we must realize that we are human creatures. To obey and suffer with generosity we must have 'a smile of joy in the way we love'.[137] Although wisdom permits a person to obey and be patient with the proverbial grain of the salt of humor, the human creature still knows that it is in exile. Having

---

[133] Nat 3.5 (SBOp 4:261–262). Cf. Div 2.2 (SBOp 6/1:81).

[134] Saint Augustine, *Soliloquies* II.1. Fathers of the Church 5 (Washington, D.C.: Catholic University of America Press, 1948).

[135] Div 2.1 (SBOp 6/1:80).

[136] Div 2.4 (SBOp 6/1:82).

[137] Div 2.5 (SBOp 6/1:82).

in mind the work of the harvest, which took a long time and was very arduous, Saint Bernard reminded his monks:

> This heavy work, brothers, makes us think seriously about our exile and our poverty, but also, of course, about the wrong we have done. Why, in fact, *are we put to death all day long* (Ps 43:22), *fasting so often, frequently keeping vigil* (2 Cor 11:27), weighed down by toil and worries? Is it for this that we have been created? Certainly not! Because while it is true that *a human being is born for toil* (Jb 5:7), it was certainly not for toil that he was created.[138]

Alluding to the time of the first creation,[139] when neither sin nor suffering existed, Saint Bernard then places the monk—the spiritual person—between two tables. The monk has been fasting, and with two very different kinds of desire he looks at, on one hand, the table of those who take great pleasure in enjoying the good things of this world perceptible to the senses; and, on the other, the table set by Christ in his kingdom, the eschatological table. I cannot sit down at table with those who are enjoying themselves, even if I am sometimes tempted to do so, and I cannot share in the heavenly table as long as I am still in this life. As soon as I become aware of the ambiguity of my situation, I see only one tenable attitude: the decision to bear it patiently for the sake of love. But this is only the attitude of a beginner, because our whole desire will very quickly turn towards the table of the Kingdom. And if being deprived of the

---

[138] *In labore messis* 2.1 (SBOp 5:220). Cf. E. Lévinas: 'In spite of all its freedom, effort reveals a kind of condemnation. It is fatigue and suffering . . . Also, it is above effort properly speaking-in an attitude of reflection on it-that the entire mysticism of work which exploits the themes of joy or freedom through work is situated. It is never in work itself that joy resides. The happiness coming from work or duty well accomplished, the heroism of sacrifice and of surmounting difficulty, is nourished by other considerations . . . In work freely accepted, in the most spontaneous effort, there is a moment of unremitting commitment, without possibility of redemption. The ancient curse of work does not stem only from our need to work to earn our bread: it is found wholly in the instant of effort', *De l'existence à l'existant* (Paris: Vrin, 1978) 44–50. [*Existence and Existants* (The Hague: M. Nijhoff, 1978)].

[139] Cf. Hum 10.30 (SBOp 3:39); Sept 2.2 (SBOp 4:350–351).

table of sensible joy has made a monk weep, those tears will soon
come from the fountain above, and he will say: *How unfortunate I
am! My exile goes on and on* (Ps 119:5).[140]

Lay people have the responsibility of feeding and looking after
a family, pleasing a spouse and taking care of business matters
and commerce.[141] But the abbot of Clairvaux severely judges a
monk who forgets the priority of spiritual things to devote himself
completely to manual work or physical penance. Quoting Saint
Paul, he reminds such a monk that *physical practices are of little use,
but the usefulness of piety is unlimited, since it holds out the promises of life
here and now, and of future life as well* (1 Tm 4:8).[142]

For Saint Bernard, the balance between the three benedictine
occupations—prayer, reading, and work—is often summed up
as the labor of contemplation,[143] and he puts a strong accent
on eschatological tension. This marks the horizon of a monk's
life, which can be blurred when something closer is sought or
something more humanly or passionately motivated. Wisdom is
found in suffering when suffering, work, effort, all toil and all pain
are spiritualized in the sacrifice of Christ and become themselves
sacrifices of redemptive love. Max Scheler seems to have echoed
Saint Bernard's thought, when he wrote

> It is only by situating the reality of pain and suffering in the
> light of the idea of sacrifice, as Christianity was the first to do
> with the thought that God himself suffered freely by love for us
> and that he put himself in the human being's place by sacrificing
> himself . . . that we will arrive at a more profound theodicy of
> suffering. . . .[144]

---

[140] *In labore messis* 2.2–3 (SBOp 5:221–222).

[141] Div 2.1 (SBO 6/1:80).

[142] SC 33.10 (SBOp 1:240–241); Apo 6.12–14 (SBOp 3:91–94); Csi I.8.9–10 (SBOp 3:404–405).

[143] Cf. J. Lacroix: ' If the modern world is tempted to make laborious activity an end in itself at the same time as it has made it most oppressive and despiritualizing, it is no doubt to try-in vain-to fill the emptiness left in people's hearts by the absence of contemplation,' *Le sens du dialogue*. (Neuchâtel: La Baconnière, 1955). 'Travail et contemplation', 84.

[144] M. Scheler, *Le sens de la souffrance* (Paris: Aubier, 1936) 11–12.

7. SOLITUDE AND SILENCE, TO FIND GOD

If the cistercian life is wholly orientated towards the Creator's encounter with his spiritual creature, then it goes without saying that Saint Bernard, like all masters of monastic spirituality, attributes very great importance to solitude and silence. Seeking God always presupposes internalization and recollection; by them a tacit and secret accord of the divine and human wills may come about in our actions as well as in contemplation. Recollection within our own consciousness is necessary if, in meeting God, we are to go beyond, to pass from the Word-flesh to the Word-holiness (see Chapter IV). So we ought to give this aspect of solitude and silence a special place in treating the various motivations for practising them. A monk's solitude and silence are a conscious and willed preparation for the visit of the Word, who comes to a soul disengaged from all other preoccupations. Commenting on the verse of the *Song of Songs* which makes allusion to a turtle dove (I. 9), Saint Bernard points out that, like this timid little bird who hardly ever mixes with others and is satisfied with one companion, we ought to live alone for God:

> You ought to sit alone, like a turtle dove. You have nothing in common with the crowd . . . A holy soul ought to remain alone and keep itself entirely for him alone whom it has chosen in preference to all others. Flee from the crowd, even from your relatives. Leave your friends. Don't you know that you have a Bridegroom who is so shy that he will always refuse to meet you in the presence of someone else? Stay alone, not physically but by your intention, by your gift of self, in spirit. For the Spirit, Our Lord Jesus Christ, is there before you, demanding solitude, not of body but of mind. It may happen that it is also profitable for you to be alone physically, especially at times of prayer . . . But outside of this case, only solitude of mind and soul is recommended to you. Now, you are alone as soon as your thoughts are not attached to banal preoccupations, when you are not anxious for news, if you scorn the crowd's idle talk, or if you find tiresome what everyone else is so avidly interested in. You are alone when you avoid quarreling, if you are not hurt by offenses inflicted on you and if you forget spitefulness.

Otherwise, even in physical solitude you are not alone. Don't you see that you can be alone in the midst of a crowd and, on the contrary, find yourself engulfed in the crowd even when you are physically alone? Even if the crowd is all around you, you are alone on condition that you are not too curious about what other people are doing, and that you do not rashly judge them.[145]

In this passage we again find Saint Bernard's undeviating teaching on the close relationship between mysticism and ethics. The allusion to the Holy Spirit, present before our spirit like a jealous bridegroom demanding all our attention, is followed by a description of what really encumbers our consciousness: the swarm of sentiments and judgments which invade it and create an uproar. Silence is an important cistercian observance, one of the six jars of Cana whose water ought to become the wine of charity:

Now in regard to the tongue: does anyone not know how badly idle remarks, lies, detraction, flattery, malicious words and boasting contaminate us (cf. Jm 3:6)? To remedy all these, the fifth jar is clearly necessary: that is, silence, the guardian of religious life. Therein lies our strength.'[146]

We can make bad use of speech for various reasons: to amuse ourselves,[147] presumptuously to impose our own ideas,[148] to brag,[149] deviously to slander another person,[150] to complain about the food,[151] to feign humility by confessing our faults[152] or to attract attention to ourselves.[153]

Saint Bernard also knew that there are reprehensible kinds of silence just as there are worthwhile kinds of speech. He knew the

---

[145] SC 40.4–5 (SBOp 2:26–27).

[146] P Epi 2.7 (SBOp 4:325). See also: Div 55.1 (SBOp 6/1:280). Bernard also described the evils of idle talk, detraction and calumny when he returned from one of his trips to Rome: SC 24.2–4 (SBOp 1:152–156).

[147] Hum 12.40 (SBOp 3:46–47).

[148] Hum 14.44 (SBOp 3:50).

[149] Hum 13.41 (SBOp 3:47–48).

[150] SC 24.4 (SBOp 1:154–156).

[151] SC 30.10 (SBOp 1:216–217).

[152] SC 16.10 (SBOp 1:95).

[153] Hum 18.46 (SBOp 3:51–52).

advantages of replacing criticism and murmuring with thanksgiving and reconciliation with our brother.[154] Speaking can be just as useful and valuable as it can be harmful and deadly. It is not only the time subtracted from our life that is lost in idle talk, but also life itself and the life of others.[155]

There are people who are readier to speak than to listen, to teach than to learn, and who, although unable to govern themselves, presumptuously claim to be our guides. Instead of storing up water like a reservoir, and letting the surplus overflow, they are nothing more than canals, letting the water spill over almost as soon as it flows into them, and so they remain empty.[156] As Heidegger rightly pointed out, the most important thing about idle chatter is that somebody keeps talking. Since what is being said has lost all connection with the reality of what is being talked about, such communication does not consist in an appropriation of reality, but only in the transmission and repetition of a discourse whose authority increases as it spreads more widely.[157] Contrariwise, a wise person who, thanks to silence, has heard an important truth, keeps it in his or her heart, also thanks to silence.[158]

The ascesis of solitude and silence is indispensable in a life devoted to seeking God. It is a daily struggle against the distractions which the mind uses to try to escape what is essential. How often monks could repeat these lines written by a modern author:

> From then on, we talked just to say nothing. We saw a screen coming between us, made up of glossy words and the noisy echoes of daily life, of the verbal liquid people feel obliged to use to fill up silence, without knowing why. With stupefaction I discovered that talking is, in fact, the best way to silence what is essential.[159]

---

154 Nat BVM 14–15 (SBOp 5:285–286); SC 29.4–5 (SBOp 1:205–206).
155 Div 17.4 (SBOp 6/1:152).
156 SC 18.3 (SBOp 1:104).
157 Cf. M. Heidegger, *L'être et le temps* I, 36 (Paris: Gallimard, 1964) 207. [Being and Time].
158 SC 57.5 (SBOp 2:122).
159 A. Makine, *Le testament français* (Paris: Mercure de France, 1995) 156.

For a monk, observing silence means being attentive to what is essential. Saint Bernard gave his community an example of this in his funeral eulogy for Clairvaux's prior:

> If you follow his example, you will not easily stumble into trivial thoughts and idle conversations, into joking and foolishness (because by those things you will lose a lot of your life and time) . . . I know very well that it is hard for a talkative person to bear silence and for a wandering mind to remain fixed on something . . . The man we are burying—I know this myself—had to struggle hard in the beginning against this same tendency, which he finally conquered. The good habit he formed became so natural to him that he would have been unable to let his mind stray in such silliness.[160]

The cistercians thought of solitude and silence as two strong points in their reform. Saint Bernard fully adopted this attitude and developed an extensive spiritual teaching on them. To waste one's time and life in idle chatter not only exposes a person to disparagement and detraction, but it is depersonalizing: the mind goes blank and the heart dries up. Meditation becomes difficult and prayer loses fervor because of all the things we have said or heard.[161] Solitude and silence are effective means of arriving at a truly humble self-knowledge. For a monk, maturity results from the capacity to renounce the superficial and vain 'I'. To speak before understanding the truth is to speak about something one does not know. Truth reveals itself only to a pure heart, which does not seek its own interests but communicates truth generously. Here again, it is the wisdom of love which enlightens our vision and enables us to speak about what we can know only by experience.[162]

For Saint Bernard, silence is a kind of eschatological perfection, and words are an imperfect but necessary means not only of communicating with others but also of speaking with oneself. I speak to myself as I would to another person when I am estranged

---

[160] Humb 8 (SBOp 5:447).

[161] Div 17.5 (SBOp 6/1:154).

[162] SC 62.8 (SBOp 2:160–161).

from myself and anxious to come back to my heart, to regain my interior unity and find God there. And yet, one day all words will be superfluous:

> Because even among ourselves words will no longer be necessary, when we all come together to form one perfect human being (cf. Eph 4:13). Then, quite rightly, *tongues will cease* (1 Cor 13:8) and we will not need an intermediary interpreter, for by love the one sole Mediator will have utterly done away with all go-betweens (*medium*).[163]

Divine love, permeating everything, will do away with every mid-ground. Space and distance will be transcended. Love—the agreement of wills—spans distance. Far from hardening hearts and isolating consciousness, solitude and silence nourish true charity because, more than words, they develop our compassion, that true knowledge of others which is for Bernard the foundation of the fraternal relationships we are now going to speak about. Even more than solitude and silence, and nurtured by them, fraternal charity is the supreme observance; the ones we have already mentioned simply prepare the heart for this.

8. PRACTISING FRATERNAL CHARITY

For the Creator and his spiritual creature in their search for one another, there is a *locus* particularly favorable to their meeting: another spiritual creature, a fellow human being. Because every human person is made in the image of God-Charity, this image ought to be discernable on every human face. More than once Saint Bernard underscored his conviction that social love has a mediating role as a passageway from love of self to love of God. Love's wisdom reveals itself in a zest to share with another person what I cannot be content to love alone without its becoming insipid. Love of others is not necessarily something illusory or calculated; it is not subtle self-seeking or self-interest. With the help of grace, love's natural goodness should regain the purity of its driving force and

---

[163] Div 110 (SBOp 6/1:384–385).

become free of whatever fetters it, that is to say, opposing passions. Using a vocabulary very different than that found in later theological formulations, Saint Bernard affirmed that nature exists in grace by its very creation; it is therefore fundamentally good, and the same grace heals the image's disfigurement resulting from sin.[164]

It was on the foundation of this still basically good human nature that Saint Bernard was able to describe the journey towards love of God which begins with love of self and develops through love of neighbor. The ordering of love is possible only if love is disposed by nature to love of neighbor. So we love our neighbor by 'association of nature' (*propter naturae societatem*).[165]

Saint Bernard very clearly recognized a natural goodness in the human soul: it loves itself and, when not impeded by sin, spontaneously loves others as it loves itself.

> Fraternal love is surely born in the most secret affections of the human heart. It is from a certain kind of inherent tenderness which a human being experiences in innate love for self that fraternal love germinates and grows. It is like the humus of fertile soil which brings forth fruits of piety when grace blows on it from above. We do not believe, therefore, that what we desire naturally for ourselves can justly be refused to another human being, who as a sharer in humanity seems to have some right to it. We will even offer it willingly, joyfully, whenever and however this is possible.[166]

So there is in the human heart an ointment of natural goodness and tenderness[167] which spreads naturally into love of others, provided that self-centeredness and envy do not corrupt it. There is a 'beauty of our social and common nature', a 'social grace', which

---

[164] See P. Delfgaauw, *Saint Bernard, Maître de l'Amour divin* (1952). (Paris: FAC-éditions, 1994) 175–185.

[165] Cf. Div 50.3 (SBOp 6/1:272). See also: 'In themselves, elementary passions (*affectiones*) are in us by nature, as coming from us. What is additional comes from grace. It is therefore quite certain that grace simply sets in order what has already been given to us at creation, so that virtues are nothing but well-ordered passions (*affectiones*)', Gra 6.17 (SBOp 3:178).

[166] SC 44.4 (SBOp 2:46–47).

[167] Cf. SC 23.6 (SBOp 1:142).

is a sign of wisdom and maturity, but which is lost by dryness of heart and proud contempt of others.[168]

How can this completely human love of self become love of neighbor and God? Recall, as we have just done, that natural goodness towards self and others is inherent in all human beings, yet is not enough. It is important to know what kind of love of self and others is meant. Knowledge and love of God, who is Truth and Love, can attain their object only by conformation to this Truth and Love. (See above, Chapter IV). To arrive at this Truth we must pass by truth about ourselves, which is true love of self, no matter how unpleasant a light humility casts. From self-knowledge, true knowledge of others flows naturally, and that is compassion. In Saint Bernard, fraternal charity more often than not carries the overtone of compassion.[169] To suffer with another with 'sympathy' means to know better and love truth more, to purify one's heart and open one's eyes.[170] Humility and compassion go together and make the heart pure. In this way an authentic love of self leads to perfect charity.

---

[168] SC 44, 5 (SBOp 2:47). On the contrary, Pascal said: 'All humans hate each other naturally', *Pensées* (451, Brunschvicg's edition). As for Lévinas, he is obviously very close to Saint Bernard when he considers the Other as a primordial exigency even before any commitment of free will. Paradoxically, he wrote : 'The person called to exist replies to a call which has not been able to reach him, because, issued from nothingness, he has obeyed before hearing the order . . . The responsibility for another person, which is not an accident reaching a Subject, but precedes the Essence in him, has not waited for the freedom by which commitment to another person would have been made', (*Autrement qu'être*, [La Haye: Nijhoff, 1974] 54). [*Otherwise than Being or Essence* (The Hague: M. Nijhoff, 1981)]. Commenting on this text, Catherine Chalier wrote: ' If then there is in every creature some pure passivity, we must also admit the idea of an imprint of goodness on the human being, which is written in the most secret part of the human psyche as an investment by the Other, and which would establish each person in his or her individuality, without there having been time to examine the terms of the investment and measure its demands', *La persévérance du mal* (Paris: Cerf, 1987) 118.

[169] The whole *Sermon 12 on the Song of Songs* should be read on this subject, with its biblical examples (SBOp 1:60–67). Cf. J. Regnard OCSO, 'La compassion comme chemin spirituel chez saint Bernard', Coll 55 (1993) 314–323. J. Leclercq OSB, 'Saint Bernard et la tendresse', Coll 52 (1990) 1–15.

[170] Hum 3. 6 (SBOp 3:20–21).

If we follow the line of more subtle reflection which Saint
Bernard offers us in his description of the first step of love of God,
we again find fraternal love as a necessary passageway to divine
love. He asked himself whether love of God precedes or follows
love of neighbor. His answer depends on the point of view from
which one looks at it. He says that we begin to love God before our
neighbor, but that this love for God can be perfected, nourished,
and increased only by love of neighbor. When love is newborn, love
of God is first; as it grows, love of God is preceded and nourished
by love of neighbor.[171]

Let us take a look at how Saint Bernard explains the dynamic
of the first step of love in his treatise *On Loving God*.[172] Because
love is a natural sentiment, using it to serve God, the author
of nature, would be only right and in keeping with the first and
greatest commandment: *You will love the Lord your God* (Mt 22:37).
Once this principle is established, we must look at things concretely
and recognize that, in actual fact, 'because nature is too fragile
and weak [to do this], necessity obliges it to serve itself first'.
The reasoning underlying the whole development that follows is
based on two scripture texts: *What was animal came first, then what is
spirit* (1 Cor 15:46), and: *You shall love your neighbor as yourself* (Mt
22:39). Now, we can really love our self only by loving our neighbor,
and no one can love his or her neighbor perfectly without loving
God. As often happens in Saint Bernard, there is a step backward
here, and the need to love God logically concludes a journey which
began with self-interested love, that is, a kind of self-preservation
instinct. But to love self as we should, in a completely true way,
presupposes a certain degree of moderation. This is the case not
only in christian morality but in that of the Stoics as well. Natural
self-love usually exceeds what necessity requires and, overflowing

---

[171] Sent 1.21 (SBOp 6/2:14–15).

[172] For the explanation which follows, see: Dil 8.23–25 (SBOp 3:138–140).
This development of the first step of love is not in the first, shorter version found
in Saint Bernard's *Letter to the Carthusians*, which he inserted in the treatise Ep
11 (SBOp 7:52–601). Cf. Dil 15.39 (SBOp 3:152–153). His second reflection
is no doubt significant.

like a river in flood, it goes to waste in the plains of pleasure. What saves nature then is a balanced love for another person who shares the same nature and 'especially for this grace which is inherent in nature'. This vocabulary, very disconcerting to scholastics, signifies that love, in so far as it is the original grace given to a spiritual creature, cannot of necessity not be shared. Anyone who would be satisfied with using it only in a self-centered way would run the risk of damnation. Sharing makes for balanced and just love. 'So it is that carnal [naturally egocentric] love becomes social love when it broadens out in view of the common good.' Sharing what is superfluous is therefore salutary, because what is superfluous puts a person in danger of damnation. It may, however, happen that by sharing, a person will lack what is necessary. We must take the risk in faith[173] and seek the kingdom of God so that what is necessary may be given to us as well. In any case, our neighbor has a right to what nature bestows on us. It appears that, for Bernard, this love of neighbor is not yet perfect, because there is still self-interest about one's own salvation. It is here that the transition from social love to love of God occurs. God creates and protects nature, so in order for our love of others to become perfect, we must love our neighbor in God. And so that the creature will not forget this, God in his providence and plan of salvation has it undergo testing. Experiencing its limits, the creature calls on God for help, in reply to his invitation: *Call upon me in your trouble, I will rescue you and you shall honor me* (Ps 49:5). Did we not see this same psalm verse being quoted by Bernard in his description of what he considers 'the fundamental experience of the beginning of conversion' (above, Chapter II.5)? We find the same experience here, provoked by the demands of authentic love for others.

Saint Bernard then saw fraternal love as inherent in the search for God. 'In what,' he asks

---

[173] Cf. 'Communication with another person can only be transcendent when it is like a danger in life, like a beautiful risk to run. These words take on their whole meaning when . . . they express the gratuitousness of sacrifice . . . It is there alone that the Other, absolutely exterior, comes so close as to become even an obsession,' E. Lévinas, *Autrement qu'être*, 154. [*Otherwise than Being or Essence*].

does justice consist, if not in rendering to each what is his due? Do not be attentive only to God. You owe it also to those who have a responsibility for you, and to your brothers as well.[174]

Fraternal love is a necessary step on the way to union with God. In the twenty-third *Sermon on the Song of Songs*, Saint Bernard develops his thought on three concrete ways of loving others in three different kinds of relationships.[175] First of all, we do well to notice that to portray this school of charity he uses the image of cellars or storerooms, which in the *Song of Songs* narrative is found along with that of a garden and the king's bedroom (1.4–6). He distinguishes three storerooms: for spices, for ointments, and for wine, and in them he discerns three forms of ascesis proposed to those who, while already forming part of the Church (the garden), pursue further their search for ultimate peace in God (the King's bedroom). This same idea of going-beyond was analyzed in Chapters I.1 and IV.1. The three storerooms correspond to the three steps of truth. The storeroom of discipline, where seeds are pounded by the pestle of obedience to a superior, recalls the tart knowledge of self that comes from humility and crushed pride. The storeroom for ointments or of 'nature', because of our natural agreement with our peers who share the common lot of our human condition, resembles the second step of truth, that is, compassion. Finally, the storeroom for wine, where certain persons are called upon to guide those who submit to their authority, represents as it were a kind of fullness of fraternal charity through a forgetfulness of self and self-interests which imitates charity in its divine truth.[176] The three storerooms can likewise be taken as parallel to the three forms of love: of self, of others, and of God. The spiritual value of fraternal love comes from its eschatological quality. By virtue of it, the brothers participate in Christ's mediation in the Body of Christ, the Church and the monastic community, regardless of

---

[174] Quad 4.2 (SBOp 4:369).

[175] SC 23.5–9 (SBOp 1:141–145).

[176] SC 19.4 (SBOp 1:118–111). It is from love of Christ, the Wisdom of God, that all power comes and it is this love which preserves superiors from the serious temptation of abusing this power by self-will or vanity.

their functions and the relationships which unite them (see above, Chapter III.6). The spiritual or material services rendered through fraternal love are consequently even more important than seeking God by the practices of the interior life.[177] Fraternal love empties the heart of all self-seeking and opens it to the Spirit of love. Just as Saint Thomas was unable to see the risen Lord because he distanced himself from the college of the apostles, anyone who withdraws from community exercises and loses zeal for the common life cannot please Truth or see Christ according to the Spirit.[178]

So fraternal charity is a perfect expression of the search for God. It is the practice of the charism which is far superior to all others (*charisma peroptimum . . . incomparabile*), and in a way it is the characteristic feature of cistercian spirituality.[179] We can also see in it the full realization of the progressive evolution from eremitism to the ideal of cenobitism, in which the priority of explicit fraternal charity is the central preoccupation of daily life in community.[180] The place of fraternal charity in Saint Bernard's spiritual teaching has been the object of two studies which set it in its doctrinal context and analyze key texts.[181] What interests us more particularly in this

---

[177] Div 101 (SBOp 6/1:368). Cf. H. de Lubac sj: 'Charity has not to become inhuman to remain supernatural; like the supernatural itself it can only be understood as incarnate. He who yields to its rule, far from giving up his natural qualities, contributes to those societies of which he is by nature a member an activity that is all the more effective because its motive is more free. No human problems, no human anxiety can find him a stranger: all of them awake within him an echo that is all the deeper for his realization of their eternal consequences', *Catholicism*, translated by Lancelot Sheppard (London: Burns & Oates, 1962) 207.

[178] Asc 6.13 (SBOp 5:157–158).

[179] Cf. SC 29.3–4 (SBOp 1:204–206).

[180] Cf. J. Pegon: 'Thus the ideal of the monk, which has always been and still is perfect imitation of Christ and conformity to the Gospel, appears in the cenobitical formula with more interior and more social features. Love of neighbor and the spirit of prayer, which give even the most banal actions a supernatural value, have an important place in their practical preoccupations, perhaps the central place', in the Introduction to Maximos the Confessor, *Centuries sur la Charité*. SCh 9 (Paris: Cerf, 1943) 13–14.

[181] B. Olivera ocso, 'Aspects of Love of Neighbor in the Spiritual Doctrine of St Bernard', CSQ 26 (1991) 107–119 and 204–226, and M. V. de Sallier-Dupin ocso, 'Saint Bernard et la charité fraternelle dans les sermons sur le *Cantique des cantiques*', Coll 58 (1996) 111–124.

bernardine synthesis is the role of truth fraternal charity plays in our going-beyond to God-Truth. It begins with humility, that is, truth about self and authentic love of our real self.

Right away an objection crops up: the brother we love—do we love him for himself or for some other reason? Do we love him for ourselves, or because thanks to him we may attain perfect union with God alone? In either case, it would be not love but still self-seeking. Moralists have unmasked the deceit of self-interested altruism, when someone else is used for personal self-satisfaction.[182] For Saint Bernard, not only is self-love of the same nature as love of neighbor, but both are of the same nature as divine love. When he speaks about willingly giving up the tranquillity of reading, meditation, and prayer,[183] he means the spiritual practices we have described (see Chapter V.2, note 46) and not interior charity, which is the motivation for the monk's whole life. He also said, in connection with his attachment to his brother Gerard, that it is, of course, impossible for someone who cleaves to God to be conscious of or to taste anything but God alone; but because God is charity, the more we are united to him the more we are filled with charity. And he added that although God cannot suffer he can compassionate[184] and He invites us to be compassionate as well. Fraternal love is never simply a means for us to achieve something else, not even love of God; it is already participation in divine love. Saint Bernard points out three ways of practising love of neighbor: bringing it to life; helping it to grow; and cultivating it so that it does not deteriorate. He concludes: 'Anyone who practises this kind of love of neighbor with a pure heart can be sure that he or she also grows in love of God'.[185]

To love our self well we must love our neighbor, and fraternal love can be true and disinterested only if it is founded on nature and confirming grace. There are three kinds of natural gifts: health of

---

[182] Cf. J.-J. Rousseau: 'Pity is sweet, because when we put ourselves in the place of someone who suffers, we nevertheless have the pleasure of not suffering', *Emile ou de l'éducation* IV (Paris: Garnier-Flammarion, 1966) 287.

[183] Cf. SC 51.3 (SBOp 2:86); 52.7 (SBOp 2:94–95).

[184] SC 26.5 (SBOp 1:171).

[185] Div 96.6 (SBOp 6/1:360).

body; purity of heart; and peace with one's neighbor. Our sensibility as well as our reason is at all times aware of these gifts in ourselves and all around us, remarks Saint Bernard, even though they are no longer at our command because of the original wound. It is because we are beings attracted to social relationships and capable of them (*quia sociale animal sumus*) that we owe peace to those who participate in the same nature we do: this is the natural law of any society.[186] Yet we can give peace only if we are at peace with ourselves. 'Charity begins at home.' This saying may have come from Saint Bernard. Another, more recent, phrase expresses the same reality, when it is correctly understood, which is to say, as its author—Sartre—understood it: 'Hell is other people'.

> But 'Hell is other people' has always been misunderstood . . .
> If our relationships with others are twisted and vitiated, then
> the other person can be pure hell. Why? Because deep down
> other people are what is most important in ourselves . . . This
> means that if my relationships are bad, I put myself in a position
> of total *dependence* on others. Then I really am in hell . . .
> What I wanted to point out was precisely that many people
> are incrusted in a series of habits, of customs; they have made
> judgements about others which have made them suffer, but they
> do not even try to *change* them. And these people are as if they
> were dead . . . Whatever circle of hell we live in, I think we are
> free to break through it. And if people do not break through it,
> it is because they stay there willingly. So they freely condemn
> themselves to hell.[187]

If we look again at the fundamental principle of bernardine anthropology, we can see very clearly that in the area of relationships with others there is still a question of freedom or *dependence*.[188] Sartre wanted human freedom to be totally, absolutely, autonomous and to be a law unto itself. As we can see, he arrived at absolute

---

[186] Div 16.3 (SBOp 6/1:146).

[187] J.-P. Sartre, Preface to *Huis clos* (1944). The first title of this work was: '*Les autres*', in *Un théâtre de Situations* (Paris: Gallimard, NRF, 1973) 238–239. [*No exit* (New York: A. A. Knopf, 1947)].

[188] See above, Chaptre I.3.

heteronomy where he was totally dependent. How could he find a way to break through the circle which imprisoned freedom? Sartre went so far as to speak of an evolution of *conversion*. Isn't this the twisted soul Saint Bernard described when he spoke of a soul that had lost its original simplicity? How, he asked, can we base anything at all on the inescapable state of confusion that causes our suffering: the very fact that we are composite beings whose simple nature has been corrupted by duplicity? 'Find me a son of Adam who can bear, much less want, to be seen for what he is.'[189] Didn't Saint Bernard also describe the hellish circle in which the person whirls whose love wears itself out in endless dissatisfaction with what is merely finite good? If we do not love others in God, they remain finite, limited, and dissatisfying beings. Total freedom without dependence on the Creator of our nature cannot lead to brotherhood. Without a Father there are no brothers. Without transcendence and without dependence on infinite freedom, finite freedom remains totally dependent on other freedoms, no matter what it does.[190] Fraternity is possible only within a mutual dependence based on common obedience to recognized values. Among these values is that of the Other who is divine Love, the Infinite. There has to be a conversion.

The paradise of the cloister is the place where the monk seeks God while sharing the same way of life with others in obedience to a Rule. He acquires a form of life: Truth in dependence on brothers who by the great variety of their gifts lead him to the holiness of charity:

> Look! One monk weeps over his sins, another exults in God's praise; this one serves everyone else, that one forms and instructs others; one prays, another reads; one shows mercy,

---

189 SC 82.3 (SBOp 2:293–294).

190 Sartre's failure to establish a moral foundation is clearly expressed in the following lines, where we can also see a justification for the monastic community . . . : 'Sartre, pondering on the question of the constitution of a moral subject, asks himself if he has not failed because, ontologically, he has missed relationship to others . . . And is it not necessary to discover a constitutive bond between the subject and another person in order to develop a moral teaching? It would then no longer have freedom alone as the source of all values, but would include also the demands of fraternity', J. Colombel, 'La recherche d'une morale impossible', in *Magazine littéraire* (November, 1990) 63.

another punishes sins; still another has ardent charity; another stands out by his humility; another is humble when he succeeds, another shows his noble spirit in adversity; another is energetic in the active life, another remains quiet in the contemplative life . . . This is nothing less than a house of God and gate of heaven.[191]

Fraternal relationships require conversion of the affections, the kind of conversion Sartre needed to break through the circle of his hell. Consequently, there will be mutual exchange among the brothers, who will give and take in an atmosphere of kindness.[192] Such real communication is part of a community's formation and its unity in communion. There is no reason to worry about experiencing, or not experiencing, affective emotions. Love is an act of the will, a disposition of willingness, both with regard to one's brothers and to God.

To our brothers with whom we live we are obliged by the law of fraternity and human solidarity to give advice and help. And we also want them to be generous with theirs to us: advice to instruct our ignorance, help to make our weakness easier to bear.'[193]

In all circumstances, fraternal love needs practice. This is how Saint Bernard speaks of it in a letter to Suger in which he lists the tools of monastic ascesis.[194] Whether we are speaking of salutary love of self, love of neighbor, or love of God, moreover, love always requires an effort; it is a demanding effort.[195] Saint Bernard does not neglect to ferret out charity's great enemy in community: self-will, which seeks only its own interests. He gives a humorous description

---

[191] Div 42.4 (SBOp 6/1:258).

[192] See communication among equals in the storeroom of ointments, SC 23.6 (SBOp 1:142): *insuper et libenter communicans in ratione dati et accepti.*

[193] Adv 3.5 (SBOp 4:178–179). In his French translation of this sermon, Fr. P. Y. Emery pointed out that 'help and advice' (*consilium* and *auxilium*) are terms taken from feudal vocabulary: what a vassal promises to assure to his lord. See *Saint Bernard, Sermons pour l'année*, note 11, page 58.

[194] Epi 78.4 (SBOp 7:203–204).

[195] Cf. Sent 3.120 (SBOp 6/1:219–221). On pages 226–227 we again find the symbol of the three storerooms.

of the fourth of the kinds of monks who, he says, exist in our monasteries:

> The fourth kind are the sarabaites, who love their own selves and seek only what is to their advantage. Two, three or four strong, they run counter to the common rule of the monastery. In their attempt to impose new ideas which are simply their own they create cliques and division in the community. They defend their wrongs and continually cause trouble for the Lord's flock.[196]

The diversity of types of persons can either favor the development of relationships of fraternal love or throw up obstacles to unity of hearts. In the first case people grow, thanks to their dependence on the common will; in the second case, they lose their personality by complicity in a display of false autonomy.

When he arrives at the goal of the loving adventure of the Creator and his spiritual creature, Saint Bernard teaches us in *Sermon 85 on the Song of Songs* that from one common source—God, to whom the soul is united—proceed two acts: apostolic or charitable activity; and the heart's union with God in the peace and joy of loving. One and the same fruitfulness, resulting from union with God, produces these two fruits which, as Bernard sees it, have the same value and efficacy of mediation in the Body of Christ. If there is a difference, it consists in the pleasure God gives the soul in the act of contemplative prayer, by making it feel already the corresponding happiness of eternity's plenitude, even if the experience is rare and brief.[197] Often, moreover, there is an alternation and interaction between these two forms of love:

> After a good action, one rests more peacefully in the sleep of contemplation. When one is conscious of not having failed in works of charity by love for one's own tranquillity, it is possible to return more confidently to meditation on the divine mysteries.[198]

---

[196] Sent 3.31 (SBOp 6/2:85).
[197] SC 85.13 (SBOp 2:315–316).
[198] SC 47.4 (SBOp 2:64).

Ideally, says Saint Bernard, it is desirable that both joy in contemplating God and solicitude in helping and being useful to one's neighbor be united in every soul. In community at least, he adds, let these manifestations of love be harmoniously proportioned.[199]

The same teaching is found in his commentary on the following verse of the *Song: He has led me into his wine cellar: he has given me the sense of charity* (Sg 2:3).[200] Today, to avoid reading these words in a sense quite different from what Saint Bernard intended, we need first to take a look at the end of *Sermon 50.*[201] There is a wisdom of love, a divine wisdom, which enlightens and impels our desire towards fullness in God. In the spiritual creature, therefore, love is the vestige of the divine image tending towards likeness, even to deification. Here again are two ways of loving: the one foreordained for us in eschatological vision and the one required of and accessible to us here below. Affective charity and charity in action. The first will be freed from all earthly limitations only in eternity. Yet while it is progressing towards perfection, this charity, which requires attentive effort and constant laborious self-giving, is already directed by the taste for wisdom experienced in the heart (*gustum sapientiae afficientis*). In a phrase whose very conciseness makes it a bit mysterious, on earth there is already 'love of love' (*amor amoris*), but it makes us desire its fullness, that is to say, the love without mediation which is possible only by deification. During our lifetime, preoccupied as we are with temporal cares, we sense only a foretaste of this and then only at rare, brief moments.[202] By love of neighbor, which we practise in virtue of divine charity, we have a foretaste of God whom we can dimly perceive in this love of others. God's advent in the world of human beings is the miracle

---

[199] SC 57.11 (SBOp 2:125–126).

[200] 'He has shown me the sense of charity' translates here '*ordinavit in me caritatem*', it signifies love's orientation, its 'ordering'. The original Hebrew permits this unusual translation.

[201] SC 49–50 (SBOp 2:73–83).

[202] We can compare this teaching with the one given in *Sermon 8 on the Song of Songs*, where Saint Bernard speaks in the same way about 'the kiss of the kiss' (*osculum de osculo*), SC 8.7–8 (SBOp 1:40–41). Cf. Saint Augustine, *On the Trinity*, VIII.8.12. Fathers of the Church 45 (Washington, D.C.: Catholic University of America Press, 1963).

of the Incarnation, and Saint Bernard's thought constantly centered on it. From that moment on, the meaning of all true love is linked to its completion in Christ, Wisdom of God, Wisdom of Love.[203] We truly love ourselves, therefore, when we see that all love comes from God. We love our brother, 'who because he is a human being is what you are', better and more than we could by a love deprived of this taste of eternity, this infinite horizon and sense of the absolute. Even if the delight of loving is complete only in personal and direct union with God, charity is practised just as effectively in exterior action as in interior prayer. So it is that this very beautiful prayer to Wisdom concludes these two sermons:

> O Wisdom! . . . guide our actions as our temporal life requires, and guide our affections in the ways of your eternal truth, so that each of us may say in complete tranquillity: *He has given me the sense of charity* (Sg 2:3).[204]

Between affective (contemplative) charity and active charity (service of one's neighbor) there is interaction. Union with God gives active charity its value, and its exercise—because it is grace—makes the soul tend towards its total and perfect fulfillment beyond the limits of our human earthly condition.

Saint Bernard has given us a surprising example of the relative equality of divine and human love. The same image he uses for rapture, 'sober inebriation', he boldly applies to fraternal charity. We have already seen him compare the water in the jars at Cana to cistercian observances, and assert that this water is changed into wine by the monks' loving obedience (above, Chapter V.2). The practice of fraternal love, the paramount observance, will likewise by transformed by the presence of Christ.

In the treatise *On Loving God*, Wisdom presides over a triple banquet of charity. The third is eschatological, it will take place after the resurrection of the body, when we will experience 'this sober

---

[203] Cf. C. Bruaire: 'All among them (Christians) who separate the plan of salvation from human action simply apply the practical consequences of the teaching of the Nestorians, who held that the divine and human are foreign to one another', quoted by A. Gesché, *La destinée* (Paris: Cerf, 1995) 155.
[204] SC 50.8 (SBOp 2:83).

inebriation . . . which does not come from drinking too much wine but from burning with love for God'.[205] Yet even now, in the fourth degree of love—therefore in this life—'the soul is totally inebriated with divine love', even though it remains weighed down by its earthly condition, and 'what is even more constraining, is called back by fraternal charity.'[206]

And at the end of a sermon for Epiphany, Saint Bernard tells us that the water of the tears of human compassion, far from tearing us away from contemplation, is changed into the wine of divine charity:

> I would say that these tears are truly changed into wine, because when your heart goes out to your brothers in compassion your tears flow with the fervor of love. And because of this self-forgetful love you seem to be overwhelmed by sober inebriation, at least for a moment.[207]

Here we have an excellent example of the moral mysticism or holiness attributed to Saint Bernard's teaching (see above, Chapter II.8). What begins as an exercise of mutual love, an observance, can become rapture in union with God.

This will be no more frequent than the rapture of divine love, and still less will it be habitual. But it is these special moments which will give community life its value as the search for God. More ordinarily, there will be unpretentious sentiments and even suffering, but these will always be focused on the eschatological realization of perfect union. The contrast with imperfection will be a stimulating trial to be borne in a spirit of solidarity.

> You see: in our communion on earth we find no real security, perfection or rest. And yet it is also here that *it is good and pleasant for all of us to live together as brothers* (Ps 132:1). No matter what trouble befalls us, either exterior or interior, we find it easier to bear because of this solidarity with our brothers who are so close to us and with whom before God we form one

---

205 Dil 11.33 (SBOp 3:147).

206 Dil 10.27 (SBOp 3:142). Cf. SC 7.3 (SBOp 1:32).

207 Epi 3.8 (SBOp 4:309).

heart and one soul. How much more pleasant, more delightful and joyful will this union be when there can be no suspicion and no occasion for dissension, and where perfect love will gather all the brothers in an indissoluble covenant. As the Father and the Son are one, so we will be one in them (cf. Jn 17:22).[208]

Peace, the fruit of the practice of fraternal love, is also the goal pursued by the monk. It remains for us to see how the wisdom of love leads us to final, eternal peace.

---

[208] OS 5.6 (SBOp 5:365).

VI

WISDOM OF THE HEART ON THE PATHWAY OF PEACE

1. WISDOM: TASTE FOR TRUTH AND GOOD

ALTHOUGH SAINT BERNARD is not systematic in the way he taught, he does nevertheless often come back to what constitutes the heart of his doctrine, from which everything radiates and towards which everything converges. As we are about to show what he considered the goal of the adventure of human life as he lived it and presented it to his monks, we should take as point of reference one of his all-encompassing intuitions. Three interventions by grace in free choice trace God's advancing search for his spiritual creature. All three are signs of his desire for his creature: creation; reformation; and the state of consummate perfection. All three of God's interventions in human destiny are accomplished through the grace of Christ, through which is brought about the human person's restoration as the image of God. Freedom in turn, in its response to grace, passes into action in the humble obedience of the practices of cistercian life. This purifies the intention and appeases the conscience through mastery of the passions. And when the passions—especially love—are re-orientated towards their authentic final goal, they lead the soul to union with God.

> Bent down under earthly cares, intention rises up again, little by little, from the depths to the heights; affection, weakened by desires of the flesh, gradually becomes stable in spiritual love;

memory, defiled by the degeneracy of former deeds, regains the purity of new, good acts. It becomes more joyful each day. Interior renewal consists in these three things: rightness of intention; purity of affection, and mindfulness of good actions thanks to which memory, with clear conscience, becomes full of light.[1]

There is a *locus*, we might say, which the Creator has chosen as his meeting-place with the spirit he has created: it is peace. But God, who waits in peace for his creature, has endowed us with a gift which is capable of leading us to personal encounter with him. This is wisdom, an interior relish that comes from him who said: *Taste and see that the Lord is good* (Ps 33:9). These two themes will be interwoven in the last pages of our synthesis, because if peace is the *locus* to which Saint Bernard wants to lead us to meet God, ultimately wisdom alone will enable us to find this peace, in a patience and perseverance consented to with pleasure. Fullness of knowledge is in fact this wisdom, this 'sapience', this seventh gift of the Holy Spirit which at the summit of moral progress corresponds to the seventh Beatitude; blessed is the peacemaker. 'For those whose souls are peaceful and serene have a keener taste for things above and see them more penetratingly. The more patient one is in times of trial, the more one is shown to be wise.'[2]

In his conversion, a monk will acknowledge having received a twofold gift: for knowledge, fullness of knowledge (*id est caritatem*); and for understanding knowledge, an understanding of wisdom and wisdom itself.[3] To set affectivity and understanding in opposition, as has too often been done, is to misunderstand what Saint Bernard meant. We have already alluded to this error (above, Chapter II.5). The distinction is not between ignorance and knowledge, but between wisdom and knowledge. Wisdom is a broadening and deepening of what we know, along with an attraction which

---

[1] Gra 14.49 (SBOp 3:202). The adverbs *paulatim* (little by little) and *sensim* (gradually) already quoted no doubt come from Cassian, who spoke of the spiritual ascent this way in *Conference* 10.8.
[2] Sent. 3.7 (SBOp 6/2:245).
[3] Par 7: The eight Beatitudes (SBOp 6/2:300–301).

knowledge exercises as it procures for us the happiness of loving Truth. Jean Gerson, the chancellor of the university of Paris (†1429), who can hardly be suspected of obscurantism, described this bernardine wisdom very well:

> The holy doctors, especially Saint Bernard, make an important distinction between knowledge and sapience, because knowledge belongs principally, and, as it were, only to understanding, and sapience to affectivity; sapience is more important because it is savory knowledge, as its name suggests. Savor has to do with a person's affections, desire, appetites, and will. Someone can have a great deal of knowledge and education but little or no sapience, because he or she finds no savor or attraction in what is known.[4]

Gerson then gives two examples: honey and sickness. Using books, we can know the nature of honey, but never its taste. By experiencing pain ('savoring' it, is the expression in old French), patients know it much better than do their doctors with all their scientific knowledge. In speaking of God's sweetness—for which we must have a taste if we are to contemplate him—Saint Bernard distinguishes it from the kind of erudition which teaches nothing without anointing, and from knowledge which lacks comprehension and the awareness of conscience.[5]

Since Saint Bernard said that charity is at one and the same time God and God's gift,[6] we can say that for him wisdom is God and God's gift.[7] So we must start from above if we are to grasp the meaning of wisdom, because although Saint Bernard is more concerned with the human situation than other ancient writers, he never thinks of it apart from its relationship with its

---

[4] Jean Gerson, *La montagne de contemplation* (5). Oeuvres complètes VII (Paris: Desclée et Cie, 1966) 19.

[5] Conv 13.25 (SBOp 4:99–100). We find an echo of this in the advice given by Gargantua to his son Pantagruel, a student in Paris: 'Because knowledge without conscience is ruination for a man, and *sapience does not enter a cunning soul* (Ws 1:4)', F. Rabelais, *Pantagruel* VIII. *Oeuvres complètes* (Paris: Gallimard, NRF, 1955) 206.

[6] Dil 12.35 (SBOp 3:149).

[7] SC 85.7 (SBOp 2:311).

Creator and Redeemer. When he describes freedom's disastrous situation and the disfigured, degraded, deformed image of God in the human being, he shows that a human being could never have regained form and beauty if Wisdom had not restored wisdom to its whole being, the wisdom which transforms and conforms it to the Wisdom itself which originally formed it.[8] Saint Bernard recognizes Wisdom first of all as incarnate Wisdom.[9] The Incarnate Godhead is God's Wisdom who enlightens the eyes of the heart and leads it to faith.[10] In incarnate Wisdom, mercy and truth meet.[11] At Christmas, Saint Bernard exclaimed: 'O veiled Wisdom, truly incarnate! . . . O human being, Wisdom reveals itself to you in the flesh. See how what was formerly hidden now penetrates the very senses of your flesh. "Flee pleasure . . . do penance", because that is how the Kingdom comes.'[12]

By becoming incarnate, the Son, God's Wisdom, manifested the Father's power through his works and the Holy Spirit's goodness through the forgiveness of sins, 'but what is properly his, or better, what he is in himself (that is, wisdom), he hid . . . Supreme power became weakness; and we might say—yes, if we may say so, but with respect—Wisdom became foolish'.[13]

In the remarkable compendium which constitutes *Sentence Seventy* of the Third Series, Saint Bernard allotted wisdom the place of saving taste. After calling to mind the doctrine of the restoration of God's image in the human person thenceforth endowed with gifts of the Spirit, he comments on the gift of wisdom. In the Body of Christ, that is, the Church of the Old as well as the New Testament, its head has from all eternity had four spiritual senses: sight (the angels), hearing (the patriarchs), smell (the prophets) and touch (common interpretation). But before the Incarnation it was as if the members of the body were languishing and lifeless because the

---

[8] Gra 10. 32–33 (SBOp 3: 188–189). For form, see above, Chapters III.1 and V.1.

[9] Asc 6.10 (SBOp 5:155).

[10] Pasc 1.10 (SBOp 5:87).

[11] SC 6.7 (SBOp 1:29).

[12] Nat 3.2–3 (SBOp 4:259–260).

[13] Div 57.1 (SBOp 6/1:286–287).

fifth sense, taste, was missing. Without taste, nothing could do the body any good. 'The Man Christ Jesus has made wisdom tasty to us through a kind of interior taste of divinity, he who for us became Christ, God's wisdom.'[14] In the mutual quest of Creator and spiritual creature, the taste which arouses desire plays a determinative role. Wisdom of the heart is precisely this meeting point and this secret complicity with Incarnate Wisdom which comes into contact with us in our true and entire physical being.

Incarnate Wisdom has conquered spiritual malice.[15] This is how Saint Bernard paraphrases Wisdom 7:30, and he continues by commenting on the following verse (8.1), which was very dear to him: *so as not only to deploy strength from one end of the earth to the other, but also to order all things gently.* This is the gentleness He revealed during his life on earth, a gentleness of total humility and peace.[16] Wisdom is not in opposition to intelligence, or to knowledge or to strength—all of which it lets participate in its fullness; but it is radically opposed to malice of spirit or a spirit of maliciousness (*malitia*).[17] Within us, it is the taste and savor of what is good; it fights off and destroys the taste for evil. Its primary significance lies on the moral level, but by incarnate Wisdom's presence in it this moral wisdom has also become, as we have often pointed out, morality enlivened by faith and by the flowering of faith which is the mystical life, God's folly.

The steps of spiritual progress are aptly described in *Sermon 23 on the Song.*[18] To the bride's words: *The king has brought me into his storerooms* (1:3), Saint Bernard adds two images taken from other passages of the sacred text: the garden (5:1) and the king's room (3:4). In the garden, God first found the soul when he saved it by the mystery of salvation: creation, redemption, and glorification (see

---

[14] Sent 3.70 (SBOp 6/2:102–107). Cf. Div 49 (SBOp 6/1:269–270). Other characteristics of the five spiritual senses: SC 28.5–10 (SBOp 1:195–199) and Div 10.2–4 (SBOp 6/1:122–124).

[15] Cf. Par 7 (SBOp 6/2:300).

[16] Miss 2.13 (SBOp 4:30).

[17] Sent 3.4 (SBOp 6/2:66), quoting *Wisdom* 7:30.

[18] An abridgement is found in the treaty *On the Steps of Humility* : Hum 7.21–22 (SBOp 3:32–34).

Chapter I.1). But he did this to make himself sought through self-transcendence, in the life of grace which takes place in the three cellars, or storerooms, where active social charity is purified by discipline, fraternal love, and the service of responsible authority (see above, Chapter V.8). From the level of this moral meaning, Saint Bernard goes on to the meaning of contemplative charity (*in theoricae contemplationis arcano*). But these continue to be simply two stages leading to admittance to the king's room, about which we will speak further on (Chapter VI.5). We have in these descriptions of ordinary mystical experience what some modern authors have interpreted as the purification which precedes perfect union. Saint Bernard's sober style, filled with imagery and supported by scriptural texts, seems to me to have the advantage of setting in bold relief God's initiative in the steps towards interior encounter. God leads the spirit into a deep and secret place so it may apply itself to seeking him, with pleasure, of course, but it is still a place in which the spirit cannot yet find rest.[19] It remains anxious in its holy curiosity and tires itself out with it, because whatever it grasps constantly slips away from it. The alternation of pleasure and anxiety makes it impatiently desire the peace that is above and beyond these vicissitudes.[20]

The last trial the contemplative spirit must undergo in its search for divine peace is the enigma of the tenacious presence of evil. Saint Bernard described the soul's terror in terms no less expressive than those used by Pascal or Kierkegaard. He says that he is horror-stricken when he repeats the words of *Ecclesiastes: No one knows if he is worthy of love or hate* (9:1 Vulgate) and, concretely, has in mind those unworthy, lusty clerics whose scandalous ways so grieved

---

[19] This refers to the rare and fleeting character of mystical experience, which, like every intense experience during a person's life, is rare and brief. Saint Bernard could have been thinking of Venerable Bede's commentary on the *Song of Songs*, which in those days was read in cistercian refectories: 'The pleasantness of interior contemplation . . . is but brief and rare (*brevis et rara*) because of the lethargy of the spirit weighed down by the burden of the body.' Bede, *On the Song of Songs* I.2.8; Corpus Christianorum 119b (Turnhout: Brepols, 1983) 218.

[20] SC 23.11 (SBOp 1:145–146). Of his main experience of the Word's presence within him, Saint Bernard likewise said: 'Trouble and remorse in the dark depths of my conscience made me admire the profundity of his wisdom'. SC 74.6 (SBOp 2:243). Among the four 'dimensions' of God, Wisdom is also his depth. Csi V.13.29 (SBOp 3:491–492).

him. David himself, whom he calls that 'great contemplative', was indignant at seeing sinners hardened by pride. And yet, he cries out, the place where this evil reigns is the house of God and gate of heaven. In the midst of the anguish at the trial brought on by the enigma of evil, wisdom does not enlighten our intelligence, as was the case in the preceding stage, because there is no explanation. But it touches our heart and inspires salutary fear.

> It is true to say that fear of God is the beginning of wisdom, because the soul begins to sense God's savor only when God touches it to make himself feared, and not when He instructs it to make himself known.

Knowledge prepares us, but at the risk of letting us become puffed up with pride, whereas in humble and religious fear God gives us access to wisdom, which opens the door of peace to us and gives us the certainty which comes from a foretaste.[21]

In harmony with the gifts of counsel and intelligence, the gift of wisdom makes what we have learned penetrate our heart (*affectus*), letting it acquire a taste for it. And so our heart finds pleasing and attractive what had until then seemed hard and unbearable.[22]

Wisdom, in Saint Bernard's work, has an extremely vast and varied significance.[23] Before theology became a branch of knowledge, wisdom was its principal mode of expression. In the notion of wisdom reason is dominant at one moment, love at another, and studies have been done on the respective value of reason and affectivity in Saint Bernard's conception of religious experience.[24] It would be interesting to see whether wisdom, which is after all a gift of the Holy Spirit, has some role in bringing about a sanctifying

[21] SC 23.13–14 (SBOp 1:147–148). Cf. SC 54.9 (SBOp 2:108–109); 74, 6 (SBOp 2:243). Certitude is linked to a very basic fear, the fear of making experience futile. 'This paradoxical and permanent linking together of certitude and fear . . . is the expression of the christian mystery in our wayfaring lives, and it develops and flowers in humble, fearful, and invincible hope', J. Mouroux, 'The Criteria of Spiritual Experience according to the *Sermons on the Canticle of Canticles*, in *Cistercian Studies* 2 (Berryville, Virginia: 1962) 34.
[22] Sent 3.4 (SBOp 6/2:65–66). Cf. And 1.2 (SBOp 5:428).
[23] Because it is so rich in myriad meanings, as he himself said: '*Cum multis modis sapientia intelligatur*', Div 52.1 (SBOp 6/1:274).
[24] Cf. Van Hecke, *Le désir dans l'expérience religieuse*, 79–84.

synthesis of the two. When Bernard speaks of the relationship between knowledge and affectivity in the day-to-day life of the monk,[25] he does so to show that the kind of knowledge which contributes nothing to spiritual progress would be superfluous, insipid, and utterly tasteless for the monk, no matter how useful it might otherwise be. Father R. Fassetta grasped the abbot of Clairvaux's thought when he wrote:

> Routine and dryness of heart are a threat not only to the practice of God's commandments, but also to prayer and *lectio*, the very areas where the soul ought to be able to renew itself. This is why we must beg Christ, our Spouse, to give us a *kiss of his mouth*, as the *Song* says (1:2), that is, to grant us his Spirit of wisdom and intelligence: intelligence to attain and comprehend, wisdom to taste what we will have thus understood. Taste, *gustare*; this is Bernard's key word.[26]

There, in the heart, we again find what Saint Bernard has already told us about union with God by conformity of will. 'Mystical' union, in the ordinary sense of the adjective, takes on for him, more than for others, an affective tone, but it means cleaving totally with all one's being to infinite Wisdom.

> Wisdom is truly this form, distinct in a sense from primitive nature, by which the soul acquires its rectitude and its true greatness. The perfection we then obtain is truly ours, like a completely interior form, but it is communicated to us by the One who himself became our wisdom . . . The divine impulse is in the heart.[27]

---

[25] For example, in Sermons 3 and 6 for the Ascension (SBOp 5:131–137 and 150–160); Sent 3.111 (SBOp 6/2:188–189); SC 69.2 (SBOp 2:202–203), Ep 18.1–3 (SBOp 7:65–68).

[26] F. Fassetta OCSO, 'Le rôle de l'Esprit-Saint dans la vie spirituelle selon Bernard de Clairvaux', in *La dottrina della vita spirituale nelle opere di San Bernardo di Clairvaux* (Rome: Edizioni Cistercensi, 1991) 371. This passage refers to the two lips of the soul: intelligence and wisdom: SC 8.6–9 et 9.2–3 (SBOp 1:39–42 and 43–44).

[27] Aimé Forest, 'La sagesse du coeur', in *Saint Bernard, homme d'Eglise* (Paris: Desclée de Brouwer, 1953) 204–205. Forest has shown the remarkable likeness of

The spirit of wisdom confers perfect purity of heart and love.[28] It is by the heart that a person becomes more polished *(erudiat)* in wisdom,[29] and subtlety of spirit is one of the windows through which a ray of wisdom enters to enlighten the heart.[30] But just as with Pascal, this heart is the very depth of one's being, the point where our intention and the commitment of our freedom are joined. Contrary to malice, the epitome of evil which plunges a person into deepest despair, wisdom is the perfection and consummation of all the virtues; it gives life and assurance to those who are tending towards the kingdom.[31]

When Saint Bernard spoke to us about the Form by which we shall be reformed, becoming as we were originally formed by God's hand, he told us that this Form coming into the world was Wisdom. 'Conformation' to this Wisdom means that the image accomplishes in the body what wisdom does in the world, *deploying its strength from one end of the earth to the other, and ordering all things gently* (Wis 8:1). The same should be true for free choice—the divine image within us. It will seek gently to govern the whole body, and in this manner recover the pristine beauty of its being.[32] It surprises us to see in this text that restoration of the image is situated in the body. Another text, just as surprising, shows us the idea of the body Saint Bernard may have had, according to a certain tradition. 'By a human body I mean the whole rational creature, the soul which lives in it and gives life to all things, that is to say, God's strength and God's wisdom'.[33] In this text we also encounter the role of taste in physical healing, as a symbol of wisdom's role in the renewal of the entire human person: body, soul, and spirit. Once again we find the prerogative of freedom, the free choice which by grace works itself free from everything that weighs it down, and with strength

---

thought on this point between Pascal and Saint Bernard: 'Pascal et saint Bernard', *Giornale di Metafisica* 12 (1958) 409–424.

[28] Sent 1.34 (SBOp 6/2:19).

[29] Ep 170.2 (SBOp 7:384).

[30] Sent 2.109 (SBOp 6/2:45).

[31] Sent 3.89 (SBOp 6/2:137–139).

[32] Gra 10.33–34 (SBOp 3:189–190).

[33] *De septem donis Spiritus Sancti. Sermones varii* 5 (SBOp 6/1:47).

and gentleness regains its likeness to the divine image. Strength
(*virtus*) and gentleness are complementary in this free response to
grace.[34] Freedom of the will and the taste offered it by wisdom give
Saint Bernard's moral theology a very modern character, as Bernard
Piault has observed:

> So, according to Saint Bernard, a moral (resolute) conscience
> is the very condition for the goodness or malice of an act . . .
> Contrariwise, to do good without willing to accomplish a good
> act does not stem from wisdom, because it is not wisdom which
> inspires it . . . No act is good which does not proceed from
> love: once more, the augustinian principle inspires the abbot
> of Clairvaux. Yet he gives it mystical connotations: it is in the
> union of love, and under the guidance of wisdom and faith, that
> the true ways of virtue are discerned and understood. Saint
> Bernard's theology is therefore an urgent appeal to a human
> being's two highest faculties: intelligence, which ought to let
> itself be reformed by faith, and will, which finds fulfillment
> in love.[35]

The same author, in discussing Bernard, affirms that, because of
lack of intention, he considered excusable an objectively bad action
coming from a mistaken conscience, but only partially excusable,
because the whole person has an obligation to renew itself unceasingly in its spirit according to wisdom. On the subject of moral
conscience, what distinguishes Saint Bernard from someone like
Abelard is that, for him, continual renewal of the spirit is precisely
what constitutes the reason for the existence of monastic life. What
he especially reproached the peripatetic theologian for was that he
had forgotten this obligation to continual conversion, even though
he was himself a monk.

---

[34] Cf. SC 85.7–9 (SBOp 2:311–313).

[35] B. Piault, 'Le désir de la sagesse. Itinéraire de l'âme à Dieu chez S. Bernard
dans le sermon LXXXV sur le *Cantique des cantiques*', Coll 36 (1974) 24–44; see p.
36. Cf. Sent 3.92 (SBOp 6/2:147–148), where Saint Bernard speaks again about
the distinction between carnal and spiritual love, saying that the latter comes
from reason or wisdom, which makes the soul sensitive (*sapit*) to everything it
owes to its Creator and Saviour.

Furthermore, moral reformation is always centered on the mystery of the Incarnation, and Saint Bernard liked to refer to Mary's role in the accomplishment of the restoration of wisdom in the spiritual creature:

> The serpent's malice which succeeded in outwitting Eve robbed us of our taste for good. But malice sees that it is conquered for eternity on the same ground that it believed for a while it had won. Look! Wisdom has again filled the heart and the body of a woman, so that we who were deformed and deprived of wisdom by one woman may be healed and led back to wisdom by another woman. Henceforth, wisdom triumphs over malice in the souls it penetrates; it drives out their taste for evil and replaces it with a better savor.[36]

Unlikeness was caused by the loss of original simplicity: duplicity.[37] It is therefore by simplicity that the divine likeness can be regained. Saint Bernard has, in fact, described a wise person as 'someone for whom each thing tastes like what it is'.[38] His first biographer tells us that Saint Bernard was in the habit of repeating this principle, based on his own experience.[39] The ancient wisdom of the Stoics was recast in the search for divine Wisdom.[40]

> Wisdom is manifested by a certain tranquillity of soul joined to mildness of spirit. It is interior peace. Wisdom can be defined as a taste for virtue . . . Too often we do good without tasting its savor, obeying only reason, or bowing to some circumstance or necessity. Contrariwise, many people do evil without having a taste for it, but rather under the influence of fear or some

---

[36] SC 85.8 (SBOp 2:312–313). Cf. Div 14.6: Wisdom replaces the taste for evil with the taste for good, just as one nail drives out another (SBOp 6/1:139).

[37] SC 82.3 (SBOp 2:293).

[38] Div 18.1 (SBOp 6/1:157–158). Cf. SC 50.6 (SBOp 2.81). Saint Augustine, *Christian Instruction* I.27.28. Fathers of the Church 2 (Washington, D. C.: Catholic University of America Press, 1950)

[39] Geoffrey of Auxerre, *Vita prima* III.1 (PL 185:304 B). Cf. Div 15.4 (SBOp 6/1:142); Adv 3.7 (SBOp 4:181); QH 17.2 (SBOp 4:486–487).

[40] Cf. Marcus Aurelius, *Meditations* 8.29: 'But seeing all things as they are, I make the best of each one according to its value. Remember this power you have by your nature.' See also *Meditations* 6.13.

momentary desire. If we need to know the truth, we also need to will what is good, because wisdom never enters a soul of ill-will.[41]

In Saint Bernard's works, taste for good or evil is correlative to a free and voluntary act of either love or cupidity, an act free of every other consideration but its choice. Love is the supreme simplification:

> Love is sufficient for itself. It is its own merit and its own reward. Love does not ask for any reason or fruit. Its fruit is its purpose . . . I love because I love; I love that I may love.[42]

The decisive moment of progress in love of God comes when a soul passes to the third degree of love. There, repeatedly calling upon God, it tastes him; and tasting him, it experiences his attraction and henceforth loves him gratuitously.[43]

For the eye to be simple, love must exist in our intention and truth in our choice, love of what is good and knowledge of what is true.[44] The constant balance in Saint Bernard between the two principal energies of the soul—intelligence and will—no doubt refers back frequently to wisdom, which joins them together in view of its own goal: interior peace through loving possession of the truth. Wisdom of heart seeks simplicity. God also seeks it among his spiritual creatures. '[God's] simple Nature seeks simplicity of heart',[45] and refuses not only all duplicity or falsehood, in the biblical sense of deceptive appearance, but also everything superfluous. In Saint Bernard's search for God, what most fascinated him was the attribute of divine simplicity: 'God has not been formed, he is form; he has not been moved by affection, he is love; he is not a composite being; he is pure simplicity'.[46] Cistercian simplicity finds its source here in the form that inspires all its exterior manifestations

[41] SC 85.8–9 (SBOp 2:312–313).

[42] SC 83.4 (SBOp 2:300).

[43] Dil 9.26 (SBOp 3:141).

[44] Pre 14.36–37 (SBOp 3:279).

[45] *In labore messis* 3.9 (SBOp 5:227).

[46] Csi V.7.17 (SBOp 3:480). Cf. SC 81.2: *'primum et purissimum simplex'* (SBOp 2.285).

in daily life as well as in art and architecture. With a few brief words in speaking about pruning vines, Saint Bernard formulated this imperative of simplicity: 'Take away what is superfluous and what is healthy will grow,'[47] On the moral plane, selfish desires are useless and superfluous; they suffocate the life of the soul. But 'the removal of everything superfluous', says the abbot of Clairvaux, 'is expressed by willing poverty, the toil of penance, observance of the *Rule* and everything it teaches'.[48] Wisdom has been a very good teacher, he adds, leading us to *renounce ungodliness and desires of this world, to live with sobriety, justice and piety* (Tt 2:12). This sobriety is contrasted to two kinds of intoxication; one, pleasures, is exterior, and the other, idle curiosity, interior.[49] There is a superfluous self-love,[50] but there can also be lack of sobriety in our thoughts. In the *Song*, the bride's neck does not need showy necklaces. It is beautiful just as nature made it.

> Truth is a precious necklace, as are simplicity and wisdom or moderation. The intelligence of philosophers and heretics does not possess this luster of purity and truth. This is why they are so careful to cover it up with the artificial brilliance of dazzling, affected turns of phrase and clever syllogisms. If it showed itself naked, people would no doubt see its baseness and falsehood.[51]

In the same sense, intelligence remains weak and fragile in the face of infinite simplicity. Is it not dialectical and discursive, by its very nature always in motion? Only in beatifying contemplation will it be able to fix its fine point on God without being shattered to pieces. In the final analysis it comes down not to knowing but to comprehending. Only holiness comprehends (cf. Eph 3:18). Knowledge is not enough. It is quite remarkable and in line with Saint Bernard's moral mysticism that, in the last chapter of the

---

[47] SC 58.10 (SBOp 2:134).

[48] Circ 2.4 (SBOp 4:280).

[49] Div 54 (SBOp 6/1:279). Saint Aelred of Rievaulx developed this in his *Mirror of Charity* II, Chapters 22–26. Cistercian Fathers Series 17 (Kalamazoo: Cistercian Publications, 1990) 208–218.

[50] SC 1.2 (SBOp 1:3).

[51] SC 41.1 (SBOp 2:28–29). Cf. Pent 3.3 (SBOp 5:172–173).

treatise *On Consideration,* comprehension of infinite simplicity is ultimately conformation to divine holiness. The saints comprehend, says Saint Bernard.

> Do you want to know how? If you are a saint you have comprehended; if you are not, be one and you will comprehend by experience. It is a holy disposition of heart that makes a saint: holy fear and love of the Lord . . . With these two arms the soul embraces God and can also cry out: *I held him and I will not let him go (Sg 3:4).*[52]

Wisdom has built herself a house and in it she has erected seven pillars (Pr 9:1). Wisdom's house has come to us; it is Mary. The seven pillars are the three divine Persons and the four principal or cardinal virtues.

> The Blessed Virgin Mary showed herself *strong* in what she proposed to do, *moderate* in her silence, *prudent* in her questions and *just* in her avowal: *I am the servant of the Lord* (Lk 1:38) . . . By these four pillars pertaining to her way of conduct, just as by the three pillars pertaining to her faith, heavenly Wisdom made its dwelling place in Mary. It so filled Mary's spirit that from her spiritual fullness her flesh itself became fruitful. Thus, by an exceptional grace, the Virgin gave birth to this same Wisdom clothed in our flesh, which she first conceived in the purity of her spirit.[53]

With this total number, seven, the symbol of perfection, Saint Bernard daringly alludes to the cohabitation of the three divine Persons with the four principal moral virtues. Wisdom's abode has all the beauty of a pure conscience united to the divine: Mary is the mystical and moral abode whom we are invited to imitate by our consent to grace and our purity of conscience.

Of the four cardinal virtues, justice is the most important and even enough in itself, whereas fortitude, temperance, and prudence

---

[52] Csi V.13.27 and 14.30 (SBOp 3:490 and 492).
[53] Div 52.1–4 (SBOp 6/1:274–276). On the presence of the Trinity in Mary, see Miss 3.4 (SBOp 4:38). Notice, too, this beautiful phrase: '*Sapientia paterni cordis erit fructus uteri virginalis*', 3.8 (SBOp 4:41).

are simply its helpers.[54] In a short sermon Saint Bernard ingeniously links the four major passions of the soul with the four principal moral virtues: the cause of justice is fear and its fruit is love. Now fear and love, when correctly oriented by justice, lead the soul undeviatingly to a perfect observance of the two greatest commandments, love of God and neighbor.[55] Justice, defined as rendering to each person his or her due, can almost be identified with wisdom when Saint Bernard presents it as true knowledge of the value and taste of things as they really are—for example, the human being in its state of misery and God in his mercy.[56] Justice is rectification of the will brought about by the conversion of those who have had a taste for evil.[57] Among the weapons of the spiritual combat, justice is *the sword penetrating to the point where the soul is divided from the spirit* (Heb 4:12).[58] The Virgin Mary is the seat of Wisdom because she has been enriched with the four pillars—that is, the principal virtues, which she received 'from the Bridegroom as bride, from the Lord as servant, from the Son as mother, and from the Father as daughter'.[59] The spiritual creature justified by faith also receives these gifts. *The soul of someone who is just is the seat of wisdom.* Saint Bernard often quotes this saying from Scripture (Pr 12:23 in the Septuagint and the tradition of the Fathers).[60] Each time he does this, he does it to take us back to the doctrine (so dear to him) of more intense faith and of deep and strong spiritual love for the Word-Spirit by purity and holiness of our moral life. If we are then 'burning with zeal for justice and fervently seeking truth and wisdom', it is because *Christ has become in us justice and holiness* (1 Cor 1:30). In the simplicity of love, we need only consent in order to conform ourselves to this wisdom of God by the agreement of our will with his.[61] By such

---

[54] Sent 3.21 (SBOp 6/2:77).
[55] Div 50.2–3 (SBOp 6/1:271–272).
[56] Circ 3.5 (SBOp 4:286).
[57] Sent 3.120 (SBOp 6/2:222).
[58] Sent 2.152 (SBOp 6/2:53).
[59] Sent 3.111 (SBOp 6/2:190).
[60] SC 25.6 (SBOp 1:166); 27.8 (SBOp 1:187); 63.3 (SBOp 2:163); Pre 20.61 (SBOp 3:293–294); Pur 1.4 (SBOp 4:337).
[61] SC 20.8 (SBOp 1:120). Cf. above, Chapter IV.1.

conversion of life, like that of the sinful woman, the entire space of our interior freedom becomes permeated with the fragrance of grace and recovers its capacity for the infinite and peace.

2. PACIFIED MEMORY

In antiquity, memory was considered a constituent of the soul just as much as intelligence and will.[62] Following Saint Augustine, Saint Bernard sees in these three spiritual realities an image of God in three Persons. He attributes each of them to one of the divine Persons. Memory resembles the Father in his eternity. It is a reflection of the eternal, passing over time. Whereas intelligence is subject to error and will to the passions, memory is liable to forgetfulness. Yet by the soul's restoration as image of God, it cleaves eternally to the inexhaustible wellspring which is the Father.[63] A human being is time (Heidegger), and the depths of memory unify the spiritual creature. It remembers God—that is its way of seeking him and desiring his presence during the intermediate period of life on earth.[64] Memory turns towards the future when our heart waits with assurance for the peace promised to it.[65] In the same folds of memory, in the depths of one's consciousness, simultaneously dwell remembrance of God and remembrance of our past life in which, according to Saint Bernard's thinking, our sins occupy a large place. Here again, the contrasting opposition between God's presence and sin, a refusal of God, is a cause of suffering, but a good kind of suffering which leads the contrite heart to salutary confession.[66] Memory then opens itself to God's forgiveness in the sacrament of reconciliation. We should not forget, however, that confession of faults assumed also other forms at Clairvaux.[67]

---

[62] Conv 6.11. *'Denique tota ipsa (anima) nihil est aliud quam ratio, memoria et voluntas'* (SBOp 4:84).

[63] SC 11.5 (SBOp 1.57). Cf. Gra 14.49 (SBOp 3:201–202).

[64] Div 18.2 (SBOp 6/1:158). Memory plays an important role in contemplative meditation, as we pointed out above in Chapter III.5: Memory and presence.

[65] Div 19.6 (SBOp 6/1:164).

[66] Div 87.6 (SBOp 6/1:332). Cf. Div 40.3 (SBOp 6/1:236).

[67] Cf. J. Leclercq osb, 'Saint Bernard et la confession des péchés', in *Recueil d'études sur saint Bernard et ses écrits* V, 171–180.

Depth psychology and psychoanalysis have rediscovered memory's important role in the field of consciousness. We are saturated with more or less conscious memories which influence our self-knowledge and behavior. Our memory has been wounded by traumatic experiences, of greater or lesser seriousness.[68] In the following long quotation from the sermon *On Conversion* which we are going to read, we will recognize points of comparison with modern thought, even if the research methods and the goal are different. We will also see how the sacrament, the grace of forgiveness, is located directly and effectively at the heart of the experience of freedom in a person's conscience. While reading this passage, we should picture in our minds a scribe holding his pen in one hand and in the other a scraper for making corrections:

Once the will is changed and the body subdued, when the fountain of evil has been dried up and the breaches by which it flowed in filled, a third thing still remains to be done and it is not the least difficult: the memory needs to be purified, the sewer cleaned out. But how can I cut my life out of my memory? The flimsy thin parchment on which it is written has soaked up so much ink that it is impregnated with it. How can anything be rubbed out? It is stained not only on the surface but all the way through. It would be useless for me to try to scrape it away, because the parchment would be torn before the miserable characters would be obliterated. Forgetfulness can blot out memory—if, for example, I had a mental lapse I would not be able to remember what I had done. But what scraper can I use to keep my memory intact and still make the stains disappear? There is only *the living and effective Word, more penetrating than any double-edged sword* (Heb 4:12): *Your sins are forgiven* (Mk 2:5). Let the Pharisee mutter and say : *Who can forgive sins but God alone?* (Mk 2:7). The One who said these words is God, and no one else can do it . . . His pardon wipes away sin, not of course that he cuts it out of the memory, but what used to stick to the memory and stain it no longer darkens

---

[68] Cf. D. Linn SJ and M. Linn SJ, *The Healing of Memories* (New York: Paulist Press, 1974).

it, even though it is still there. We then remember numerous sins committed by others or by ourselves, but only our own trouble us, whereas those of others do us no harm. Why is this, except that it is our own sins which make us especially blush with shame, because we are afraid that we will be reproached for them. Take away condemnation, take away fear, take away confusion—full pardon does all that—and then our faults do not weigh on us but work together for our good, enabling us to give thanks to him who has forgiven them.[69]

Although Bernard says elsewhere that the remembrance of our works of darkness is an undying worm in our consciousness of the past,[70] the soul 'recovers the past by tears of penance, according to these words: '*In your presence I will go back over all my years, in the bitterness of my heart* (Is 38:15 Vulgate)'.[71] Confession of faults is viewed then in the objective and dynamic perspective of consciousness' progress towards definitive peace. Made in God's likeness, it strives to adorn itself interiorly and is renewed from day to day, with the assurance that nothing pleases God more than to see his own image restored to its primordial beauty.[72] We must prune the vine of our conscience unceasingly. Winter ends along with its rains, that is, our tears of anguish which the bitter memory of our sins wrests from us. For most of you, Saint Bernard tells his monks, I am certain that these rains are already over and that springtime with its flowers is now here, the sign that fear has given way to love. These flowers in your hands are the acts of your joyful obedience.[73] Saint Bernard compares pardon to a kiss of peace, because if *our sins separate us from God* (Wis 1:3), then as soon as what is between him and us disappears, he gives us his peace.[74]

---

69 Conv 15.28 (SBOp 4:102–104). The remembrance of our sins was previously mentioned in Conv 3.4 (SBOp 4:74–75); 5, 7 (SBO 4:79); 6.11 (SBOp 4:84).
70 Csi V.12.25–26 ((SBOp 3:488–489).
71 OS 1.14 (SBOp 5:340). Cf. Div 113: *mundatur memoria per confessionem* (SBOp 6/1:391); Ded 2.3 (SBOp 5:377).
72 SC 25.7 (SBOp 1:167).
73 SC 58.11 (SBOp 2:134).
74 SC 4.2 (SBOp 1:19).

The simple avowal of our misery is enough to attract the Saviour's merciful attention to us. There we are sure to meet him. Humble confession of what we are obliged to suffer arouses God's compassion; what is more, it was he who inspired our tears.[75] For misery itself is true poverty of spirit when it recognizes itself as such. It receives the beatitude of the kingdom. 'Misery is mercy's natural place.'[76] Perhaps the most intimate relationship my conscience can have with him who alone can penetrate it arises from salutary reflection on what estranges me from God, so that he may come to meet me.

> To be justified, it is enough for me to have the favor of the One alone whom I have offended . . . Not to sin is the prerogative only of divine justice, whereas human justice is God's indulgence. I have observed this and have understood the truth of these words: *Anyone who is born of God does not sin, because a heavenly birth preserves him* (1 Jn 5:18). This heavenly birth is our eternal destiny in Christ . . . If such persons have sinned in time, their sins do not appear in eternity.[77]

Saint Bernard commented on these words of Scripture in various ways, but always with the same certainty of faith in infinite mercy.[78] There is one passage, however, where this citation from the *First Letter of Saint John* is unusually forceful, because it is found in a context where Saint Bernard outdoes himself in his theological synthesis, his great skill in choosing the biblical texts which are literally interwoven into his writings, and the irresistible thrust of his hope and desire. So we must read this passage attentively and with fervor.

> His divine gaze has been fixed on us since the creation of the world, *that we may be holy and irreproachable in his presence, in love* (Eph 1:4). *We know, in fact, that whoever has been born of God does not sin, because this heavenly birth preserves him* (1 Jn 5:18).

[75] Ded 5.8 (SBOp 5:394).
[76] Conv 7.12 (SBOp 4:86).
[77] SC 23.15 (SBOp 1:148–149).
[78] Sept 1.1 (SBOp 4:344–345); Gra 9.29 (SBOp 3:186).

This heavenly birth is eternal predestination, by which God foresaw *conforming us to the image of his Son* (Rm 8:29). None of these persons sins (1 Jn 3:6), that is to say, none persists in sin, because the Lord knows those who belong to him (2 Tm 2:19) and *God's plan remains unalterable* (Heb 6:17). Although David could be burned interiorly and deeply marked by the most horrible crimes, although Mary Magdalene could have a band of seven devils in her (Lk 8:2), although the prince of the Apostles could sink into the depths of denial (Mt 26:29), no one could snatch them from God's hand (Is 43:13). *Those whom he has predestined, he has also called; and those whom he has called, he has also justified* (Rm 8:30).

Does our whole happiness not consist in cleaving to him (cf. Ps 72:28)? Seek, brothers, *seek the Lord and his strength* (Ps 104:4). *Seek the Lord and let your soul live* (Ps 68:3). *My soul will live for him* (Ps 21:31); it is dead to the world. For the soul who lives for the world does not live for God. Let us seek him then so that we may seek him always, and so he will be able to say about us when he comes to seek us: *This is the generation of those who seek the Lord, who seek the face of the God of Jacob* (Ps 23:6). And *may the eternal gates open then, and may the King of glory enter* (Ps 23:7), and we with him, because he is *God, forever blessed* (Rm 9:5).[79]

God's gaze fixed upon us is his love. Our love responds to it and, in this sermon where it is compared to other forms of relations, our love is recognized as the strongest, surest, and truest means of union with the One who sought us first. Here again we find the theme of conformity to Christ and, by concrete examples taken from the Gospel, the reality of the unfailing and reciprocal search by God and the race of those who are seeking his face. As soon as the gaze of God—who has released me from the prison of my finite condition—rests on me, there is no longer any unhealthy feeling of guilt. Neither my own shame nor fear of being stared at by others can paralyze me, because my conscience is set at ease by the very fact that my freedom is humbly subject to the compassionate gaze of Him

---

[79] Div 4.5 (SBOp 6/1:97).

who has saved me from my misery. By this Other, my conscience has broken loose from the finite state of what is 'the same' to let itself be penetrated by the Infinite.

In this broad vision of the reciprocal loving search by the Creator and his spiritual creature, evil and sin are integrated into the pursuit of good. As Saint Bernard says:

> A just person falls into God's hands and, in some marvelous way, even his sin contributes to his justice. *For we know that everything works together for the good of those who love God* (Rm 8:28). Does not even this fall contribute to our good by making us more humble and more cautious? And is it not the Lord who raises up anyone who has fallen and has been raised up by humility? . . . That is why it is important for every soul to keep its attention turned towards God at all times . . . Who, in fact, could ever be negligent if his eyes were unceasingly fixed on God who is looking at him?[80]

For a monk, the search for God is the whole meaning of continual conversion. Memory (this mixture of eternity and time) links together the important moments of return to God. The initial experience in this return was knowledge of self. Stricken with distress, the monk turned to the Lord and became conscious of the grace of liberation. That experience was remembered, and in humble prayer the monk continued to ask to receive this grace again (see above, Chapter II.5). In the transition from the second to the third step of the love of God, greater familiarity with God still came about by the practices of the ascetical life and contemplation. Then God came to be loved for himself (see above, Chapter V.2). Even at the height of mystical union Saint Bernard confessed his misery and at the same time begged God to come back and let him feel his presence in face of this misery (see above, Chapter V.2).

So it is that mindfulness of myself as a sinner and mindfulness of God progressively come into harmony in my memory through the meeting of truthful avowal and loving pardon. Mercy means that God is with us at heart in our misery, pacifying our conscience and

---

[80] QH 2.2–3 (SBOp 4:390–391).

drawing it to himself. Memory then turns into thanksgiving. And when the soul comes to look back over its life on the last day, it will be at peace before the Son of man, who will come like the fawn of a doe. For it is this little child who has been born for us (Cf. Is 9:5), this child born of a woman, who will judge us.[81]

3. THANKSGIVING AS A STATE OF GRACE

Before going further along this pathway of peace on which Saint Bernard has guided us this far, let us recall our starting point. From the remoteness of unlikeness to the nearness of likeness, the soul has returned to God by recovering its freedom, which had been screened from itself by separation from the source of its creation. Established again in radical dependence on its Creator, the soul is now settled in the truth of humility and no longer blinded by pride. It is free to love God in contemplation and other human beings in compassion. This return or conversion of freedom has been the effect of Christ's grace, which brought the human will—as well as its desire and seeking—into agreement again with the divine will, even to the point of transforming union. The mutual seeking by the Creator and his spiritual creature has assumed a concrete form and has been confirmed by the practice of the monastic art: its ascesis and its spirituality. Confident that it is loved, and loving with wisdom and peace the One who has sought and found it, the incarnate soul of the monk intelligently and fervently follows the God who by his Incarnation has come near us to communicate life in the Spirit. Thanksgiving for this work of grace is thenceforth the best aspect of the monk's prayer. Grace has restored freedom, which now gives thanks. The first time, Saint Bernard explains, God gave me to myself by creating me; the second time—which took longer and was more painful—he gave himself to me. And by giving himself to me, he gave me back to myself. Given and given back, I owe myself to him twice. But what shall I offer to God for the gift of himself, for what am I before God?[82]

---

[81] SC 73.4 (SBOp 2:235–236).
[82] Dil 5.15 (SBOp 3:132). Cf. SC 11.7 (SBOp 1:58–59); QH 14.3 (SBOp 4:470).

The relationship has thus become accustomed and easy. An intimate conversation, which consists essentially in astonished reflection on God's action in the monk's life, now goes on in the depths of consciousness. So Bernard can say that 'the Word's language is the gift of grace (*infusio doni*) and the soul's response is its surprise, which is expressed in thanksgiving'.[83] As long as it responds the soul is in a state of grace, because it converses with God and counts on him for interior support as it continues to advance towards the point which can never be reached in this life, but which gives life its whole meaning and dynamism. Thanksgiving expresses the peace and joy that result from the active and effective presence of grace, from its voice in our heart in the midst of life's trials.[84] It is the highest form of prayer. Saint Bernard expressly affirmed this in speaking about the four forms of prayer distinguished by the early Christians, as we find them in the *First Letter to Timothy* (1 Tm 2:1). First of all, there is the prayer of supplication to a mediator; then direct recourse to God for forgiveness of sins; confident petition; and finally thanksgiving. The last type seems to go even beyond or before prayer. Let us quote a particularly meaningful text:

> As to the fourth form of prayer, thanksgiving, I believe that few reach it. It is all the more precious in being more infrequent. It is an abundant grace which a human being who has arrived at this point finds in God directly, in virtue of God's promise to answer even before being invoked (*Rule of Saint Benedict,* Prologue 18). The Spirit received from God attests to this person's spirit that its desire has been heard. Then one can stop entreating and give thanks with perfect confidence. So it was that, when he raised Lazarus from the dead, before asking anything in prayer, the Lord cried out: '*I thank you, Father, because you have heard me* (Jn 11:41).[85]

Because grace indwells such a soul by the very act of thanksgiving, just as it indwells Jesus, a person who is united to Christ is

---

[83] SC 45.7–8 (SBOp 2:54–55).
[84] SC 32.7 (SBOp 1:230–231).
[85] Div 25.6 (SBOp 6/1:191–192). Cf. Div 107.1 (SBOp 6/1:379–380).

like him and with him in an attitude of thanksgiving. Gratitude saves
what is best in us from vanity, and somehow makes it sacred. When
even those who are wise in the ways of this world (wrote Bernard
to his friend Peter, bishop of Palencia) keep engraved in their hearts
every kindness they have received, is it not right for us to know how
to keep in our hearts what we have received, so that God's grace
will not be barren in us? So that it may abide in us at all times, let us
give thanks to the Lord our God at all times.[86] Thanksgiving gives
us assurance that we will receive the gift of grace again. About the
bride's words in the Song,: *His right hand will embrace me* (Sg 2:6),
Saint Bernard points out that she uses the future tense. 'She does
not say: his right hand *embraces me*, but *will embrace me*, so that you
may understand that she is far from being ungrateful for the first
grace and anticipates a second grace by giving thanks.'[87] Humility,
which is true knowledge of self and of pride's subtle ways of seeping
in, is directly linked with grace and in this sense it plays an essential,
irreplaceable, and continuous role throughout the entire journey of
the search for union with God. Pride inevitably deprives us of grace
by vitiating our intention or making us complacent about some good
action of our own which it has failed to prevent. In this case, it is a
matter of freedom pretending to act only by itself. Fear of God is the
water of humility which fills the jar of the heart and leaves no more
place for pride. Grace can then make this water taste like wine and
fill a perceptive and transparent heart to the very brim.[88] In a way,
the persistent practice of the prayer of thanksgiving characterizes
transition from an initial degree of prayer to Jesus crucified, the
object of which is conversion, to a second degree, which is praise
and contemplation of the glorified Christ.[89]

As it becomes increasingly aware of the action of grace within
itself, the soul becomes humbler and, like the humble Virgin Mary,
it voices its thankful praise for what God is accomplishing in
it.[90] Following Origen, Saint Bernard says that only after having

---

[86] Ep 372 (SBOp 8:334).
[87] SC 51.5 (SBOp 2:87). Cf. Nat BVM 15 (SBOp 5:285).
[88] SC 54.9–12 (SBOp 2:108–111).
[89] Div 123.1 (SBOp 6/1:400).
[90] O Asspt 12 (SBOp 5:271–272).

become detached from the world with the book of *Ecclesiastes*, having progressed in its moral life according to *Proverbs*, and having become spiritual and contemplative, can the soul live habitually in grateful praise as in the *Song of Songs*, Solomon's third book.[91] More excellent than the other canticles in Holy Scripture, the *Song of Songs* is the symbolic song of praise which celebrates the loving union of Christ and the Church. It is also the song of the soul's desire quickened by the Spirit. It is the wayfarer's song of those who are experiencing combat and victories, and most particularly it is the song of cordial agreement of wills, divine and human.[92] A conscience that is troubled and discouraged, tepid or in the grip of evil passions, is incapable of praise. It cannot give thanks until memory has been freed from the past which weighs it down.[93] But 'nothing on earth gives us such a good idea of what our heavenly home is like as the happiness of those who praise God'. Praise is equally 'a good way to make the sorrows of this life more bearable'. It gives a monk joy in fraternal communion because, freed from sin, which results in isolation, 'those who lead a life of thanksgiving contemplate God and think of him alone; consequently they truly live together in unity'.[94] In his profound analysis of the pharisee's false thanksgiving, Saint Bernard demonstrates how he prayed in vain because of his self-sufficiency:

> So we can see that many people proclaim their thanks in a routine kind of way rather than by a feeling of love . . . Not just any kind of thanksgiving is pleasing to God therefore, but only the type that wells up with simplicity from a pure and sincere heart.[95]

Is the celebration of God's blessings with simplicity of heart, and above all the blessing of the Redemption,[96] not the attitude which ought to be the soul of all liturgy? Saint Bernard spoke about the

[91] SC 1.2–3 (SBOp 1:3–4).
[92] SC 1.8–11 (SBOp 1.6–8).
[93] SC 10.9 (SBOp 1:52–53).
[94] SC 11.1 (SBOp 1:54–55).
[95] SC 13.2–3 (SBOp 1:69–70).
[96] SC 11.3 (SBOp 1:56).

Eucharist only rarely, whereas his disciples developed its theology.[97]
He seems moreover to have been principally concerned with its
practical effect on moral conversion: charity and loving union with
God. Grace comes to our assistance, he says in his *Sermon for Holy
Thursday*, to heal our wound of cupidity, and we are assured of
this healing

> by the investiture the sacrament of the body and precious blood
> bestows. This sacrament has two effects on us: it abates the
> desires of our senses and where serious sins are concerned it
> quells our consent to them absolutely. If one of you no longer
> feels as often or as violently the motions of anger, jealousy,
> lust or other passions of this type, let that person give thanks
> to the body and blood of the Lord, because the effects of the
> sacrament's power are pervading him.[98]

For him the Body of Christ is above all the Church, whose
members are nourished by the sacrament of the body and blood of
the Lord.[99] On the other hand, someone who sins deliberately by
consent of the will, in spite of conscience's condemnation, is cut off
from the body of Christ.[100] We can see that with regard both to the
sacraments and to mystical experience, the accent remains focussed
on the moral aspect of spiritual union.

If, for Saint Bernard, thanksgiving is the surest manifestation
of a liberated conscience consenting to grace, it also seems certain
that for him ingratitude is proof of a conversion that didn't happen.
Let us quote a particularly severe passage:

> Even today we see many people who insistently ask for what
> they realize they need, but we know very few who give thanks

97 Cf. C. Hontoir OCSO, 'La dévotion au Saint Sacrement chez les premiers cisterciens
(XIe-XIIIe siècles)', in *Studia Eucharistica*, Antwerp (1946) 132–155. The following
are quoted (p. 132–140): William of Saint Thierry, Isaac of Stella, Baldwin of
Ford, Guerric of Igny, Gilbert of Hoyland and Gerard of Liège. Saint Bernard,
who inspired this devotion by the importance he gave to the Humanity of Christ,
appears in this article only once, in the text quoted below.
98 5 HM 3 (SBOp 5:70).
99 SC 66.8 (SBOp 2:183).
100 Div 6.3 (SBOp 6/1:106–107).

in proportion to what they have received. There is nothing reprehensible about insistent petition, but if we show that we are ungrateful we nullify the effects of what we asked for. . . . We are sorry to say that we see many [monks] who think that as long as they continue to wear the habit and are tonsured they are completely safe. They are not aware of how the worm of ungratefulness is gnawing at them inside . . . Haven't they been gradually falling away? . . . A number of them are secretly afflicted with an ulcer worse than this leprosy [of worldly life]: ungratefulness, which is all the more dangerous because it is hidden . . . When we show that we are not ungrateful for the gifts we have received, we prepare a place in ourselves for grace, so we may receive still greater gifts. It is ungratefulness, and ungratefulness alone, which prevents us from progressing in our christian commitment . . . When we are at the beginning [of our conversion] we feel like strangers (like the leper and the samaritan woman) and disclose that we are full of fear, fervor and humility. But later on we easily forget the gratuitous nature of everything we have received and become abusively presumptuous about our familiarity with God . . . What God requires of us is not words, but an *act* of thanksgiving.[101]

Thanksgiving is an activity which occupies a person's whole being and tolerates no holding back. As soon as the slightest relapse creeps into our conscience and we become self-satisfied over a gift we have received, everything is lost. 'The better one is, the worse one becomes, if what makes one good is attributed to self.'[102] When Saint Bernard opposes merit to grace, it is only the resurfacing of pride from a moral point of view. If Saint James quite rightly said that *grace is given to the humble* (Jm 4:6), this is 'because a humble soul does not let itself be preoccupied with human merit,

---

[101] Div 27.6–8 (SBOp 6/1:202–203). Cf. Quad 2, 2 (SBOp 4:361).
[102] SC 84.2 (SBOp 2:303–304). Pascal quoted this Bernardine phrase in Latin in writing about people who seek God without Jesus Christ. *Pensées* 549 (Brunschvicg's edition). In *Pensées* 551, he also quotes in Latin, but not literally, a phrase from the same *Sermon 84.6 on the Song*: 'Meriting blows more than kisses . . . I am not afraid because I love' (SBOp 2:305–306).

and consequently fullness of grace can permeate it more freely'.[103] Saint Bernard points out the two different ways the bride in the *Song* expresses herself when she speaks of her love; first in the words: *My beloved is mine and I am his* (2:16), and secondly: *I am my beloved's and he is mine* (6:3). Then, in a very significant passage, he justifies this reversal of attitude:

> Why this change? Because she wants to affirm that she has greater fullness of grace when she surrenders wholly to grace and attributes both the beginning and the end to it. Otherwise, if there were still something in her which did not spring from grace, how could she be full of grace? Grace could not enter a place already occupied by merit. Total acknowledgment of grace, therefore, is in itself a sign that grace has reached its fullness in the soul which professes it. As long as something remains which comes from the soul itself, grace has to cede its place to it. Whatever is imputed to merit is taken away from grace. I do not want a kind of merit that excludes grace. To be my own, I shrink with horror from everything that is my own, unless perhaps what makes me my own is to some extent my own. Grace restores me to myself, gratuitously justified and freed from bondage of sin. For *where the Spirit is, there is freedom* (2 Cor 3:18).[104]

We needed to quote this text in full to show Saint Bernard's insistence and precision when he speaks here again about grace and freedom. He sees merit as a refusal of grace, in the sense that it is a kind of self-sufficient freedom. This makes us think back to the first moment when we lost the divine likeness when, to be precise, human liberty refused to depend on God's grace and posed as autonomous. In the passage quoted above, when the Creator and his spiritual creature have both arrived at their point of meeting,

---

103 Ann 3.9 (SBOp 5:40).
104 SC 67.10 (SBOp 2:195). Cf. SC 68.6 (SBOp 2:200). On the way Luther used Saint Bernard's teaching on this point, see B. Mousnier, 'Saint Bernard et Luther', in *Saint Bernard, homme d'Église* (Paris: Desclée De Brouwer, 1953) 166–168. [See also Franz Posset, *Pater Bernhardus, Martin Luther and Bernard of Clairvaux* (Kalamazoo 1999)—ed.]

the creature, by its admission that it belongs to divine love, regains its identity as image of God and also its freedom in grace; this is a matter of divine Love. These considerations on merit, in which Saint Bernard sees the danger of a subtle form of pride, also show how important humility is in his teaching.[105] In a beautiful meditation on Mary's words, *He has looked upon the humility of his handmaid* (Lk 1:48), in which each word must be weighed, Saint Bernard comments that Mary in fact means that God made her humble by looking on her by his grace, and made her his in order to accomplish through her and in her his work of salvation.[106] For, he repeats, without denying a just person's merit, 'it is humility which purifies the intention; it is humility which acquires any merit, all the more truthfully and effectively because it never thinks about attributing merit to itself'.[107]

Thanksgiving is an activity. It is the state of grace in action, in the whole life of a person whose freedom has been converted to grace by humility. Gratitude is the gift of self, responding to God's gift.[108]

At the end of his treatise *On Grace and Free Choice*, Saint Bernard sketched out a kind of spiritual route, as he often did, and his summary of this journey very clearly shows the place the prayer of thanksgiving holds in it. Being created, existing, being saved and justified can be attributed only to grace. Thanksgiving itself is also a gift to us, because we can receive the chalice of salvation, the Saviour's blood. We ought then to acknowledge the threefold work of Christ's grace: creation; reformation; and the state of consummate perfection. Only reformation, which takes place with our voluntary consent, will be considered as owing to our merits, and these merits are the life of obedience and monastic *ascesis*. They

---

[105] Cf. SC 54.10 (SBOp 2:109).

[106] Sent. 3.127 (SBOp 6/2:246–247). Cf. Nat BVM 8 (SBOp 5:280).

[107] QH 14.10 (SBOp 4:475).

[108] Cf. G. Marcel, *Le declin de la sagesse* (Paris: Plon, 1954): 'It is all too clear that there is an inner relationship between gratitude and grace. In French, the expression "*action de grâce*" suffices to show it. One could say, I believe, that the gift, as such, can in no way be separated from gratitude for the gift.' [*The Decline of Wisdom* (Chicago, Henry Regnery, 1955)].

result in interior renewal consisting in rightness of intention, purity of affection, and mindfulness of good deeds, thanks to which our conscience becomes luminous. These are God's gifts because this is the Holy Spirit's work in us; they are also our merits because this work cannot be accomplished without our assent. Yet God is also the source of merit, because it is he who sets the will in action and sustains it.

> Furthermore, if we give what we call 'merits' their proper name, they are seed-beds of hope, incentives to charity, portents of a hidden predestination, and harbingers of future happiness, the road to the kingdom. In short, *those whom God has justified—* not those whom he found already just—*he has also glorified* (Rm 8:30).[109]

Thanksgiving is not only a continual call to grace, it is our life's endless striving towards fulfillment. To focus on self and our own personal merits would, in a way, be like having a paralyzed conscience or withered freedom. The road broadens out ahead for anyone who knows that he or she is on the way to the kingdom along which grace guides our freedom, and on the pathway of peace where the seeds of hope grow.

4. THE WISDOM OF ENDLESS DESIRE

Created freedom, which, through separation from its Creator, had turned in on itself and become suffocated by its inability to accomplish the good which it could no longer see because of its aberrant pride, has by grace gradually regained its beauty as image of God. Saint Bernard has described this recovery of the soul whom the Spirit, like a physician, has visited and healed by giving it a taste for God and the joy of his forgiveness. Immediately the soul comes back to life; it thanks God and praises him for breaking its chains. Then it takes up the practices of the monastic life and prayer. Soon it reaches contemplation and seeks God more and more interiorly. Charity flows into the heart and fills it completely. The soul achieves

---

[109] Gra 14.46–51 (SBOp 3:199–203); CF 19A ¶51, p. 111.

fulfillment, because love is the fullness of the law and also of the heart. *God is love* (1 Jn 4:8) and nothing in the world can totally satisfy a creature made in God's image but the God of charity, who alone is greater than the soul.[110] In another sweeping summary, Saint Bernard shows how a soul escaping the ancient conspiracy which darkened creation first experiences the false day which the saints cursed: the day of the spirit's harassing struggle with flesh and death. Then at last it breathes freely in the light of true day, which is the Saviour himself. He who by his grace breathed life into our body has restored breath to *the inner person who is renewed day by day* (2 Cor 4:16) in the image of the Creator, and it is He who will also raise us up in the glory of the resurrection.[111]

Quoting Job, *Why have you set me against you, why have I become a burden to myself?* (7:20), Saint Bernard shows what the consequences are when a creature tries by perverse intention to imitate its Creator's infinite freedom without depending on Him and to be deified apart from God. It no longer has any law but its own, which has subjected it to the law of fear and self-interest. Charity converts the soul by setting it free, but it does not do away all at once with those fears and desires, like those of a slave or hireling, within us. It pacifies, assuages, purifies and orientates them towards promised fulfillment.[112]

Although the spiritual creature's encounter with the Spirit who created it brings about their complete union, the search cannot end there. In truth, *God is love* (1 Jn 4:8), and although our power to love tends towards the infinite, it remains limited. So we find this beautiful prayer:

> My God, my help, I shall love you as I am able for your gift. My love is less than is your due, but not less than I am capable of. For even if I cannot love you as much as I should, still I cannot love you more than I can. I shall be capable of loving you more only when you graciously grant me greater love, and yet it will never be what you are worthy of. *Your eyes will see my*

---

[110] SC 18.5–6 (SBOp 1:106–108).
[111] SC 72.8–11 (SBOp 2:230–233).
[112] Dil 13.36–14.38 (SBOp 3:150–152).

imperfections, but in your book all shall be inscribed (Ps 138:16): all those who do what they can, even though they cannot do all that they should.[113]

Is this not the meaning of the words Saint Bernard addressed to Eugene III?

> What is God? Are you not perhaps going to think that I have asked this question too often already? Are you not perhaps going to despair of finding the answer? And yet I tell you, holy Father Eugene, it is only God who can never be sought in vain, even if he cannot be found. Your experience will teach you, but if it has not, believe someone who has had this experience; not me, but the holy man who said: *You are good to those who hope in you, to the soul who seeks you* (Lm 3:25).[114]

In this passage, which brings to our mind the reciprocal relationship between experience and Scripture, we also find once again the theme Seek-Find, which is the very life and paradox of love (see above, Chapter I.1 and 2). Here, however, the union is not between two equals, and yet there is fully shared love. More than ever, this is a matter, not of understanding, but of recognizing these sentiments in oneself by conformity of being.[115] From the radical inequality between a spirit with a capacity for God and God himself, who is infinitely beyond all human capacity, two experiences ensue. The first is the realization that the only perfection possible in this world is to know that we are imperfect. 'In his goodness God habitually disposes things so that, even in the highest degree of the spiritual life, the more we progress the less the impression we have that we are making progress.'[116] Consequently, says the abbot of Clairvaux, refusal to advance on the road of life means mere stagnation and even worse, retreat. We make real progress only when we bear

---

[113] Dil 6.16 (SBOp 3:133). Cf. S. Augustine, *Confessions* XIII. 8. 9 (Fathers of the Church 21 [(Washington, D. C.: Catholic University of America Press] 1953).

[114] Csi V.11.24 (SBOp 3:486).

[115] SC 67.8 (SBOp 2:193–194).

[116] Div 25.4 (SBOp 6/1:189–190).

in mind that we have not yet comprehended, and when we strive onwards and expose our imperfections to divine mercy.[117]

The second experience that ensues from inequality between a loving soul and its God is the experience of desire. But he means a desire without need, plenitude without satiety, a desire that is fully gratified yet remains desire.

> Here is satisfaction without disgust, insatiable curiosity without restlessness, the eternal desire which cannot be satisfied and yet knows no want, and finally that sober intoxication athirst for truth and not for pure wine. It comes, not from too much wine, but from burning with love of God.[118]

At this fourth step of love of God, what he means is surely a rare and fleeting experience of God, but does true, religious, and profound desire not always tend towards the infinite? In this sense different from need, desire feeds on itself, as Lévinas saw in his philosophy of love.[119] It not only feeds on itself, but when it is satisfied, it remains desire.[120] The patristic idea that happiness consists in fulfilled desire which remains desire is often repeated by Saint Bernard. It is by desire that the soul seeks God,[121] he says, and the happiness of discovering him, far from putting an end to desire, increases it.

---

[117] Pur 2.3 (SBOp 4:340). Cf. SC 58.12 (SBOp 2:135); Ep 34.1 (SBOp 7:90); Ep 91.3 (SBOp 7:240) Ep 254.3 (SBOp 8:158).

[118] Dil 11.33 (SBOp 3:147).

[119] Cf. E. Lévinas: 'I think that the relation to the Infinite is not something one knows, but a Desire. I have tried to describe the difference between Desire and need by the fact that Desire cannot be satisfied; that Desire, in some manner, feeds on its own hunger and increases by its own satisfaction; that Desire is like a thought that thinks more than it thinks, or more than what it thinks. This is no doubt a paradoxical structure, but not more paradoxical than this presence of the Infinite in a finite act.' *Éthique et Infini. Dialogue avec Philippe Nemo* (Paris: Fayard, 1982) 97.

[120] R. Char: 'A poem is the fulfilled love of desire which has remained desire.' *Partage formel*. Oeuvres complètes (Paris: Gallimard, 1983) 162. Cf. P. Claudel: 'Let no one gag and blindfold me with a kind of happiness that takes desire away from me!', *Le Père humilié*. Acte III, scene 2. Oeuvres complètes, tome X (Paris: Gallimard, 1953) 263.

[121] SC 74.2 (SBOp 2:240–241).

Does consummate joy consume desire? On the contrary, it is oil poured on the flames. This is certainly how it is. Joy will be complete, but that will not put an end either to desire or to the search. Think, if you can, of seeking eagerly without any impression of lacking something, of desire without anxiety. It is a paradox, but fullness and desire are not mutually exclusive.[122]

The wisdom of this desire, which is both aroused and unceasingly satisfied by grace, consists in understanding and having a taste for the things of heaven—the goal and the meaning of any christian and monastic spiritual life. In these happiness is found, as Claudel claimed when he wrote of monks: 'blessed are those who live in a "hidden" place! . . . that they may unimaginably inhabit plenitude, and that this may be their lot: to have no other joy than Joy'.[123] A certain assurance about being in conformity with God gives the heart peaceful joy and enables it both to converse familiarly with him and to consult him about everything. This heart-to-heart contact makes the monk even bolder in his desires, because he understands them better.[124] 'For Saint Bernard,' wrote Jean Mouroux, 'the christian life is inconceivable without the living security which God gives to his own.'[125] From among the bernardine texts this theologian quotes to describe the quality of such confidence, which is neither empirical nor experimental, but experiential, let us quote the following:

> When does God leave his elect without testimony? Or, when they are tossed about anxiously between hope and fear, what encouragement can they have if they receive absolutely no evidence of being chosen? . . . Now if, as is certain, sureness is utterly denied us, would we not be far happier if we could discover at least a few signs of our being chosen?

---

122 SC 84.1 (SBOp 2:303). Cf. 31.1 (SBOp 1:219–220); QH 11.10 (SBOp 4:455), then QH 17.6 (SBOp 4:490–491); OS 1.11 (SBOp 5:336); Div 94.2 (SBOp 6/1:352).

123 P. Claudel, *Le Repos du Septième Jour*. Acte III. Oeuvres complètes, tome VIII (Paris: Gallimard, 1954) 241.

124 SC 83.3 (SBOp 2:299).

125 J. Mouroux, *L'expérience chrétienne* (Paris: Aubier, 1952) 348.

Yet, continues Saint Bernard, 'witnesses of salvation *are* given to us' and in his conclusion to a long series of scriptural texts on the three witnesses on earth: *the Spirit, water, and blood* (1 Jn 5:8), we find this sentence which is very characteristic of his whole spiritual doctrine: 'A new way of living gives completely sure evidence that a new spirit has come upon us'.[126]

In the christian way of speaking, is desire for the infinite not hope's desire? Bernard's series of *Sermons on Psalm 90* provides a running testimony to the dynamic of love: hope striving totally towards liberation by the Resurrection. After reminding us how important it is for each soul to turn its attention to God who gives it his attention, Saint Bernard has the soul express its genuine hope:

> Such a person can very rightly affirm: *My God, I will hope in him* (Ps 90:2). Notice that he did not say: 'I have hoped' or 'I hope', but 'I will hope'. In other words, this is my promise, my resolution, the firm intention in my heart. This hope— my hope—has been put in my breast like a pledge and I will persevere: I will hope in him. No, I will not despair or hope in vain, because cursed is anyone who sins by abuse of hope, and equally anyone who sins by lack of hope. I do not want to be among those who do not hope in the Lord: *I will hope in him*.[127]

As a truly spiritual man and christian monk, Saint Bernard knew that there is a vital bond between trials and hope, and that hope is limitless. It hurls itself unceasingly towards life.[128] Let us quote the following, one of a great number of passages having a fervent eschatological tone:

> It is in tribulation that hope of glory is found. Still more, glory itself is found in tribulation like hope of fruit is found in the seed, and like the fruit itself is in the seed.
> Notice how the kingdom of God is already within us, an immense treasure . . . hidden in a field of no value. It is here, I

---

126 O Pasc 2.3 and 5 (SBOp 5:119–121).

127 QH 90.2–3 (SBOp 4:391).

128 Hell is the opposite: it is immobile despair: *Ibi mors immortalis, defectus indeficiens, finis infinitus.* Sent. 3. 91 (SBOp 6/2:142).

say; yes, but hidden. Happy the person who has found it. Who is that person? The one who was more concerned about the harvest than about sowing.[129]

We must be *like servants waiting for their master to return from the wedding feast* (Lk 12:36), says Saint Bernard. If we see someone with his hands on a plough or on the way to market to buy or sell, we do not ask him what he is expecting. But if someone is standing in front of a door, looking up at the windows, it is obvious that he is waiting for something. To wait is to keep oneself free in prayer, as a psalm invites us to do: *Be free and see that I am God* (Ps 45:11).[130] To reflect on our goal is a salutary pause when we are waiting for the One who is the Way and Life.

All the graces of divine presence which the soul can experience soon disappear—to our sorrow. Our joy will never be complete, and the soul will be subject to the alternation of presence and absence until the end of life on earth.[131] Yet this gives us a reason to long for the beatific vision. 'Which of us,' cries Bernard, 'burns with a love so holy that desire to see Christ makes all the shining colors and glitter of earthly joy seem drab and tiring?'[132] When speaking of christian mystics' realism, Bergson remarked:

> Truly, if we were sure, absolutely sure, that our life would continue after death, we would no longer be able to think of anything else. Pleasures would remain, but they would be dull and drab, because their intensity comes only from the attention we fix on them . . . Pleasure would be eclipsed by joy. And joy, in fact, would consist in the simplicity of life which a diffused mystical intuition would propagate in the world. . . .[133]

The simplicity of life to which Bergson invited humankind—already then overly keen on technology (*méchanique*)—should, in his

---

[129] QH 17.3 (SBOp 4:488).

[130] O Epi 1.1 (SBOp 4:314–315).

[131] SC 32.2 (SBOp 1:227).

[132] SC 28.13 (SBOp 1:202).

[133] H. Bergson, *Les deux sources de la morale et de la religion* (Paris: Félix Alcan, 1932) 342–344. [Translated by R. A. Audra and C. Brereton as *The Two Sources of Morality and Religion* (New York: Henry Holt, 1935)].

opinion, be born of a mystical conviction, as cistercian simplicity had been.

Simplicity also reveals itself in perseverance, because the wisdom of infinite desire puts the interior life first and enables one to rise above the inevitable fluctuations of time, which remains the measure of motion and change. Little by little the soul acquires some equanimity.

> No matter what source temptation comes from, the soul has only to remain steadfastly and calmly fixed in God. Yes, I repeat, this advice is for those who are perfect, those who by their way of living already imitate the state of existence reserved for them in eternity.[134]

Saint Bernard was convinced, as we have seen over and over again in other texts, that the moral, ascetic, monastic life is already eternal life. He says so clearly: 'Perseverance is a certain image of eternity. In fact, it is to perseverance that eternity is given, or rather, it is perseverance alone that confers eternity on a human being.'[135] In his panegyric for Humbert, who had been prior at Clairvaux and abbot of Igny, Bernard stressed his simplicity and equanimity, qualities that lead to perseverance:

> More than all the other men I have met these days he was continually himself, unified and constantly the same, persevering at all times and at every hour. He followed unhesitatingly in the steps of the Lord Jesus until the day he came to the end of his journey.[136]

Saint Bernard was a great realist. After insisting on fidelity to spiritual exercises in moments of weariness or repugnance, and finding no pleasure in anything, he sets before his monks the beauty of perseverance. In the unstable alternation of adversity and happiness, he tells his brothers, you will somehow preserve an image of eternity—I mean to say the unwavering evenness of an intrepid

---

[134] Div 84.2 (SBOp 6/1:326).
[135] Csi V.14.31 (SBOp 3:492–493). Cf. Div 111.7 (SBOp 6/1:389).
[136] Humb 5 (SBOp 5:444).

heart. The sign of the renewal of the spiritual creature made in the image and likeness of its Creator is this: it refuses to conform itself to this unstable world. Still more, it obliges this world to become conformed to it so that all things work together with it for good and, thanks to it, recover their original harmony. Saint Bernard continues along the same line of thought, affirming that the poor in spirit will possess not only heaven but even what is good on earth, and all the more because they will be less greedy. The whole earth, with both its successes and its misfortunes, is at their service to assist them for their good.[137]

After experiencing the Word's presence within himself and also His departure, Saint Bernard prays for Him to come back to him 'full of grace and truth'. Again he mentions the image of the doe and her fawn which he had been discussing in his commentary, and reminds us how necessary it is for us to have the gravity of a mature doe with regard to truth and reality—even bitter reality—when we receive the grace of a fawn's youthful gladness.[138] This balance between grace and humble faithfulness in all we do is of course one of the traits of the Abbot of Clairvaux's teaching, which is founded on humility from beginning to end. The present world is a mixture of happiness and unhappiness, sadness and joy, just as a single day is made up of morning and evening. Spiritual people cannot escape this reality; it makes them humble and patient.[139] And it is once again consideration which in moments of joy anticipates adversity, but seems not to suffer from it when it comes. In the first instance, prudence is in play, in the second, fortitude.[140] Yet the dynamic thrust of this moral balance is always a driving mystical force. It always revolves around a desire for God joined with intelligence. They are like the two wings of the seraphim who fly towards the One for whom they are burning with love. 'Look at a flame', continues Saint Bernard, 'it looks as if it is flying, whereas it is really staying in the same place. And do not be astonished that the seraphim can

---

[137] SC 21.6–7 (SBOp 1:125–126).

[138] SC 74.7–8 (SBOp 2:243–245).

[139] Palm 2.1 (SBOp 5:46); Palm 3.2 (SBOp 5:52). Cf. SC 54.9 (SBOp 2:108–109).

[140] Csi I.7.8 (SBOp 3:404).

fly without moving around or that they stay in the same place while flying.'[141] This is the paradox of the co-existence of stability and thrust in the contemplation that is love.

To maintain the absolute within the relative, the spiritual within the unspiritual, the eternal within the temporal: is this not the challenge grace proposes to freedom? In a finite and earthly existence, does the wisdom of endless desire not imply continual advancement towards the infinite, because the infinite is in the heart of every creature, just like a call from its Creator who loves it? Is this not the prophetic life which the Abbot of Clairvaux spoke to his monks about in glowing terms:

> Great, surely, is this type of prophetic life to which I see you are dedicated, great is this service of prophecy to which I see you are devoted. But in what does it consist? Indeed, if we believe the Apostle, *to prophesy is to no longer have eyes for things that are visible, but only for things that are invisible* (2 Cor 4:18). *Be guided by the Spirit* (Ga 5:16), *live in faith* (Rm 1:17), *seek heavenly things, not the things that are on earth* (Col 3:2), *strain ahead with all your strength for what is to come* (Ph 3:13). This, by and large, is what it means to prophesy. How then, if not by the spirit of prophecy, can we live in heaven?
>
> So it was that the prophets long ago lived as though they were not among the people of their time; but by the strength and a sort of impetuosity of the Spirit they leapt over those days, rejoicing to see the Lord's day. They saw it and in it found their joy.[142]

5. THE HOLINESS OF PEACE

Mutual seeking by the Creator and his spiritual creature has been the theme of the cistercian life as Saint Bernard lived and taught,

---

[141] 1 Nov 4.1–2 (SBOp 5:315–316). 'This problem of the relationship between stability and motion, so central to the spiritual life, had already preoccupied the Fathers.' P. Y. Émery gives several references in the note which accompanies his translation of this passage. See *Saint Bernard, Sermons pour l'année*, 751, note 2.
[142] *In labore messis* 3.6 (SBOp 5:225–226).

and over and over again we have developed it, approaching it from various angles and tracing its successive stages. From the beginning it has been clear to us that the search for God can be identified with a search for peace. In the divine image, which the human person is, likeness to God has had to be restored in freedom, truth and love. Incarnate Wisdom gave the spiritual creature back its original form. Christ himself has raised our merely human love for his visible nature to spiritual love for his invisible nature. By the agreement of our will at its deepest level with his, faith has discovered a contemplative dimension of holiness. Thus love has inspired a whole life of *ascesis* based on a spiritual intention, a moral mysticism. *Ascesis*, in turn, has protected the life of the spirit: active charity, in permanent contact with humble human reality, both personal and social, has supported spiritual effort and given it a concrete character. But the search has been unceasingly orientated towards encounter with God. A kind of peace is offered to the faithful soul. Its taste for good is restored; memory regains peace with itself and with God. The peaceful accord of freedom with grace is then spontaneously expressed in a prayer of thanksgiving, and the heart's unshakeable desire also finds itself assured because it is continually fulfilled. The loving quest for God is itself encounter. Is this not how we ought to understand what Saint Bernard said at the end of his life: 'Only God can never be sought in vain, even if he cannot be found'?[143] Does God not always remain the present object of a desire that is coextensive with our very existence? For Saint Bernard, seeking is the first, the best, of God's gifts, and no end can ever be set to this search.[144] Did he not say about his own search for God, mingling study with his personal experience:

> We dedicated ourselves to the goal of seeking him whom until now we have discovered only imperfectly, who can never be sought too much. But it is possible that prayer is more suited to this than is analysis, and an easier means of finding him. So let this be the end of this book, but not the end of the search.[145]

---

[143] Csi V.11.24 (SBOp 3:486).
[144] SC 84.1 (Quoted above, Chapter I.1).
[145] Csi V.14.32 (SBOp 3:493).

A book devoted to seeking God in the form of seeking peace never ends, because for Saint Bernard peace is the pure simplicity of love, which can never exist unalloyed on earth. Like every true and lasting friendship, this one, which unites a spiritual creature to its Creator, is never static, it is always progressing in intimacy and authenticity; it is constantly creative.

The abbot of Clairvaux was attracted by the symbol of the kiss, in the medieval sense of the word. For him a kiss is a sign (a sacrament) of love as agreement of wills.[146] In the case of a soul who returns to God, it means first of all conversion (the kiss of the feet), then spiritual progress (the kiss of the hands), and finally the attainment of union with God (the kiss of the mouth).[147] These kisses are kisses of peace. Saint Bernard applies this symbol to the two most sublime christian mysteries: the Incarnation and the Trinity. The kiss is Christ, in whom divinity and humanity are united, the sign of God's loving will which fulfills his promises of peace.[148] But the kiss to which the creature aspires and which is bestowed on it 'is the Holy Spirit, who is the imperturbable peace of the Father and the Son, their unalterable bond, their undivided love, their indissoluble unity'.[149] The love of the Father and the Son is revealed and transmitted to the human spirit by the Spirit. The spiritual life has no other source. To receive the kiss of the Spirit, which is at one and the same time the *spirit of wisdom and understanding* (Is 11:2), the soul should welcome it with fervor and intelligence. Here Saint Bernard comes back again to his teaching on the perfect balance between intelligence and affectivity as a condition for the pursuit of peace.

> Let neither those who understand truth without loving it nor those who love it without understanding it think that they have received the kiss. Truly, in this kiss there is no place for error or lukewarmness.

[146] See above, Chapter IV.4, note 51.

[147] SC 3.1–6(SBOp 1:14–17).

[148] SC 2.1–9 (SBOp 1:8–14). Cf. C. Dumont OCSO, 'Noël, baiser de paix d'après saint Bernard', in *Une éducation du coeur*, ch. VI. Pain de Cîteaux 10. 3rd Series (Oka: Abbaye-N.-D.-du-Lac, 1996) 109–122.

[149] SC 8.2 (SBOp 1:37).

To receive it, the created spirit should offer its two lips to the uncreated Spirit, 'its reason to receive the gift of understanding, its will to receive the gift of wisdom'.[150] The ascetical and spiritual journey Saint Bernard traced out always leads to the spirit of peace. The path we have followed through the storerooms and the ascent to the king's room leads in the end to the God of peace who pacifies all things and communicates his peace to us when we contemplate Him.[151] The experience of the fullness of divine peace is of course always rare and fleeting in our human situation, but to be disposed to it is already to know it. Saint Bernard expressed this with realism and faith:

> Furthermore, when I say that we must either keep our will in suspense or subject it to the divine will, I am not speaking simply about the instinctive tendencies of our desires or the ups and downs of our sensibilities. That is, in fact, impossible as long as the soul is retained in this body of sin, this body of death. If we could follow God's will in all things and with all the strength of our affections, what else would that be but eternal life? But it is our consent which we must submit to God's will if we desire to have eternal peace and to have it now, already, as is written: *I give you my peace, I leave you my peace* (Jn 14:27).[152]

Saint Bernard—passionate, hyperactive, and hyperemotional as he was—reached peace only at the end of a long struggle with himself, and he did it by unremitting reflection, thanks to the secondary type of his personality, which disposed him to meditation. On a verse of Isaiah: *It was in peace that my bitterness was most bitter* (Is 38:17), he said with simplicity:

> Bitter was the bitterness which I endured for my sins at the beginning of my conversion . . . more bitter still the bitterness

---

[150] SC 8.6 (SBOp 1:39–40). Cf. Asc 3.1–2 (SBOp 5:131–132); Asc 6.5 (SBOp 5:152–153).

[151] SC 23.15–16 (SBOp 1:148–150). Cf. Dante, *The Divine Comedy: Paradiso* 30.
'A light is there which makes
The Creator visible to this creature,
Who only by beholding him finds its own peace.'

[152] Div 26.4 (SBOp 6/1:196–197).

which came from the terrible dread I experienced during my conversion . . . But now that my sins have been expiated by penance and the dread which so often assailed me has been stilled, now in this peace I must bear the bitterest of bitternesses because of the shortcomings of my contemplation.[153]

These words are true and express the seriousness of a life committed to seeking truth. In your monastic life, Bernard wrote to the monks of Tre Fontane at Rome, before everything else have humility, above everything else have peace, because God's spirit rests only on someone who is humble and at peace.[154] The bond between humility at the foundation of any spiritual edifice and the peace at its summit must never be forgotten. As far as the summit of peace in mystical union is concerned, that is, the Word's spiritual marriage with the soul, Saint Bernard told his monks (and in a way these were his last words) that if they wanted to know what this kind of language cannot express, they were to have recourse to the grace of humility which freely gives what cannot be taught, because that is God's plan.[155] Here again it is a question of experience, because humility and love cannot exist apart from experience but are formed reciprocally in the soul. The importance of peace as a goal unremittingly pursued through the entire journey progressing towards divine union has often been pointed out by scholars who have studied Saint Bernard's spirituality. The reflections of two of them follow. First, Aimé Forest:

> Peace is the constant theme, or rather the only theme of his sermons. The spiritual sphere to which Saint Bernard wants to lead us is peace. The whole significance of his doctrine and the richness of his experience may be expressed by these words from Claudel's *Hymn to Saint Benedict*: 'He consents to peace'. Peace is metaphysical consciousness of self. This gives us the most profound reply to the questions raised today in the philosophy of the spirit. Bernard shows us a kind of peace

---

153 Div 3.7 (SBOp 6/1:91).
154 Ep 345.1 (SBOp 8:287).
155 SC 85.14 (SBOp 2:316).

which somehow enables us to create ourselves, because we cannot reach fulfillment without acceding to it.[156]

Father Maur Standaert had much the same thought. He envisaged peace as the goal of the principle of order which was so dear to Saint Bernard. 'For Saint Bernard, it seems, peace and tranquillity quite frequently represent, we might say, the final goal to be attained in the spiritual life.'[157]

Peace is the goal of every monk, of no matter what era or religion, yet only gradually and imperceptibly does it take possession of the depths of the heart. Saint Bernard, as usual, distinguishes three steps. In commenting on the beatitude of the peacemakers, by which one becomes a child of God, he says that there is first of all the person who is pacified (*pacatus*), who repays good for good insofar as possible and has no desire to harm anyone. Then there is someone who is patient (*patiens*), who does not repay evil for evil and can even bear being harmed. And lastly there is the peacemaker (*pacificus*), who pays back good for evil and spontaneously does good to someone who does him harm.

The peace of the first is fragile; the second preserves peace of soul; the third not only remains at peace, but communicates peace to many other people. Such a person is thus a child of God because, reconciled with self, he or she reconciles others with the Father.[158]

On the subject of this reconciliation, let us quote a beautiful passage on the Eucharist in which Saint Bernard once again expresses his faith and sense of realism in the context of a moral teaching intimately bound to mystery.[159] When asked whether someone

---

[156] A. Forest, 'Saint Bernard et notre temps', in *Saint Bernard théologien*, 298–299. Cf. A. Forest, 'L'expérience du consentement selon saint Bernard', in Coll 18 (1956) 269–275.

[157] M. Standaert ocso, *Le principe d'ordination dans la théologie spirituelle de Saint Bernard*. Doctoral dissertation (in typescript) (Louvain University, 1944) 4.

[158] Conv 18.31 (SBOp 4:107–108). Cf. Div 98 (SBOp 6/1:364–365); OS 1.14 (SBOp 5:340).

[159] Cf. H. U. Balthasar: 'For Origen as well, the moral sense of revelation is not juxtaposed to its mystical sense, that is to say, to its profound spiritual influence; it expresses the penetration of this influence, which goes right to the heart of the spectator: "Because here there is no place which does not see you. You must

whose heart is filled with resentment can receive communion, he replied:

> I can only say that I pray God may keep me from ever approaching the peaceful victim with a heart in turmoil, or from receiving with a soul full of hate and anger the sacrament by which we know God has reconciled the world to him. And since it is certain that my offering will not be accepted at the altar until I have made peace with my brother whom I remember has something against me, how much less will it be accepted if I am not at peace with myself.[160]

When Saint Bernard brings out the contrast between wisdom and strong virtue (*virtus*), he quotes the latin version of *Ecclesiasticus*: *The scribe's wisdom comes by leisure* (38:25).

> The works of wisdom are therefore leisure. The more at leisure wisdom is, the more active it is in its own way. The force of virtue, on the contrary, wins acclaim by being practised and proves itself by its acts. If anyone wanted to define wisdom as love resulting from virtue, I think he would not be far wrong. Yet, where there is love there is no toil, but instead taste, the taste for good.[161]

The soul progresses towards the peaceful practice of the spiritual art as an artist progresses by mastery of artistic technique. About the same verse: *Anyone who reduces his activity will receive wisdom*, Saint Bernard says that Mary, the contemplative, remained seated and was silent, completely absorbed in her interior desire for God.[162]

If contemplative peace is indeed the monk's vocation, it is so on earth, in the expectation of something better. Saint Bernard associates the *Glory to God in the highest and peace on earth* (Lk 2:14)

---

change your way of life" (Rilke),' *La gloire et la croix* (Paris: Aubier, 1965) tome 1:20. This also applies of course to Saint Bernard.

[160] Pre 19.58 (SBOp 3:291).

[161] SC 85.8 (SBOp 2:312).

[162] Asspt 5.7 (SBO 5:254–255).

of Christmas with Isaiah's words: *I will not yield my glory to another*
(48:11). But the human creature craves its own glory and replies
to God:

> 'So what then will you give us?' And God answers: '*I give you
> my peace* (Jn 14:27).' 'That is enough for me,' says the human
> creature. 'I gratefully accept what you leave me and I leave to
> you what you keep for yourself. That way I am pleased, and I
> do not doubt that it is good for me. From now on I renounce
> all claims to glory, for fear that by usurping what you do not
> grant me, I may deservedly lose what you offer me. It is peace
> that I want, peace that I desire, and nothing more. Anyone who
> is not satisfied with peace is not satisfied with you, for you are
> our peace . . . Yes, Lord, all glory remains yours; as for me, all
> will be well if I have peace.'[163]

If a human being's 'life is temptation', it is good for a person
to seek, not glory, but peace: peace with God, peace with others,
peace with oneself.[164]

The discernment made by wisdom, which knows things by
savoring, tasting what they really are, is found here as it was
in *Sermon 50 on the Song of Songs*, where the difference between
active charity and affective, or contemplative, charity is shown.
Our circumstances in this world oblige us to be more concerned
with peace on earth than with glory in heaven.[165] Fullness of peace
exists only in hope, as Saint Bernard often repeats:

> There is peace even now on earth, of course, for people of
> good will; but what is that peace in comparison with the super-
> eminent fullness of peace? That is why the Lord himself said:
> *I give you my peace, I leave you my peace* (Jn 14:27). You are
> not yet capable of receiving my peace, which surpasses all
> understanding and is peace surpassing peace. What I do give

---

[163] SC 13.4 (SBOp 1:71). Cf. Nat 4.2 (SBOp 4:265); Div 7.1 (SBOp 6/1:107–
108); Conv 10.21 (SBOp 4:93); Ep 126.7 (SBOp 7:314–315).
[164] OS 5.8 (SBOp 5:366).
[165] SC 50.5 (SBOp 2:80–81).

you, however, is the land of peace, and what I leave to you for the time being (*interim*) is the pathway of peace.[166]

Is the pathway of peace not the Lord himself, the Mediator, the path on which the soul and God meet? He is our peace and this peace is our holiness to the extent that our will is in agreement with his by humble love, which is transforming vision.[167] Commenting on the words of the *Letter to the Hebrews*, *Pursue peace and holiness, without which no one can ever see the Lord* (12:14), Saint Bernard asks himself why holiness is not enough. No, he says, we also need peace—that is, the peace found in the holiness of fraternal charity by which Jerusalem, 'the vision of peace,' is built. Without peace no one can see God, because such a person would be outside the mystery of love.[168]

We are on the pathway of peace and our goal is Jerusalem, the vision of peace, but it remains a distant far off vision of a peace not yet in our possession. 'So if you do not have peace— or rather, because you cannot possess perfect peace in this world but can only see it—then fix your gaze, your attention, and your desire on it.'[169] The eschatological tension within the spiritual life is strongly accentuated by Saint Bernard, as we have often seen in this synthesis. There is, moreover, perhaps no other basis for a synthesis of his writings than the affective dynamism which animates his thought by unifying the experience in which it is founded. The impetus of desire bridged the stages of his ceaseless lifelong striving towards the fullness of peace into which he had already entered by the ordered and continuous progress he made in his search for God. Some ten times Saint Bernard quoted this saying of Job: *Man, fleeting*

---

[166] V Nat 4.8 (SBOp 4:225–226). Cf. *In tempore messis* 1.1 (SBOp 5:217); Gra 14.51 (SBOp 3:203): *via regni, non causa regnandi.*

[167] SC 82.8 (SBOp 2:297); 7.7 (SBOp 1:35); 26.5 (SBOp 1:173); 31.3 (SBOp 1.221).

[168] QH 17.6 (SBOp 4:490–491). Cf. R. Maritain: 'The mystic's fullness of peace, whether it is triumphant or underlies terrible combats, proves that he or she has not been wrong in striving to attain truth by the ways of holiness', *Magie, poésie et mystique*, Oeuvres complètes XV (Paris: Éditions St Paul, 1995) 693.

[169] V Nat 2.1 (SBOp 4:204).

as a shadow, never remains in the same state (14:2).[170] This is the reason
why, once on the way, a person who no longer wants to advance is
going backwards. Happy the man who guards in his heart the desire
to ascend. In his heart, in other words in his will.[171] On the feast
of the Ascension which Saint Bernard particularly loved, he felt the
need to share with his monks what was in a way his fundamental
insight:

> Christ descended; it is also he who ascended (cf. Eph 4:10).
> These are the words of the Apostle. For my part, I believe
> that his very descent was an ascension, because Christ had to
> descend to teach us to ascend. We are, in fact, eager to go up;
> all of us desire to be raised up. We are noble creatures, gifted
> with such a greatness of soul that our natural desire consists in
> seeking what is above.[172]

Isn't this the essence of the drama lived out by a person created
in the image of the Most High but having a proclivity towards what
is lower and just as natural a desire to ascend towards God? This
'noble creature' ought to seek its happiness in the part of itself by
which 'a human being surpasses what is human'.[173]

For the procession on Candlemas Day, Saint Bernard again
speaks of this impetus, which is indispensable to the life of the
spirit. We must go on, singing as we advance in the ways of the
Lord, because the fruit of love is joy in the Holy Spirit. To cease

---

[170] For example: Ep 254.3–5 (SBOp 8:158–159). Quoted by Saint Francis of
Sales in a 1619 letter to Angélique Arnaud, abbess of Port-Royal: 'Ma Fille,
estre en ce monde et ne sentir pas ces oinclinations de passions sont choses
incompatibles. Nostre glorieux saint Bernard dit que c'est hérésie de dire que
nous puissions perseverer en un mesme estat icy bas, d'autant que le Saint
Esprit a dit par Job, parlant de l'homme, que *jamais il n'est en mesme estat* . . .
Ces inclinations d'orgueil, de vanité et de l'amour propre se meslent par tout,
et fourrent insensiblement et sensiblement leurs sentimens presque en toutes
nos actions; mayis pour cela ce ne sont pas les motifs de nos actions », *Oeuvres
complètes*, tome XIX (Lyon: Vite, 1914) 51.
[171] Div 124.1 (SBOp 6/1:402–403). Cf. Ep 91.3 (SBOp 7:240); 254.3 (SBOp
8:158–159); 385.1 (SBOp 8:351–352).
[172] Asc 4.3 (SBOp 5:139–140).
[173] Dil 2.2 (SBO 3:121).

to advance on the way of life, to stop making progress, is to go backwards, for nothing can continue in the same state.

> As for our progress, it consists in this (as I recall having often said to you): we should never think that we have already comprehended, but always strive forward towards what is ahead (cf. Ph 3:13); we should unstintingly try to do better and continually lay our imperfections open to the eyes of divine mercy.[174]

To seek God is to seek peace. *Seek peace and pursue it* (Ps 33:15). 'In other words,' comments Saint Bernard,

> to seek peace we have to follow it and pursuing it once we have found it means to seek what must be tasted and to taste what we have sought: *the realities above and not those on earth* (Col 3:2).[175]

Isn't this the whole wisdom of Christianity and monasticism? We have to persevere on the pathway of peace with the full strength of our spirit and the thrust of our desire. The peace of God which surpasses all understanding also surpasses anything anyone can say about it, says Saint Bernard earnestly, because 'no one ought to try to speak about something no one has experienced'.[176]

This peace which surpasses all understanding has come to us and we have received it. 'The Son has come forth from the Father into the world; he who was first a plan of peace in the Father's heart became in Mary's womb our very peace.'[177]

When we shall have come along the pathway of peace to the end of life's road, when we shall have entered port and the portals will open, when we shall be judged by Mary's child, let us hope that he will appear to us full of grace and truth, with the grave eyes of a doe and the grace of a young fawn:

> May he appear bearing peace, smiling and joyful, yet grave and serious, so that while subduing my arrogance by the stern gaze

---

[174] Pur 2.3 (SBOp 4:340).

[175] Asc 6.5 (SBOp 5:152–153).

[176] OS 4.3 (SBOp 5:357).

[177] Ben 10 (SBOp 5:9).

of truth, he may purify my joy. May he come . . . rejoicing and in splendor, as he proceeds from the Father; [and yet] gentle and mild, who did not disdain to be called—and really to become—the Bridegroom of the soul that seeks him, even though he is God, above all things and blessed forever. Amen.[178]

---

[178] SC 74.11 (SBOp 2:246).

Epilogue without Conclusion

AT THE END OF THE fifth book of his treatise *On Consideration*, which treats of God, Saint Bernard tells us that he has reached the end of the book, but in no way the end of his search. How, in fact, could anyone finish seeking the Infinite? To conclude the present synthesis would be to deny what constitutes its whole beauty and unity: sustained and constant seeking for God.

As I come to the end of this study, I would like to begin it over again, because as I got further into it, I became increasingly aware of the internal cohesion of Saint Bernard's thought and life. Unity is found at every instant in motion, desire, aspiration, and eschatological tension. The mutual seeking by the Creating Spirit and the created spirit acquires its dynamic force from the desire of approaching one another they experience. But it is God who first desires and accordingly moves the soul even to the Infinite.[1]

To conclude this synthesis of a search by beings who love one another would be contradictory. Let us hope that a new synthesis will be undertaken some day, as if by a relay runner. Throughout this whole journey, it would perhaps have been preferable to show its close link with the patristic doctrine of the progressive restoration of God's image in the human creature. If it is principally by freedom that a person resembles the Creator, it is also true that the soul's dynamic force is situated from conversion until deification in the human will seeking to free itself in order to become conformable

---

[1] To the scholastic adage inspired by Aristotle: *Deus movet sicut desideratum*, we should dare to add, following Saint Bernard: *Deus movet sicut desiderans*. It is the only formula 'which furnishes the supreme explanation of his spirituality', Cf. M. Dumontier, *Saint Bernard et la Bible* (Paris: Desclée de Brouwer, 1953) 39.

to the divine will. The accord that unifies will be brought about by love, which bridges the distance between the finite and the infinite. But there is no love without humility. In Saint Bernard's work from beginning to end, humility underlies the life of love; it is its truth. Like love, humility is above all an experience, the experience of created freedom's radical dependence on its Creator, in an obedience which does not seek its own self-interest. It is a matter of fundamental choices which animate one's entire being by conforming all one's thought, desires, and actions to the divine will.

Even Saint Bernard's style often reveals this continuous movement towards a goal never attained but always in sight. While I was writing Chapter VI, I read as Lenten book the *Homilies on Ecclesiastes* by Gregory of Nyssa. There I found the same thrust of passionate seeking for God, often in the same words:

> To find him is to seek him unceasingly, because seeking is not one thing and finding another, but the gain born of seeking is the seeking itself. Do you wish to learn what moment is best for seeking the Lord? I can tell you in a few words: throughout our whole life.[2]

Yes, a Cistercian's whole life is motivated, ordered and orientated by search for God in the midst of life's vicissitudes and the continual change it implies. The description of fixed steps of spiritual progress ('degrees') should not make of this permanent motion something static. 'Little by little', 'unexpectedly': these adverbs which, as we have seen were used several times by Saint Bernard, characterize above all the mobility of the interior search itself. When Saint Bernard describes the various steps of a ladder, he always sees the motion as a whole. Each step points to the summit, not to the following step. 'No one arrives at the summit all at once. We must go up, but not fly. We must go up on our own two feet: reflection (meditation) and prayer. Reflection shows you what you lack, prayer obtains what you lack.'[3]

---

[2] Gregory of Nyssa, *Homilies on Ecclesiastes* VII.5. SCh 416 (Paris: Cerf, 1996) 361.

[3] And 1.10 (SBOp 5:433).

This passage also shows us that ascension by steps is constantly linked to reflection and prayer. The three steps of truth express particularly well this continuous motion towards the summit which is always in sight and is the sense of the whole itinerary. This is because in every christian soul divine truth exists inchoately in the truth as found in the first two steps, knowledge of self and knowledge of others. Regardless of how interesting these two are in themselves from a psychological or moral point of view, for Saint Bernard they are two steps towards contemplation of Truth in itself, towards union with God. They are, above all, sources of progress.

This continual motion of going beyond is found in many parts of the present synthesis. Several titles or subtitles bear this out: Memory and presence (Chapter III.5); from the Word-flesh to the Word-holiness (Chapter IV); from merely human love to spiritual love (Chapter IV.1); experience of love as progress in faith (Chapter IV.5); eternalization of time (Chapter V.4); death, port and portal of life (Chapter V.5.5); the wisdom of unending desire (VI.4); the holiness of peace (VI.5), always a far-off vision.

This going beyond is found in faith in Christ, which develops in contemplation, in a moral life which is open: a 'mystical morality',[4] and also in an eschatological perspective.

The theme 'image and likeness' is also related to this motion of transformation. The search we are speaking about changes in form, color, and character following time, personal fervor or lassitude, and the alternation of our appeals to God and his replies. As soon as presence gives way to absence, Saint Bernard cries, 'Return!'

Change, alternation, and the motion of going beyond have their philosophical foundation—because Bernard was a philosopher in spite of himself—in the mutability of being. 'What is invariable is incomprehensible',[5] he said. Being changes constantly; it is always in motion, as Heraclitus long ago affirmed. When Saint Bernard spoke of immortality as being the characteristic trait of divine likeness in

---

[4] The expression '*moralisme mystique*' was coined by Henri Bremond, in *Histoire littéraire du sentiment religieux en France,* tome 5, ch. 6 (Paris:Bloud & Gay, 1920), especially pages 286–287 and 307. This reference was furnished by Fr Gaëtano Raciti of Orval.

[5] SC 51.7 (SBOp 2:288).

the soul, he said that it is completely relative because all movement is an imitation of death. Everything which moves passes from one condition to another. What *is* must die in a certain way so that what is not may begin to exist.[6] Sartre said the same thing in his own way: 'I am what I am not and I am only because I am what I am not', which signifies that human consciousness is always ahead of itself, in pro-ject, ex-istential. It is also, on another level, ec-stasy or the *ex-cessus* which Saint Bernard spoke about.

The meaning of life's motion, its guiding thread, can come only from accord between grace and freedom. A life has meaning and unity only by reason of fundamental obedience or creative fidelity, which are the heart's response to an interior call from God who desires to unite this heart to his. The monk prays every day that God's will may be done, that is, that the monk's will may be in agreement with God's will. '*Magna res amor* . . . Love is a great reality, provided it returns to its origin, going back to its source to draw continually afresh from it and thereby flow forth unceasingly.'[7]

The symbol of a river, then, expresses the continuity of this love which goes beyond and transcends the intermittences of the heart described by Proust. Theologically, this is the unfailing aspiration called hope, about which Saint Bernard spoke so well in the seventeen *Sermons on Psalm 90*. Balance in this progress towards peace is emphasized by the contrasts Saint Bernard so clearly distinguished between pleasantness and bitterness, joy and sorrow, anguish and hope, fear and confidence. As Claudel had the aged Anne Vercors say:

> Peace—for anyone who knows it—joy
> And sorrow enter there in equal part.[8]

Wisdom, a synthesis of intelligence and affectivity, helps us to enter into peace, and this peace is found in seeking God because the search unifies and simplifies our existence. One thing alone is necessary, everything else is secondary and contingent.

---

[6] SC 81.5 (SBOp 2:287). Cf. also SC 82.3 (SBOp 2:294).

[7] SC 83.4 (SBOp 2:300).

[8] P. Claudel, *La jeune fille Violaine*, 2nd version, Act IV. Oeuvres complètes, tome VII (Paris: Gallimard, 1954) 425.

Both the greatness and the small side of human conscience, as well as its striving and failings, are untiringly looked upon with the same gaze, now admiring, now compassionate. Through these highs and lows, these moments of enthusiasm and fatigue, the trek continues upwards towards Jerusalem, vision of peace, which the pilgrim never loses from sight for fear of falling into despair. The far-off vision sustains us as we advance. A type of freedom which would not seek peace of heart would remain indecisive, unsatisfied and anxious.

As the Cistercian Order, which Saint Bernard marked so strongly, enters the tenth century of its history, it may well question itself about its future, and it is not failing to do so. In the past its vitality has been largely due to the influence which the doctrine of 'the most typical representative of monastic theology' (in the words of that great monastic historian, Dom Penco) has had on its members. 'It is with Saint Bernard', Dom Penco said, 'that the benedictine tradition attained its summit . . . traditional monastic spirituality reached its full-flowering in the Cistercian School.'[9]

Certain people, however, in this age of interplanetary communications and increasingly sophisticated technology, may think that Saint Bernard is obsolete and out of date. That was perhaps the opinion of Julia Kristeva. Yet, in her research on love she could find nothing better than Saint Bernard!

> Love, as Saint Bernard saw it, is—to sum up—the hyphen which constitutes the specificity of a human being as nature-senses, body-ideality, sin-divine grace . . . The heterogeneity maintained by these rims, and at the same time their indisputable subordination to the essential priority of divine ideality, make cistercian mysticism—more than any other doctrine—the adequate and powerful means of defining a human being as a loving subject. Neither sin nor wisdom, neither nature nor knowledge, but love. No philosophy can equal the psychological success of this teaching which has known how to satisfy the impulses of narcissism while raising them above their own

---

[9] G.Penco, in the *Bulletin de Spiritualité Monastique*, Coll 12 (1989), n° 693.

sphere so their rays may reach the other . . . and others: a divine expansion, surely, with the social included on the way.[10]

Saint Bernard has frequently been acclaimed as the 'doctor of love'.[11] We should also stress that his originality consists in 'an appeal to conversion of subjectivity, affective powers and sensibility . . . of desire'[12] He invites us to 'put our subjectivity in the service of faith'.[13] This is because Saint Bernard is profoundly mystical, and consequently humbly realistic.

During these last nine centuries he has taught so many men and women to understand their lives better. He has taught so many persons assailed by difficulties in their lives to look at the Star and call upon Mary, that we can be sure he will lead many others on the pathway of peace to this cistercian wisdom which the Spirit of God granted him to express with both intelligence and love.

Scourmont On the Feast of Saint Bernard, August 20, 1999

---

[10] Julia Kristeva, *Histoires d'amour* (Paris: Denoël, 1983) 211–212. To be faithful to Saint Bernard, it would be more exact to say: 'divine radiation, passing through social love'.

[11] Cf. P. Delfgaauw, *Saint Bernard, maître de l'amour divin*. Dissertation (Rome: 1952). New edition (Paris: FAC-éditions, 1994).

[12] P.-Y. Emery, Introduction to *Saint Bernard. Sermons pour l'année*, 11.

[13] P.-Y. Emery, Introduction to *Saint Bernard. Sermons pour l'année*, p. 12.

Works of
Saint Bernard of Clairvaux
in English Translation

Apology to Abbot William. In *Bernard of Clairvaux: Treatises* I, Cistercian Fathers Series, 1. Introduction by Jean Leclercq OSB. Text translated by Michael Casey OCSO. Spencer: Cistercian Publications, 1970. Pp. 1–69. Reissued as *Bernard of Clairvaux: The Apologia to Abbot William.* Kalamazoo:Cistercian Publications.

Five Books on Consideration. Advice to a Pope. Cistercian Fathers Series 37. Translated by John D. Anderson and Elizabeth T. Kennan. Kalamazoo: Cistercian Publications, 1976. Pp. 222.

In Praise of the New Knighthood. Bernard of Clairvaux: Treatises 3. Cistercian Fathers Series 19. Translated by Conrad Greenia OCSO. Introduction by R. J. Zwi Werblowsky. Kalamazoo: Cistercian Publications, 1977. Pp. 113–167. Reissued as *Bernard of Clairvaux: In Praise of the New Knighthood.* Cistercian Fathers Series 19A. Kalamazoo: Cistercian Publications, 2000.

The Letters of Saint Bernard of Clairvaux. Translated by Bruno Scott James. London: Burns and Oates—Notre Dame University Press, 1953. New edition with a new Introduction by Beverly Mayne Kienzle. Cistercian Fathers Series 62 (Kalamazoo: Cistercian Publications—Stroud: Sutton, 1998) Pp. 544.

The Life and Death of Saint Malachy the Irishman. Translated and annotated by Robert T. Meyer. Cistercian Fathers Series 10. Kalamazoo: Cistercian Publications, 1978. Pp. 170.

Magnificat. Homilies in Praise of the Blessed Virgin Mary, by Bernard of Clairvaux and Amadeus of Lausanne. Translated by Marie-Bernard Saïd OSB. Introduction by Chrysogonus Waddell OCSO. Cistercian Fathers Series 18. Kalamazoo: Cistercian Publications, 1979. Reissued as *Homilies in Praise of the Blessed Virgin Mary*. (1993) Cistercian Fathers Series 18A. Pp. 96.

On Grace and Free Choice. In *Bernard of Clairvaux: Treatises* 3. Cistercian Fathers Series 19. Translated by Daniel O'Donovan OCSO. Introduction by Bernard McGinn. Kalamazoo: Cistercian Publications, 1988. Pp. 1–114. Reissued as *Bernard of Clairvaux: On Grace and Free Choice*. Cistercian Fathers Series 19A.

On Loving God. Translation by Robert Walton. In *Bernard of Clairvaux: Treatises* 2. Cistercian Fathers Series 13. Kalamazoo: Cistercian Publications, 1974. Reissued with an analytical commentary by Emero Stiegman, as *Bernard of Clairvaux: On Loving God*. Cistercian Fathers Series 13B. Kalamazoo, 1995. Pp. 219.

On the Steps of Humility and Pride. In *Bernard of Clairvaux: Treatises* 2. Cistercian Fathers Series 13. Introduction by M. Basil Pennington OCSO. Translated by M. Ambrose Conway, OCSO. Kalamazoo: Cistercian Publications, 1981. Pp. 1–82. Reissued as *Bernard of Clairvaux: On the Steps of Humility and Pride*. Cistercian Fathers Series 13A. Kalamazoo, 1989.

On Precept and Dispensation. Monastic Obligations and Abbatial Authority, In *Bernard of Clairvaux: Treatises* 1. Translated by Conrad Greenia OCSO. Introduction by Jean Leclercq OSB. Cistercian Fathers Series 1. Spencer, Cistercian Publications, 1970. Pp. 71–150.

Parables. In *Bernard of Clairvaux: Parables and Sentences*. Translated, with an Introduction by Michael Casey OCSO. Cistercian Fathers Series 55. Kalamazoo: Cistercian Publications, 1999.

Sentences. In *Bernard of Clairvaux: Parables and Sentences*. Translated by Francis R. Swietek. Introduction by John R. Sommerfeldt. Cistercian Fathers Series 55. Kalamazoo: Cistercian Publications, 1999.

Sermons for the Summer Season. Liturgical Sermons from Rogationtide and Pentecost. Translated and with an Introduction by Beverly

Mayne Kienzle with James Jarzembowski. Cistercian Fathers Series 53. Kalamazoo: Cistercian Publications, 1991. Pp.165.

Sermons on Conversion. On Conversion to Clerics. Lenten Sermons on the Psalm: 'He who dwells'. Translated with an Introduction by Marie-Bernard Saïd OSB. Cistercian Fathers Series 25. Kalamazoo: Cistercian Publications, 1981. Pp. 282.

Sermons on the Song of Songs, 4 volumes.

Volume 1. *Sermons 1–20*. Translated by Kilian Walsh OCSO. Introduction by M. Corneille Haflants OCSO. Cistercian Fathers Series 4. Spencer: Cistercian Publications, 1971. Pp. xxx + 155.

Volume 2. *Sermons 21–46*. Translated by Kilian Walsh OCSO. Introduction by Jean Leclercq osb. Cistercian Fathers Series 7. Kalamazoo: Cistercian Publications 1976. Pp. xxxv + 247.

Volume 3. *Sermons 47–66*. Translated by Kilian Walsh OCSO and Irene M. Edmonds. Introduction by Emero Stiegman. Cistercian Fathers Series 31. Kalamazoo: Cistercian Publications, 1979. Pp. xxxv + 207.

Volume 4. *Sermons 67–86*. Translated by Irene Edmonds. Introduction by Jean Leclercq OSB. Cistercian Fathers Series 40. Kalamazoo: Cistercian Publications, 1980. Pp. xxxv + 261.

CISTERCIAN TEXTS

Bernard of Clairvaux

- Apologia to Abbot William
- Five Books on Consideration: Advice to a Pope
- Homilies in Praise of the Blessed Virgin Mary
- Letters of Bernard of Clairvaux / by B.S. James
- Life and Death of Saint Malachy the Irishman
- Love without Measure: Extracts from the Writings of St Bernard / by Paul Dimier
- On Grace and Free Choice
- On Loving God / Analysis by Emero Stiegman
- Parables and Sentences
- Sermons for the Summer Season
- Sermons on Conversion
- Sermons on the Song of Songs I–IV
- The Steps of Humility and Pride

William of Saint Thierry

- The Enigma of Faith
- Exposition on the Epistle to the Romans
- Exposition on the Song of Songs
- The Golden Epistle
- The Mirror of Faith
- The Nature and Dignity of Love
- On Contemplating God: Prayer & Meditations

Aelred of Rievaulx

- Dialogue on the Soul
- Liturgical Sermons, I
- The Mirror of Charity
- Spiritual Friendship
- Treatises I: On Jesus at the Age of Twelve, Rule for a Recluse, The Pastoral Prayer
- Walter Daniel: The Life of Aelred of Rievaulx

John of Ford

- Sermons on the Final Verses of the Songs of Songs I–VII

Gilbert of Hoyland

- Sermons on the Songs of Songs I–III
- Treatises, Sermons and Epistles

Other Early Cistercian Writers

- Adam of Perseigne, Letters of
- Alan of Lille: The Art of Preaching
- Amadeus of Lausanne: Homilies in Praise of Blessed Mary
- Baldwin of Ford: Spiritual Tractates I–II
- Geoffrey of Auxerre: On the Apocalypse
- Gertrud the Great: Spiritual Exercises
- Gertrud the Great: The Herald of God's Loving-Kindness (Books 1, 2)

- Gertrud the Great: The Herald of God's Loving-Kindness (Book 3)
- Guerric of Igny: Liturgical Sermons Vol. 1 & 2
- Helinand of Froidmont: Verses on Death
- Idung of Prüfening: Cistercians and Cluniacs: The Case for Cîteaux
- Isaac of Stella: Sermons on the Christian Year, I–[II]
- The Life of Beatrice of Nazareth
- Serlo of Wilton & Serlo of Savigny: Seven Unpublished Works
- Stephen of Lexington: Letters from Ireland
- Stephen of Sawley: Treatises

MONASTIC TEXTS

Eastern Monastic Tradition

- Besa: The Life of Shenoute
- Cyril of Scythopolis: Lives of the Monks of Palestine
- Dorotheos of Gaza: Discourses and Sayings
- Evagrius Ponticus: Praktikos and Chapters on Prayer
- Handmaids of the Lord: Lives of Holy Women in Late Antiquity & the Early Middle Ages / by Joan Petersen
- Harlots of the Desert / by Benedicta Ward
- John Moschos: The Spiritual Meadow
- Lives of the Desert Fathers
- Lives of Simeon Stylites / by Robert Doran
- The Luminous Eye / by Sebastian Brock
- Mena of Nikiou: Isaac of Alexandra & St Macrobius
- Pachomian Koinonia I–III (Armand Veilleux)
- Paphnutius: Histories/Monks of Upper Egypt
- The Sayings of the Desert Fathers / by Benedicta Ward
- Spiritual Direction in the Early Christian East / by Irénée Hausherr
- The Spiritually Beneficial Tales of Paul, Bishop of Monembasia / by John Wortley
- Symeon the New Theologian: TheTheological and Practical Treatises & The Three Theological Discourses / by Paul McGuckin
- Theodoret of Cyrrhus: A History of the Monks of Syria
- The Syriac Fathers on Prayer and the Spiritual Life / by Sebastian Brock

CISTERCIAN PUBLICATIONS

TITLES LISTING

Western Monastic Tradition

- Anselm of Canterbury: Letters I–III / by Walter Fröhlich
- Bede: Commentary…Acts of the Apostles
- Bede: Commentary…Seven Catholic Epistles
- Bede: Homilies on the Gospels I–II
- Bede: Excerpts from the Works of St Augustine on the Letters of the Blessed Apostle Paul
- The Celtic Monk / by U. Ó Maidín
- Life of the Jura Fathers
- Maxims of Stephen of Muret
- Peter of Celle: Selected Works
- Letters of Rancé I–II
- Rule of the Master
- Rule of Saint Augustine

Christian Spirituality

- The Cloud of Witnesses: The Development of Christian Doctrine / by David N. Bell
- The Call of Wild Geese / by Matthew Kelty
- The Cistercian Way / by André Louf
- The Contemplative Path
- Drinking From the Hidden Fountain / by Thomas Spidlík
- Eros and Allegory: Medieval Exegesis of the Song of Songs / by Denys Turner
- Fathers Talking / by Aelred Squire
- Friendship and Community / by Brian McGuire
- Gregory the Great: Forty Gospel Homilies
- High King of Heaven / by Benedicta Word
- The Hermitage Within / by a Monk
- Life of St Mary Magdalene and of Her Sister St Martha / by David Mycoff
- Many Mansions / by David N. Bell
- Mercy in Weakness / by André Louf
- The Name of Jesus / by Irénée Hausherr
- No Moment Too Small / by Norvene Vest
- Penthos: The Doctrine of Compunction in the Christian East / by Irénée Hausherr
- Praying the Word / by Enzo Bianchi
- Rancé and the Trappist Legacy / by A. J. Krailsheimer
- Russian Mystics / by Sergius Bolshakoff
- Sermons in a Monastery / by Matthew Kelty
- Silent Herald of Unity: The Life of Maria Gabrielle Sagheddu / by Martha Driscoll
- The Spirituality of the Christian East / by Thomas Spidlík
- The Spirituality of the Medieval West / by André Vauchez
- Tuning In To Grace / by André Louf
- Wholly Animals: A Book of Beastly Tales / by David N. Bell

MONASTIC STUDIES

- Community and Abbot in the Rule of St Benedict I–II / by Adalbert de Vogüé
- The Finances of the Cistercian Order in the Fourteenth Century / by Peter King
- Fountains Abbey and Its Benefactors / by Joan Wardrop
- The Hermit Monks of Grandmont / by Carole A. Hutchison
- In the Unity of the Holy Spirit / by Sighard Kleiner
- The Joy of Learning & the Love of God: Essays in Honor of Jean Leclercq
- Monastic Odyssey / by Marie Kervingant
- Monastic Practices / by Charles Cummings
- The Occupation of Celtic Sites in Ireland / by Geraldine Carville
- Reading St Benedict / by Adalbert de Vogüé
- Rule of St Benedict: A Doctrinal and Spiritual Commentary / by Adalbert de Vogüé
- The Rule of St Benedict / by Br. Pinocchio
- St Hugh of Lincoln / by David H. Farmer
- The Venerable Bede / by Benedicta Ward
- Western Monasticism / by Peter King
- What Nuns Read / by David N. Bell
- With Greater Liberty: A Short History of Christian Monasticism & Religious Orders / by Karl Frank

CISTERCIAN STUDIES

- Aelred of Rievaulx: A Study / by Aelred Squire
- Athirst for God: Spiritual Desire in Bernard of Clairvaux's Sermons on the Song of Songs / by Michael Casey
- Beatrice of Nazareth in Her Context / by Roger De Ganck
- Bernard of Clairvaux: Man, Monk, Mystic / by Michael Casey [tapes and readings]
- Bernardus Magister…Nonacentenary
- Catalogue of Manuscripts in the Obrecht Collection of the Institute of Cistercian Studies / by Anna Kirkwood
- Christ the Way: The Christology of Guerric of Igny / by John Morson
- The Cistercians in Denmark / by Brian McGuire
- The Cistercians in Scandinavia / by James France
- A Difficult Saint / by Brian McGuire
- A Gathering of Friends: Learning & Spirituality in John of Ford / by Costello and Holdsworth
- Image and Likeness: Augustinian Spirituality of William of St Thierry / by David Bell

- Index of Authors & Works in Cistercian Libraries in Great Britain I / by David Bell
- Index of Cistercian Authors and Works in Medieval Library Catalogues in Great Britian / by David Bell
- The Mystical Theology of St Bernard / by Étienne Gilson
- The New Monastery: Texts & Studies on the Earliest Cistercians
- Nicolas Cotheret's Annals of Cîteaux / by Louis J. Lekai
- Pater Bernhardus: Martin Luther and Saint Bernard / by Franz Posset
- Pathway of Peace / by Charles Dumont
- A Second Look at Saint Bernard / by Jean Leclercq
- The Spiritual Teachings of St Bernard of Clairvaux / by John R. Sommerfeldt
- Studies in Medieval Cistercian History
- Studiosorum Speculum / by Louis J. Lekai
- Three Founders of Cîteaux / by Jean-Baptiste Van Damme
- Towards Unification with God (Beatrice of Nazareth in Her Context, 2)
- William, Abbot of St Thierry
- Women and St Bernard of Clairvaux / by Jean Leclercq

MEDIEVAL RELIGIOUS WOMEN

edited by Lillian Thomas Shank and John A. Nichols:
- Distant Echoes
- Hidden Springs: Cistercian Monastic Women (2 volumes)
- Peace Weavers

CARTHUSIAN TRADITION

- The Call of Silent Love / by A Carthusian
- The Freedom of Obedience / by A Carthusian
- From Advent to Pentecost
- Guigo II: The Ladder of Monks & Twelve Meditations / by Colledge & Walsh
- Halfway to Heaven / by R.B. Lockhart
- Interior Prayer / by A Carthusian
- Meditations of Guigo II / by A. Gordon Mursall
- The Prayer of Love and Silence / by A Carthusian
- Poor, Therefore Rich / by A Carthusian
- They Speak by Silences / by A Carthusian
- The Way of Silent Love (A Carthusian Miscellany)
- Where Silence is Praise / by A Carthusian
- The Wound of Love (A Carthusian Miscellany)

CISTERCIAN ART, ARCHITECTURE & MUSIC

- Cistercian Abbeys of Britain
- Cistercians in Medieval Art / by James France
- Studies in Medieval Art and Architecture / edited by Meredith Parsons Lillich (Volumes II–V are now available)
- Stones Laid Before the Lord / by Anselme Dimier
- Treasures Old and New: Nine Centuries of Cistercian Music (compact disc and cassette)

THOMAS MERTON

- The Climate of Monastic Prayer / by T. Merton
- Legacy of Thomas Merton / by P. Hart
- Message of Thomas Merton / by P. Hart
- Monastic Journey of Thomas Merton / by P. Hart
- Thomas Merton/Monk / by P. Hart
- Thomas Merton on St Bernard
- Toward an Integrated Humanity / edited by M. Basil Pennington

CISTERCIAN LITURGICAL DOCUMENTS SERIES

- Cistercian Liturgical Documents Series / edited by Chrysogonus Waddell, ocso
- Hymn Collection of the…Paraclete
- Institutiones nostrae: The Paraclete Statutes
- Molesme Summer-Season Breviary (4 volumes)
- Old French Ordinary & Breviary of the Abbey of the Paraclete (2 volumes)
- Twelfth-century Cistercian Hymnal (2 volumes)
- The Twelfth-century Cistercian Psalter
- Two Early Cistercian Libelli Missarum

STUDIA PATRISTICA

- Studia Patristica XVIII, Volumes 1, 2 and 3

CISTERCIAN PUBLICATIONS

HOW TO CONTACT US

Editorial Queries

Editorial queries & advance book information should be directed to the Editorial Offices:

- Cistercian Publications
  WMU Station
  1201 Oliver Street
  Kalamazoo, Michigan 49008

- Telephone 616 387 8920
- Fax   616 387 8390
- e-mai   mcdougall@wmich.edu

How to Order in the United States

Customers may order these books through booksellers, from the editorial office, or directly from the warehouse:

- Cistercian Publications
  Saint Joseph's Abbey
  167 North Spencer Road
  Spencer, Massachusetts 01562-1233

- Telephone 508 885 8730
- Fax   508 885 4687
- e-mail   cistpub@spencerabbey.org
- Web Site   www.spencerabbey.org/cistpub

How to Order from Canada

- Novalis
  49 Front Street East, Second Floor
  Toronto, Ontario M5E 1B3

- Telephone 416 363 3303
              1 800 387 7164
- Fax   416 363 9409

How to Order from Europe

- Cistercian Publications
  97 Loughborough Road
  Thringstone, Coalville, Leicester LE67 8LQ

- Fax   44 1530 45 02 10
- e-mail   MsbcistP@aol.com

Cistercian Publications is a non-profit corporat-ion. Its publishing program is restricted to mo-nastic texts in translation and books on the monastic tradition.

A complete catalogue of texts in translation and studies on early, medieval, and modern monas-ticism is available, free of charge, from any of the addresses above.

DATE DUE